VIRTUAL BILLIONS

VIRTUAL BILLIONS

THE GENIUS, THE DRUG LORD,
AND THE IVY LEAGUE TWINS
BEHIND THE RISE OF BITCOIN

Eric Geissinger

Prometheus Books

59 John Glenn Drive
Amherst, New York 14228

Published 2016 by Prometheus Books

Cover image © Shutterstock
Cover design by Nicole Sommer-Lecht

Inquiries should be addressed to
Prometheus Books
59 John Glenn Drive
Amherst, New York 14228
VOICE: 716–691–0133
FAX: 716–691–0137
WWW.PROMETHEUSBOOKS.COM

20 19 18 17 16   5 4 3 2 1

Library of Congress Cataloging-in-Publication Data Pending

ISBN 978-1-63388-144-0 (HC)
ISBN 978-1-63388-145-7 (ebk)

Printed in the United States of America

To Jennifer, Poppy, and Effie

I made a mistake in presuming that the self-interests of organizations, specifically banks and others, were such as that they were best capable of protecting their own shareholders and their equity in the firms.
—Alan Greenspan, October 24, 2008, to Congress

It's a bubble. It has to have intrinsic value. You have to really stretch your imagination to infer what the intrinsic value of Bitcoin is. I haven't been able to do it. Maybe somebody else can.
—Alan Greenspan, December 4, 2013, in an interview with *Bloomberg*

CONTENTS

Introduction: Spending Symbols and Buying Potatoes   9

Chapter 1: Satoshi Nakamoto: What He Invented   21

Chapter 2: Satoshi Nakamoto: How Bitcoin Works   41

Chapter 3: Satoshi Nakamoto: A Rocket-Powered Launch   79

Chapter 4: Ross Ulbricht: Into the Dark   121

Chapter 5: Ross Ulbricht: The Rise and Fall of Silk Road   157

Chapter 6: The Winklevoss Twins: Born on Third Base,
        Hit a Double   207

Chapter 7: The Winklevoss Twins: The Fog of Success   231

Conclusion: Incremental Progress   271

Acknowledgments   277

Notes   279

Index   315

SPENDING SYMBOLS AND BUYING POTATOES

Note: According to general but not yet unanimous online agreement, Bitcoin (singular, capital B) is the name of the currency, the network supporting the currency, and the payment system in general. A single bitcoin or collection of bitcoins (referring to units of the currency) uses the lower case. For example, "I sure love Bitcoin, and I bought ten bitcoins yesterday."

On January 1, 2010, all the bitcoins in the world could be had for less than a cent. By July 1, 2013, they were worth nine billion dollars. Growth at this rate is historically unprecedented: Bitcoin easily outpaced Facebook, Twitter, Microsoft, and every other technology company in its rush to a multibillion-dollar capitalization. Back in 1997, the *New York Times* called a similar technology boom the "Internet Gold Rush,"[1] as companies monetized information, sold online advertising, and made their storefronts virtual. It was slow going at first: "Digital miners are meeting with spotty success,"[2] the paper reported, with most of the big money made by companies selling internet access and hardware (primarily routers and cables). This soon changed. Once the internet's backbone had been built, a bonanza followed, and companies achieved Fortune 500 valuations in a three-year period of explosive, unrealistic growth. What became known as the dot.bomb bubble popped in 2001, and the Internet Gold Rush ended; sober businessmen moved in.

Bitcoin isn't the electronic equivalent of a dollar, transformed into bits and bytes and transmitted over the internet; it's more of a financial subsystem, an alternate payment stream, which soon ushered in a new wave of investment—a silver rush. It's hard to understand the extent of Bitcoin's growth without turning to the only comparable real-world parallel, the transformation of a bland series of rolling hills next to a modest mountain in Nevada—the uninhabited land[3] worth pennies a few years before—into a blasted landscape pock-marked with burrows and smoke, unsteady cabins and open latrines, with desperate miners striking claims and digging and fighting over square feet of turf that gleamed with the possibility of buried riches. The 1859 discovery of the Comstock lode set off a frenzy of activity: it represented one of the largest silver discoveries in the history of mankind and signaled the end of the more famous, but played-out, California Gold Rush (1849–1855).

Soon so much silver was being pulled out the Comstock mines that prices dropped worldwide and governments considered demonetizing silver currency, as it no longer had significant independent value. The Comstock Lode's social and political effects were far reaching: acting as a magnet, it deformed settlement patterns across the West, spurred Nevada into an abrupt and early statehood, drew fortune-seekers from around the globe, and caused booms in cities as distant as San Francisco and Los Angeles. Miners swarmed the landscape, cleared forests, constructed bridges, and tunneled through mountains. The lode rewarded industry and meted out heartbreak in unequal measure.[4] James Finney,[5] one of the original discoverers of the so-called "Gold Hill" strike, was an unsophisticated man who sold his share in the claim (worth tens of millions) for an old horse and a bottle of rot-gut whiskey. This sounds uncomfortably close to a folk legend, but it's certainly true none of the early miners on the scene, who should have profited most with the least work, did well for themselves—stories of heavy drinking, insanity, and suicide were common. Compared to the fate of many others, Finney's fate was a relatively light sentence for stumbling across one of the great buried fortunes in the history of the world.

The Comstock Lode was a global event. Most people didn't feel the effect of the mining strike directly, beyond a diluted bump in national prosperity, but for some it meant uprooting themselves and changing everything they had ever done and leaving behind everyone they had ever known. Mining had a reality you could sink your hands into, in fact it was required: separating silver from lumps of quartz or shovelfuls of sticky blue mud was a messy job. When it was over, and the lode was played out, something tangible had been produced, and refined, and was in use throughout the world: 192 million ounces of 99.7 percent pure silver. You could point to it and say, *Look, that's what the fuss was all about.* Something beautiful and real had been created from one of the ugliest and most sordid celebrations of greed the human race had ever enthusiastically indulged.

Yet at its height, Bitcoin's net worth surpassed, in adjusted dollars, the aggregate total of Nevada's Comstock Lode over any *five-year period.*

Bitcoin wouldn't have captured the fancy of so many tech-savvy early adopters if it had been built on an unstable or poorly designed code base, or thrived despite wary journalists telling readers as early as 2011 that Bitcoin was nothing more or less than a "bubble," liable to pop at any moment.[6] Bitcoin succeeded without a single well-known entrepreneur adopting it within the first two years of its existence. Bitcoin flourished despite lack of institutional support of any kind, its value unstable, though trending ever-upward.

Bitcoin's relentless advance, despite a complete lack of traditional financial backing, was either a fantastic coincidence or the rational consequence of the law of supply and demand (combined with perfect timing). Looking back on it, Bitcoin's rapid expansion occurred in a void, without resistant pressure. A need existed, an opportunity as yet untapped and largely unforeseen, and when Bitcoin was invented and distributed it filled the empty space effortlessly, making little noise as there was little opposition. No businesses were impacted and pushed out of the way, and nobody gave the strange startup currency much attention at all—until it was too late to stop its onrushing growth.

By 2014, dire tales of an impending Bitcoin collapse, still regularly published, began to fade into the background. Businesses all over the world were signing up to accept the currency. Conservative investors started pouring money into Bitcoin startups. In January

2014, the Sacramento Kings of the National Basketball Association became the first professional team to accept Bitcoin for ticket and merchandise sales.[7] Bitcoin had attained a tenuous though stable level of respect in the financial community, and when it's possible to buy groceries in Birmingham, Alabama, using bitcoins, without anyone batting an eye[8] . . . it's safe to say Bitcoin's moving quickly toward mainstream acceptance.

When confronted by something as miraculous and weird as Bitcoin's explosive five-year growth, it's hard to avoid the fundamental question: *How on earth did this happen?*

When I'm at a dinner party, surrounded by people desperate to know more about Bitcoin—which, now that I think about it, doesn't occur as often as it should—there's always somebody who interrupts my description of the currency and pooh-poohs the entire Bitcoin concept because, quite obviously, "Bitcoins aren't real." They're nothing more than electrical impulses flying around the internet, sensitive to magnetic fields and stymied by broken wires or overheated hard drives or misrouted signals. It's crazy to base a currency on a delicate computer network, which might suffer a catastrophic collapse at any moment. Surely Bitcoin won't last; it's a fad, and the experiment's going to end abruptly, and certainly badly.

Bitcoin's lack of mundane existence—something you can hold in your hand or stash in your mattress—is claimed to be the fundamental drawback inhibiting everyday acceptance. Nobody wants to risk investing in something that, frankly, doesn't "really exist." Right?

This is a reasonable response and a perfectly fine objection. It was also my first reaction and, if the gung-ho early adopters and the current crop of Bitcoin-crazed entrepreneurs are honest with themselves, it's an issue we all had to think about and convince ourselves wasn't a deal breaker, or even a crucial issue. To illustrate why I don't think it's a critical objection, I offer the parable of the Suspicious Salesman.

Imagine entering a used car dealership one sunny summer day. You walk in, armed only with a long series of numbers. Despite this, the sales force takes you seriously. You test drive a few classics, and finally select an expensively restored 1968 Volvo 1800p. While paying for it, you read a long series of numbers to the attentive sales associate, who types into a computer, makes a phone call, and hands you the keys. Off you drive, happy as a clam. The kicker? The string of numbers is from a credit card, and the phone call contacted the credit card company checking for credit availability (and confirmed the number hadn't been stolen).

We already exist in a society comfortable with paying with things remotely (using the internet or telephone) or symbolically (using credit cards, checks, bank drafts, etc.). We don't think twice about it. Nor do businesses. The car dealership is happy to sell the car because of the following guarantees on credit card sales, which are immensely powerful and reassuring:

1) Credit card purchases are guaranteed in the case of fraud. If the number given to the dealership was somehow hacked or stolen, the dealership isn't out any money. The credit card company guarantees they will pay the charge and are responsible for going after the grinning con man. The dealership, after a phone call and credit card number check, is in the clear no matter what happens.
2) The credit card company is not going to go bankrupt before the car dealership gets paid.

The second point is so obvious it's hardly noticed, but it's absolutely crucial. When credit card companies were getting off the ground, stores had good reason to worry about the new venture. Could they trust consumers not to spend beyond their means? Could they trust the validity of the newly issued cards? Was the "signature" security system and call-in verification sufficient to ward off scammers? If things went bad, would they really get reimbursed? Were credit cards a passing fad? Might not the credit card company go bankrupt in the middle of next month?

With Visa making over \$12 billion in profit in 2014,[9] the second issue is pretty much dead. Nobody in their right mind worries about VISA going bankrupt, and if it does it's probably in response to a global meltdown, in which case we have more important things to attend to then one or two unpaid purchases. Faith in credit card companies is a matter of financial record. Businesses look at a credit card company's size, history, and healthy balance sheet and easily convince themselves that accepting a string of numbers for a used car isn't an unwise decision—in fact, it's such a common event we don't think twice about it.

Do credit card numbers *exist* in the same way a tree does? When issued a credit card you are given a plastic rectangle featuring a signature (often checked by stores) and a hologram (sometimes checked by stores) and a long series of numbers (the important thing). The card certainly exists, you can jimmy a hotel room lock with it, but what about the numbers? Do they have an independent existence? They are listed, but are they really "real"? Taken out of context they're a meaningless series of digits. Used in conjunction with a purchase, they allow you to buy food for a month. They are "real" because they are backed by a credit card company and are part of a trusted system of exchange. The credit card company's assurance of liquidity is what lifts the numbers out of insubstantiality. We have faith and confidence in our credit cards and their nearly universal acceptability because we have faith and confidence in the issuing companies. Everything flows from this fundamental faith.

Imagine that instead of using a credit card you walked into a used car dealership with a suitcase of hundred-dollar bills. Contrary to standard economic logic, the sales force will be significantly less happy to see you compared to a credit card user, and might refuse to sell you any car at all, the presence of hard cash implying all sorts of nasty possibilities: drug deals, robberies, money laundering, etc. If the cash is drug money, it's possible (although unlikely) that purchases made with it might be confiscated by the authorities since they came from a tainted source, and in this case the car dealership loses out big time. The government seizes both the money and the car. Even if the dealership allows purchases in cash, which is far more tangible than a string of numbers (and surprisingly heavy in large amounts), does cash truly qualify as a significantly more "real" way to pay?

A Martian couldn't distinguish between a dollar bill and a soup can label. Stating what we all know but don't quite believe, a hundred-dollar bill is just a paper rectangle and has value because we collectively believe that it's worth more than other types of paper rectangles. More importantly, our collective belief is consistent. I'm not taking a risk accepting a hundred-dollar bill today because I'm convinced I can spend it safely tomorrow. In the unlikely case that tomorrow rolls around and nobody is willing to take my hundred-dollar bill, it's another one of those "end of the world" scenarios, and I likely won't care about losing a hundred dollars because everyone else will be in the same (sinking) boat.

Most people agree paper money's useful. It's light, you can fold it, you can stack it, and to use economic jargon it's both durable and fungible. The American dollar also happens to be stable even though it's not directly pegged to anything of real value. The Gold Standard, whereby a dollar could be exchanged for a sliver of gold, had a real but lessening impact in the twentieth century until the fateful moment in 1971 when the United States officially "floated" its currency free of any association with gold. At that point cash only had value because the government, and the society using it, agreed it did. Should the government, or society, suddenly lose faith in the dollar, cash would be worth nothing more "than the paper it is printed on." These sorts of disasters are unlikely but not unheard-of—cue scenes from Germany post-WWI, with wild hyperinflation, wheelbarrows of paper currency paying for a single potato, printing presses working day and night in a desperate race against looming calamity. . . . It eventually resulted in absurd issuances such as this five billion mark note:

At the time of the note's printing in 1923, five billion marks was almost enough to buy a copy of the afternoon paper. For the majority of Germans suffering through this period, paper currency became something used to start a fire or throw into the air in colorful armfuls to amuse the children or stack in the outhouse for various utilitarian uses (which also functions as a metaphor for the public's opinion of its value). These types of worst-case scenarios have a ghostly presence in our collective memory, but for most of us hyperinflation and currency collapse isn't an ongoing concern—except for "gold bugs."[10]

Gold-standard enthusiasts ("gold bugs"[11]) are extremely uncomfortable with the idea of a free-floating currency (i.e., any currency not convertible directly into gold). Back in the "good old days" you could take a twenty-dollar bill to a bank and come away with a chunk of gold, based on a conversion price the government artificially set for such transactions. Under such a scheme, cash isn't paper—it's actually a proxy for gold. If cash was converted at every opportunity, a far-sighted citizen might be in a better position following a financial crash than his more trusting peers—at the very least, he'd retain a fistful of gleaming gold.

For gold bugs and end timers and survivalists, free-floating currency is another way the world implodes, lumped together with plagues, nuclear accidents, meteor strikes, genetic mutations, and the second coming of Christ. The only solution to the problem is to convert paper bills into *things* as soon as possible, which retain their value (or at least material existence) after an economic catastrophe.

It wasn't only extremists who found fault with the new currency. Sober-minded economists worried about the government's ability to print money without, at the same time, increasing gold reserves. Wouldn't this enable endless acts of fiscal irresponsibility? What's to stop the Obama administration[12] from a) printing as much money as it wants, b) causing inflation by printing as much money as it wants, c) slowing down the economy by printing as much money as it wants, giving it more reason to d) print as much money as it wants.

For those worried about the inflationary side of the problem, the gold standard worked to restrict an otherwise out-of-control government from profligate spending, necessarily diminishing the value of existing dollars and (possibly) making us lose confidence in the dollar as a worthwhile store of value. The gold standard functioned as an irreducible lord and master; if you didn't have enough gold to support your currency, you couldn't print more of that currency. Or, if you have a more flexible view of the gold standard, you couldn't print more currency than the percent you believe would be converted into gold should times get tough and the public freak out. Either way the government isn't free to do whatever it wants.

Gold standard currencies aren't particularly flexible—by design—and as a consequence often end up exacerbating recessions and depressions. Forcing banks to keep gold equal to their currency holdings (or a percentage of their holdings) requires increasing the gold supply in order to distribute more currency and loosen lending. The government can't arbitrarily print currency to generate a stimulus of the sort widely credited with saving the American and World economies in 2009—a stimulus economists from across the political spectrum agree was both necessary and, while massive, not quite massive enough.[13] Were we still on the gold standard, this sort of structural adjustment would be impossible without a coincidental and quite unlikely discovery of a massive new source of gold, allowing the government to generate an influx of currency.

We've come a long way from Bitcoin and the dinner party and the plaintive objection, "Bitcoin isn't *real*." The objection can't be denied, because it's valid. No, Bitcoin isn't real, if you define "real" in a way excluding Bitcoin. Having a bitcoin in your Bitcoin electronic wallet (e-wallet) is roughly equivalent to holding a piece of prettily printed paper or producing a long number stamped onto a rectangle of one-cent plastic. It's true that e-wallets only exist online and if the internet were to disappear tomorrow all the e-wallets and bitcoins that ever existed would vanish in a puff of incinerated routers, leaving some that much poorer. This again presumes an "end of the world" event, in which case mourning Bitcoin will trail the hunt for food and uncontaminated water by a significant margin. Such an event would also render credit cards valueless and cash of dubious worth.

Is it even true that things that exist only on the internet lack a fundamental type of "reality"? Do people make this claim about anything *except* Bitcoin? Imagine receiving a text message that reads, bluntly and shockingly, "I'm leaving you for Pat." Does the ephemeral nature of the transmitted message, the fact that it only exists as a series of electronic impulses or magnetic 0s and 1s, make the heartbreak less immediate? As for joy, are you allowed to celebrate when you receive an urgent email from your agent offering you a supporting role in a major Hollywood production? Is the cancer scan downloaded and inspected with a software-based magnifying tool irrelevant because it consists of electronic impulses, which lack some sort of "real," honest-to-God, solid-as-Amish-furniture existence?

These types of questions aren't really very interesting. Ignore Marshall McLuhan's commonplace "The medium is the message . . ." The medium has never been the message; at most the medium changes the way the message is communicated, but that's quite a minor point compared to the message itself. You receive an email, or a text, or a tweet, or a phone call, or a printed telegram, or watch a team of semaphore experts working twenty flags simultaneously. They all communicate the same thing: *I'm leaving you for Pat*. The world shivers and shakes and reassembling it requires years—perhaps a lifetime.

What matters isn't *how* something is communicated but *what* is communicated. If you have ten bitcoins in your e-wallet you can spend them and have any number of things delivered to your door: computers and parrots and candy and tickets to a Sacramento Kings game. You can sell them on a Bitcoin exchange for gold, dollars, pesos, or francs. You can transfer them directly to a friend or associate or a blackmailer a world away. They can be used to purchase objects or services, to buy stocks or soap, and, yes, it's true that bitcoins only exist on the internet as blips of data shuttled between servers and routers and hard drives, and this, I believe, is a feature and a strength—not a limitation.

The real problem with Bitcoin isn't the fact that it's a weird ephemeral currency. The problem is that unlike the disaster examples supplied so far (a failed credit card company, out-of-control inflation created by an out-of-control government), it's easy to envision a world without Bitcoin. It wouldn't require flood nor famine nor alien invasion, just an insanely clever virus attacking the Bitcoin network and permanently scrambling its transaction list, leaving the currency ruined.

The likely effect? Nobody you know would lose any money, and the world economy would shrug its shoulders and lose a hundredth of a percent off its expected yearly growth. That's about it.

Stability is Bitcoin's fundamental problem. It's too new to offer a comforting record of success. It's too rarely used to engender much faith. It's not backed by a government or a multinational corporation with massive profits and a fleet of lawyers. It exists as a free-to-use communal online currency. Whether this is a strength or a weakness is wholly determined by Bitcoin's future growth.

Bitcoin has been forced to quickly mature. It's achieved a significant global presence in five short years—but it got off to a pretty rocky start. This book explains Bitcoin and its operation through the stories of the people behind its rise: the reclusive genius who founded Bitcoin (Satoshi Nakamoto), the Dark Web drug overlord who used Bitcoin to power his site (Ross Ulbricht), and the celebrity businessmen who struck gold twice in the same decade with Facebook and Bitcoin (the Winklevoss twins). They represent Bitcoin's childhood, rebellious youth, and painful awakening into maturity, the story not of a soulless digital currency but the dedicated people who worked and sweated to bring it into existence—one of the craziest and most improbable events in the history of the world.

CHAPTER 1

SATOSHI NAKAMOTO: WHAT HE INVENTED

WHO IS SATOSHI?

Bitcoin's inventor is an enigma named Satoshi Nakamoto. Satoshi might be a reclusive genius quietly living in rustic privacy, or a group of like-minded enthusiasts who cooperatively created Bitcoin, making it the "King James Bible of cryptocurrency."[1] Nobody really knows, and speculation about his (or her or their) secret identity hasn't been fruitful, but it's been fun for the mass media to propose and investigate various alternatives. Here are a few possibilities that have been thrown out (and shot down) in recent years:

New Yorker, 2011. Suspects: Dr. Vili Lehdonvirta and/or cryptologist Michael Clear.

Evidence: Based on mutual association and Michael Clear's experience with cryptology, peer-to-peer networks, and interest in virtual currencies.

Fast Company, 2011. Suspects: Neal King, Vladimir Oksman, and Charles Bry.

Evidence: Based on patent filings and a curious chronology related to registering the bitcoin.org domain name.

Forbes, 2013. Suspect: Shinichi Mochizuki, a Japanese mathematician.

Evidence: Based on his unusual publishing habits and evident brilliance. Plus he's Japanese.

Vice, 2013. Suspects: Gavin Andresen or Jed McCaleb.

Evidence: Both highly experienced programmers with vast experience in peer-to-peer networks. Gavin Andresen was Bitcoin project's lead developer for a long period of time; Jed McCaleb produced the Mt. Gox exchange and faded away from it just as Satoshi faded away from Bitcoin.

Newsweek, 2014. Suspect: Dorian Nakamoto.

Evidence: Widely publicized and discredited story about Dorian, an out-of-work engineer in Temple City, California. Dorian Nakamoto, who denies being Satoshi, is currently pondering litigation against *Newsweek* using a crowdsourced legal fund.

Digital Gold, 2015, by Nathaniel Popper. Suspect: Nick Szabo.

Evidence: Szabo is an experienced programmer with close ties to a pre-Bitcoin digital currency called Bit gold, and has significant ongoing involvement with Bitcoin development and startups.

Wired, 2015. Suspect: Craig Steven Wright.

Evidence: Wright's 2008 blog included posts about Bitcoin that seem to predate Bitcoin's release. *Wired* also gained access to leaked documents from business ventures and financial records that point toward Wright being, at the least, Bitcoin's cocreator; however (as *Wired* admits) all these documents could have been forged.

None of these hypothesized Satoshis have (so far) withstood close scrutiny, and having run through all the obvious possibilities it's now clear Satoshi's real identity won't be known unless Satoshi directly reveals himself. As time passes this is increasingly unlikely.

Satoshi hasn't completely hidden his tracks—plenty of conclusions can be drawn from the evidence he's left behind, and fortunately (for the sake of a good story) Satoshi is probably *not* a group of people. Language experts,[2] taking Satoshi's written corpus and shoving it through computational linguistic programs, report remarkably consistent results. The writing style of Satoshi's first few posts matches his last few posts and everything in between. Satoshi sometimes indulged in rapid-fire back-and-forth exchanges with correspondents, which would have been difficult or impossible to pull off if a committee was involved in reading and responding to every message. Satoshi writes in a natural style of English; despite his apparently Japanese name there are almost no grammatical errors in his writing and no mistakes of types often produced when native Japanese speakers learn and write English.

A survey of Satoshi's message board time stamps[3] reveals he was almost always silent between the hours of one a.m. and seven a.m. Eastern Standard Time, making it likely that he lived in the United States and wasn't writing because he was sleeping.[4] All this is speculation, of course, but based on hard evidence. More significantly, the majority of Satoshi's writings were produced when Bitcoin was far from a sure thing. In 2009, Bitcoin wasn't thought to have more than a chance in a million of surviving its first year, much less prospering. If Satoshi had purposefully altered his message board time stamps, and assiduously camouflaged his writing, he would have had to have done so from the very start—showing unbelievable prescience and patience.

Satoshi wasn't just Bitcoin's inventor; he was an early and active bitcoin miner and left traces in the public transaction ledger of the powerful machine (or suite of machines) he used to solve Bitcoin's hashing problems. Statistical analysis[5] of Bitcoin mining rewards and a detailed inspection of public data, examining what happened to the bitcoins earned by his machine's mining, reveal that Satoshi was by far the most successful Bitcoin miner the world will ever see. Not only was Satoshi mining when the mining difficulty level was extremely low, he used computers constructed with Bitcoin mining in mind. It's estimated that Satoshi mined over 1.5 million bitcoins and spent around 500,000; of those he spent, most were used as "seed" donations for Bitcoin-related projects, not converted into cash. At least a million bitcoins remain unspent. Why? Satoshi might have lost the e-wallets containing them (unlikely), or grown bored of Bitcoin as a subject (possible), or he's holding on to them hoping for further price increases (probable). Satoshi is worth somewhere north of $250 million, down from a high of at least a billion (when bitcoins traded at $1,200 each[6]), which briefly made him without doubt the most unlikely and anonymous billionaire the world has ever seen.

The Ockham's razor principle suggests giving primacy to explanations unburdened by a host of assumptions and hypotheticals. If a shed burns down, it's possible the fire was caused by a cops-vs-robbers shootout, a thwarted alien invasion, or . . . an electrical short. Yes, it's humdrum, and it's boring, but it doesn't require many assumptions. The shed had electricity, its wires were old, and something easily could have gone wrong. In this spirit, the extent of Satoshi's misdirection likely began and ended with his name. Satoshi wasn't part of a group so disciplined during Bitcoin's creation and subsequent development that nobody peeped a word about the wonderful prank they pulled on the world. He wasn't a government plant. There isn't a code-related reason the original Bitcoin client required more than one person; in the past, far more complicated programs have been written by a single programmer.

I'm not convinced it really matters if we ever discover the "real Satoshi," somebody we can shake hands with and talk to over coffee and award innovation prizes.[7] What matters most, and the reason anyone's spent a second thinking about Satoshi, is Bitcoin. That Satoshi's creation proved reliable and resilient and found an eager and interested global audience is a testament to his creativity and his programming prowess.

Satoshi walked away from Bitcoin support and development on December 11, 2010, at 11:39:16 p.m. His final message board post was in response to a proposal that WikiLeaks accept Bitcoin, since all other avenues of financial support to the site had been cut off by various irate governments.[8] Satoshi was, to put it bluntly, not interested: "It would have been nice to get this attention in any other context. WikiLeaks has kicked the hornet's nest, and the swarm is headed towards us."[9] It wasn't clear that the Bitcoin network was mature enough, or stable enough, to handle a sudden influx of attention.

Satoshi was worried the United States government might attempt to shut down Bitcoin or conduct a massive search to identify and capture its creator. Satoshi, spooked by sudden celebrity, nervous about the government's far-reaching powers, and unsure about the future, faded away—his record is afterward blank. An army of volunteers took over Bitcoin development, and Satoshi hasn't been heard from again.[10]

What we know about Satoshi comes from the Bitcoin code, the forum messages he posted, and his white paper, outlining how Bitcoin functions. From these hard data we have to extrapolate a living, breathing human being. Yet Satoshi's anonymity doesn't leave us without recourse—many argue that in Bitcoin Satoshi revealed some of the most interesting aspects of his worldview. Before Satoshi could create Bitcoin, he had to grapple with the concept of digital currency—and if such an idea made sense. Once he was convinced a digital currency was theoretically possible, Satoshi had to start the dirty work of coding it, debugging it, distributing it, and publicizing it.

Following Satoshi's lead, this chapter looks at currencies past and present and how they functioned (or failed to function), as well as the peculiar challenges presented by a digital currency, before grappling with the most obvious question of them all: *What is Bitcoin?*

A CURRENCY CONTRARIAN

Satoshi Nakamoto makes it clear from various forum posts[11] that he had thought deeply about economics and understood how currencies operate and under what conditions they were typically stable and how they occasionally degenerated into instability. He knew of Ludwig von Mises's theories, developed in *The Theory of Money and Credit* (1912), which attempted to describe the true nature of money and how a currency necessarily arises out of a barter economy.

Satoshi knew the standard theories about how currencies developed and the forms they took and the materials often used in coinage, about the necessity of strong government control and powerful and respected legal institutions and the importance of contract law and everything else that goes along with a modern Western understanding on how economies really work. What's not clear is that Satoshi believed any of it.

In order to understand why so many people rejected the possibility of a digital currency,[12] we first must consider what it means to say something is a "currency," how it might have been invented, and its various attributes (both necessary and discretionary). To illustrate the "traditional," commonsensical, and broadly accepted view of how currencies came into being, I'll run a little thought experiment following Ludwig von Mises's lead.[13] It's a scenario set in a peaceful fictional village, and it goes something like this: In the beginning there were *things*, and these things mooed or cut well or had to be eaten before they started to go bad, and people living in small communities spent a lot of time running from house to house with a perfectly useful object they wanted to exchange for another perfectly useful object. In this way a sheep breeder eventually traded a sheep for the blacksmith's sharpest axe, and the jeweler gave a pretty little necklace to an expectant mother and was rewarded with two long and warm loaves of newly baked bread. Things went on like this for a while but it sure wasn't convenient. Sometimes nobody wanted a sheep, and the sheep seller wasted a whole day finding out. Sometimes the jeweler worked for a month on an exquisite clasp without finding anyone willing to make an equal trade.

Not everyone had problems moving their goods. In this fictional world, farmers growing long ears of Indian corn always found people willing to take it, since corn was a staple and used by many households. Farmers might not trade their entire wagonload on a given day, but they were sure to move a lot of it. The ease with which they bartered away piles of corn was soon noticed. The sheep breeder, for example, was tired of trying to guess when a family might splurge on meat, or when a wedding reception would involve mounds of charred mutton. One day a sheep breeder had a *eureka* moment: even if he didn't *want* corn, he could always trade a sheep to one of the many corn farmers in the area and receive a barrel of corn in return. Since corn was always in demand, he was certain to find people willing to trade for corn. The sheep breeder traded not because he wanted corn but because he desired corn's easily traded capacity. Corn became, in essence, an intermediary; even if the sheep breeder had far more corn than he needed for cooking or for storage, it was extremely useful as a tool for making small trades. You can't trade a sheep for a washcloth, but you can trade a small bowlful of corn.

Corn became more than a simple grain. The sheep breeder soon realized he could trade all his sheep for corn and accumulate a barn stuffed with corn for later use. No longer would he be forced to wander about, hoping to find a relatively prosperous mutton-loving peasant to cut a deal with. In addition, he was able to store the corn and trade it in the winter when other, less far-sighted villagers might be running low or without corn. Corn wasn't just useful—it could increase in value, giving him more real-world goods than if he had let his sheep grow another year. Other people saw what the clever sheep breeder was doing and soon everyone was trading for corn; corn had become not only a tangible thing you could stew and eat, but a form of money. Somebody said, for the first time, "I'll pay for it with corn," instead of "I'll trade corn for it." That was it, and there wasn't any looking back. The slow movement from object to symbol had begun, and it would be a difficult (almost impossible) transition to reverse.

Corn's transformation into currency wasn't smooth nor easy: trouble soon began. The villagers quickly realized corn was far from perfect. It was better than nothing, but not much: Due to corn hoarding and corn hauling and corn selling and corn growing, the villagers soon had corn stuffed everywhere, which the rats and mice greatly appreciated. After half their collective savings disappeared in a single month, corn was traded more frequently, saved less, and eaten far more often.

Corn lacked one of the four so-called *necessary prerequisites* of any self-respecting currency: durability. Left alone, corn dried out or rotted or was eaten by bugs. Something bad always happened.

The villagers struggled, but continued to use corn as a currency until a passing troubadour suffered a heart attack in the town square and died. He was buried and his clothing and possessions were taken up and divided among the villagers and everyone realized the troubadour was much more than he seemed. Hidden in his clothing was a vast array of silver coins, each one small and shining and perfect. There were, in total, five thousand, and when distributed each family got a gleaming handful. The next day somebody gave away a silver coin in return for a small bowl of porridge—because the porridge cooker liked the look of silver so much. The next day two silver coins were traded for a tough old chicken, only good for boiling. And so it went. Silver coins slowly became valuable; people enjoyed holding them and looking at them and passing them greedily through their hands late at night. Thus was born a currency based on silver, and silver had a useful characteristic that had so fatally undermined corn: durability.

Silver was fungible (meaning, one silver coin was like all the rest). You could even divide a silver coin, chop it into little bits, and have the blacksmith melt and repour a complete coin at a later date (he constructed a mold and was happy to do it for a mug of beer). The value of the silver currency didn't fluctuate according to the amount of silver discovered or coming into or leaving the village—demand was all that mattered—and the currency was worth exactly what people were willing to give for it. Sometimes a silver coin was worth ten chickens. Other times it was worth eight. When people starting hoarding silver, a single coin bought fifty chickens. When the coins were passed around like soiled baseball cards, one chicken would suffice. Thus was born a modern commodity-based currency, growing organically out of the economic activity of a village of savvy peasants.

That's it—the evolution of currency from a useful thing to something with symbolic value. It's a nice tale (for everyone except the troubadour), and economists around the world generally accept this theory of currency development as not only canonical but as defining what it means to be a currency in the first place.[14] Currency begins with innate value. If you can eat it, like corn, or it's pretty and fairly useful, like silver in the hands of the jeweler, it has a shot at becoming more than something you trade with.

If you attempt to start a currency with something lacking innate value, this type of natural development (collect/hoard/trade) fails. Progress can't be made. Imagine hoarding deciduous leaves with an eye to trading them later in the year, hoping to get others to go along with your leaf-based currency scheme. You can be sure that in a week or a month nobody will give you anything, not even a tough half-starved chicken, for a leaf or a pile of leaves. Objection to a proposed trade: *What am I supposed to do with a pile of leaves?* Answer: *Trade them to someone else for something you want.* Objection to the answer: *You mean I have to find somebody else as foolish as I've been?* That's where it would end.

Leaves are pretty in the middle of a spectacular autumn, but they make a poor currency. Things with innate value, chock full of the "defining characteristic of currency," are going to win out in the great coinage competition versus leaves or any other common and generally useless alternatives. The standard theory of currency explains the primacy of gold so definitively that it's hard to argue against it. Let's tick off the check boxes: gold is immensely durable, failing to tarnish or rust even when submerged in salt water; it's infinitely dividable and easily remelted into a bigger unit; it's entirely interchangeable, one bit being the same as any other; and finally, due to scarcity, it's easily transportable—if it's not, you're a happy nobleman lugging around heavy canvas sacks stuffed with bullion. In nearly all ways, gold is the perfect commodity-based currency. Whether stamped and coined or used by weight, gold was the "gold standard" for currencies as long as currencies have been around.

This theory was so obvious and clear it required a leap of faith from thousands of people to prove it was wrong, or at least inadequate.

Satoshi proposed the following in a message board post, dated August 27, 2010:

> As a thought experiment, imagine there was a base metal as scarce as gold but with the following properties: boring grey in color, not a good conductor of electricity, not particularly strong but not ductile or easily malleable either, not useful for any practical or ornamental purpose. And—this is the key—one special magical property: it can be transported over a communications channel. . . .
>
> I think the traditional qualifications for money were written with the assumption that there were so many competing objects in the world that are scarce, an object with the automatic bootstrap of intrinsic value will surely win out on those without intrinsic value. But [what] if there was nothing in that world of intrinsic value that could be used as money?[15]

Here Satoshi launches a direct attack on everything we'd been taught about currency. Satoshi puts it bluntly, imagining a perfectly bland anti-gold: boring grey, useless for industry, and without practical or ornamental purpose. Its saving grace? It can be "transported over a communications channel" such as the internet, an ability no other currency (at the time) could claim. If the amount of this easily transportable material is limited by the system, forcing artificial scarceness, Satoshi foresaw something nobody else had imagined. It was infinitely unlikely that a sane person would ever accept leaves as payment for a loaf of bread—and leaves, please note, have a material existence. Yet Satoshi saw it might be possible, even rational, for somebody to hand over not only a loaf of bread but an entire bakery for a virtual handful of a virtual currency called Bitcoin.

It was ludicrous on the face of it. Why would anyone, anywhere, give up something tangible for a digital currency without "innate value," which might evaporate tomorrow due to a random electrical fluctuation? Common sense tells us it's a dotty scheme, the product of an institutionalized economist with dreams of glory. Yet our common sense often waylays us; as discussed in the introduction, we already make this leap of faith, casually, every single day.

Traditional currencies began with silver and gold, but modern currencies have cut any link to the real world. Once the transformation of an object into a fiduciary symbol has begun—once a gold coin is more than simply gold of a certain weight—it's impossible to halt the transformation. First came coins, worth more than their simple weight in material. Then came bank notes, or bank drafts, or bank guarantees, little more than written guarantees of value—so much paid by a bank on such a date or later. Eventually paper currency (backed by gold) arrived, far lighter than metal and easy to fold and carry, and capable of being turned into gold by taking it to a convenient bank. What was the next step? Paper currency *not* backed by gold but by the strength of a governmental promise.

Satoshi, in a rare public pronouncement on February 11, 2009, described his currency criticisms to the P2P foundation message board in this revealing way:

> The root problem with conventional currency is all the trust that's required to make it work. The central bank must be trusted not to debase the currency, but the history of fiat currencies is full of breaches of that trust. Banks must be trusted to hold our money and transfer it electronically, but they lend it out in waves of credit bubbles with barely a fraction in reserve. We have to trust them with our privacy, trust them not to let identity thieves drain our accounts. Their massive overhead costs make micropayments impossible.[16]

The final, fully symbolic stage of currency's evolution is called *fiat* currency and requires complete faith on the part of its users—a faith sometimes misplaced. It's important to look back at an early, canonical example of fiat currency to understand why it developed, why it was considered a useful invention—and why Satoshi thought it so dangerous, requiring a digital currency "solution."

JOHN LAW AND FIAT CURRENCY: *LET IT BE DONE!*

Fiat in Latin means "let it be done," bringing to mind a king lazily leaning over his throne, surfeited from an elaborate feast, issuing the latest of a long series of absurd and arbitrary orders. *Why* should it be done? The king says so, therefore *it is done.* If the king proclaims the color red no longer exists it no longer exists by fiat. A clothing manufacturer could be taken to court for marketing and selling a red tunic—charged with false advertising—because, despite the evidence, red no longer exists in the eyes of the government. In court, that's what matters.

Fiat currency is typically defined as a currency not backed by any solid, real, "innate" stuff of value. No gold, no corn, no beans, not even lowly lead. Fiat currency is currency printed on paper worth, to the untrained eye, exactly as much as a bit of printed paper. The reason it's worth more is because a king or an emperor or the Dauphin or a democratically elected government says it is and everyone had better get used to it. Have faith. Trust us. For many, it sounds like a pretty iffy proposition. Tell people something without value is worth something? Is that all that's required to *create* value? Isn't there deep trickery involved here; isn't it a fundamentally unstable scheme? These are not trivial objections, and the development of fiat currency featured a disastrous early example, which certain segments of the population—the incredibly vocal gold-standard crowd—won't let anyone forget.

It all began in 1671 when John Law, destined to become an economist of legendary creativity, was born in Lauriston Castle.[17] Law, an acknowledged cousin to the Duke of Argyll and Greenwich (through his mother's side), was triply blessed: he had wealth, family, and connections. After a relatively blameless childhood, John Law arrived at maturity with a vengeance, loudly rejecting his family's boring and hugely profitable banking business, instead taking a trip to London where he gambled away much of his inheritance.[18] Pretty soon he gave offence, or took offence, regarding Elizabeth Villiers, Countess of Orkney, the acknowledged mistress of two English kings. A glove was removed and smartly slapped against a closely shaven cheek. Law and his opponent took swords in hand and went to a newly scythed field suitable for such a contest. After a little preparatory back-and-forth, matting the low grass, Law dispatched his opponent in one bloody pass. Law fell afoul of the law and was arrested, thrown into jail, charged with murder, convicted, and sentenced to hang. Things looked dire, but Law soon managed an absurd escape to Amsterdam, allowing the slow-moving English legal system enough time to degrade his murder charge into a simple fine—it *had* been a duel, after all.

Then things got really exciting.

For ten years Law traveled around Europe, writing books on economics and playing cards (successfully) against wealthy merchants and the minor nobility. An eager student of both gambling and human nature, he became spectacularly successful at extracting money from anyone sitting across the table from him. Unlike almost everyone he played against, Law knew how statistics worked and how they applied to cards and dice, and he was capable of complex mathematical calculations on the fly. Law developed a nearly unbeatable statistical style of play, reliant upon probability and wholly independent of "feel" or "intuition," putting him at a serious advantage against everyone else playing in the period. Law won millions and had the good sense not to squander it away in profligate celebration.

As Law grew more wealthy he entertained more lavishly and slowly ingratiated himself with those in power. He wrote books, lectured, and proposed an "outlandish" scheme to create a national Bank of Scotland, which the Scottish parliament politely considered but, ultimately, rejected. Law was rich and successful and had what many would consider a luxurious and enviable life. But he never stopped pushing for new economic schemes, petitioning governments and writing pamphlets and attempting to change what he viewed as calcified and inefficient ways of business into something vastly more productive. His audience listened politely, read his pamphlets, and talked about his books, but few of his economic ideas were put into practice. Theory unapplied is nothing more than speculation, and Law grew increasingly strident in his attempt to inspire economic change and induce large-scale economic experimentation. To little effect: Law continued to win money at the gambling tables and entertain lavishly, but his true intellectual passion was thwarted. Fortunately for Law, and unfortunately for the rest of Europe, the longest-reigning monarch of France was on his death bed.

The Sun King, Louis XIV, died in 1715, leaving the French economy in debt and ruin after a long series of wars and royal extravagance. Upon hearing the news, Law mounted a horse and made his way to the French court as quickly as he could. The Duke of Orleans, now regent of France, knew Law personally and respected his economic theories. The duke was willing to listen to Law's proposals about how to fix France's economy and open-minded enough to grasp what he was saying. Law initially presented a series of proposals for creating a National Bank of France, which would collect taxes, print and control the supply of paper currency, and in general stimulate the anemic French economy, riddled with outdated institutions and hampered by a suspicious and long-suffering public. The Royal Council of Finance, listening with increasing shock, was horrified by what they viewed as Law's outrageous ideas and flatly refused to have anything to do with them.

Law took a few days to ratchet down the originality of his proposal, making it more digestible to the conservatives in power, and came up with something far more modest: he would personally finance and run a "bank of discount," giving out loans based upon drafts, promissory notes, bonds, or other securities (for a reasonable fee). Crucially, his bank would issue notes redeemable by the customer in a fixed rate of coin, a rate that didn't change as the value of coins went up or down. If Law's note said it was worth one hundred coins, then one hundred coins is what you got, even if those coins were worth a lot more than when the note was issued.

Even this modest injection of new banking ideas into the system was welcome, and thanks to the note's fixed coinage value merchants, bankers, and the government itself were soon buying and selling and holding and swapping Law's notes. The public noticed. People liked this new type of paper note, which was always worth a fixed amount of coin, immediately supplied upon request by one of Law's bank branches. Soon Law's bank was prospering and became a symbol for a new way to conduct business. It was time to let go of the old and bring in the new. A year later Law again presented his original proposal before the new king, and this time everyone was on board. The little bank had worked; what could possibly go wrong with a bigger version backed by the state?

It's not clear that anyone knew what they were getting into—except possibly Law. He had spent twenty years thinking about establishing a national bank, and he leaped at the opportunity. He sent specie (gold or silver coins) to the far reaches of the French provinces, followed by new bank notes, which could be instantly redeemed for the newly distributed specie. Merchants and farmers soon discovered they could consistently and safely exchange these notes for coins, which increasingly gave them no reason to do so—it was easier to keep the bank notes. After a few months, transfer of specie inside the country ground to a halt. Despite having only six million in gold reserves, Law was soon issuing sixty million in notes while declaring publicly that any banker issuing more notes than he had gold reserves "deserves death."[19] This was banking as a high-wire act, but a good gambler trusts not only the odds but his understanding of human nature. Since everyone believed in the bank notes, and any minor conversions would be covered by the six million in reserve, the chance that the issuing bank would face a big run on the notes was extremely low—since everyone believed in the bank notes. It was circular, but it was also true. As long as nobody panicked there wasn't any reason to panic. It could continue forever. Law thought the system stable, despite gold being leveraged ten times. *How high could such leveraging go?*

Naturally, Law wanted more. He had waited all his life for such an opportunity and wasn't going to squander it. Law wished to establish not just a national bank but a bank capable of printing the national currency, of collecting and spending tax money, of taking part in monopolistic commercial ventures . . . *everything*. As luck would have it, a French explorer in the unclaimed (by Europeans) interior of North America stumbled across a river "ten miles wide," a slow-moving muddy mass we now call the Mississippi, and spent the next two months happily floating down it to the Gulf of Mexico. He claimed all the land he had passed through, on either side, as property of the French king, and he gave it a name—*Louisiana*. Law immediately saw the beckoning opportunity: why not create a commercial company based on commerce along the Mississippi, from the Gulf of Mexico all the way to the fur-rich Canadian Rockies? The king, who thought Law could do no wrong, made it happen by fiat, and thus was born the Mississippi Company, granted sovereignty over all Louisiana.

Law immediately issued a vast number of company notes (stock) backed by this huge grant of land. Slow to take off despite heavy lobbying by Law, the king, and their various toadies and supporters, early speculators eventually realized small profits, which stimulated a rush to buy more notes, increasing the price, which made the public pay attention and buy, further increasing the price. Soon it was an all-out speculative frenzy. All of Law's plans came to fruition. Everything he touched turned to gold. The economy was booming, and notes were being traded at astronomical values. Merchants purchased villas; coachmen were in a position to hire coachmen. Real estate values spiked, rents soared, and still the Mississippi bubble inflated. Apocryphal stories abounded: Over the course of a few days a humpback man accumulated 150,000 livres by letting out his hump as a writing desk to the brokers in the speculation-besotted Rue Quincampoix.[20] At the opera one night, Mademoiselle de Begond, observing a magnificently dressed lady entering the theater gleaming with an array of thick diamond necklaces, politely asked her mother if that fine woman wasn't, in fact, their cook Mary? Indeed—she had traded in her Mississippi papers and was ready to enter high society.

The king saw it happening and, unwisely but many would argue inevitably, went over Law's head and issued millions of additional notes. The temptation was too great: what better way to pay off the debts of his profligate father than to print notes to pay his creditors? The king wasn't able to resist. Many claim it's absurd to expect any government to resist. If you don't want to tax your subjects but want to give them what they desire, why not print more money? What's the downside?

Law had long ago given up any hope of keeping reserves equal to the outstanding notes for either the national bank or the Mississippi Company. At some point the speculators, grown rich beyond their wildest dreams, began to "cash in" their Mississippi notes for tangible things such as castles, estates, jewels, gold plate, and other grandly material items. They also started sending their wealth to other countries, enriching their relatives or using these investments as a hedge against "something bad happening." This proved prophetic because something bad soon did: The Prince de Conti and the Prince de Conde, aristocrats a bit more clever or suspicious than most, thought things had gone too far and went to John Law's bank with all their outstanding bank notes. They wanted them converted into coin immediately, as promised by the note. Law had enough reserves to cover their demands (barely), but the king was informed of the princes' actions, and he made it clear he wasn't happy with their overt lack of faith in the banking system. A portion of the coin was eventually returned to the bank, and the two princes were given fresh bank notes. But it made people wonder: what's the big deal?

Inflation, already a serious problem, became runaway. There was so much money flowing into the economy that chickens were going for one hundred livres each. Printing presses ran all night to handle the demand for new notes. Things were completely out of control. Soon there was a run on the bank, leading to another run. Law's bank could not supply sufficient specie for paper. Suddenly the Mississippi Company stock bubble popped, and Law's bank went bankrupt. People shook their heads to clear away the mass hysteria and realized the notes in their hands, once worth hundreds of millions of livres, were probably worthless.

Law was a gambler, and every gambler knows there's always a chance, however miniscule. He had one last card to play and he played it, hoping to trump the public panic. Through the king and his own position as controller general, Law abolished coins as a medium of exchange and made it illegal to own gold. He closed the borders, barred travel, and declared that the paper currency of France was the only way to pay for things despite it lacking substantive backing. There was no gold, no specie, and no promised land in Mississippi. This was the true birth of fiat currency: currency declared to have value because the government says it had value. Six months later France was in ruins, paper money was worthless, and Law fled to Italy, a pariah. But Law managed to sneak off with much of his wealth intact—surely not the first banker to ruin a country and, afterward, retire in Venetian luxury.

This exciting, tragic, and horrifying tale is a truncated account of what many economists (and libertarians) consider to be *the* canonical example of fiat currency failure. The lesson to be learned is simple: You can't base a currency on nothing. At some point people will realize it's just paper and ink and will desperately attempt to convert it into something else before everyone else realizes it's worthless as well. When *that* happens, it's over for everyone.

A bit of reflection pokes holes in this foundational tale of over-reach. Yes, it was a terrible thing for John Law to create fiat currency in the way he did, after a disastrous bubble and widespread panic and confiscation of gold and the outlawing of everything sensible, and yes the currency failed . . . but how could it possibly succeed given the circumstances? Did Law's fiat currency fail because it was fiat, or because of the overwrought state of public opinion following Law's recent failures? Was it a crisis of theory or a crisis of trust?

Law became a hated figure in the French popular imagination, spawning foul-minded songs and bawdy tales, as well as endless satir-ical poems, printed in newspapers across the country:

> *The Genealogy of Law's System, and its End*
> Beelzebub begat Law
> Law begat Mississippi,
> Mississippi begat The System,
> The System begat the bank,
> The bank begat the stock,
> The stock begat the dividend,
> The dividend begat the banknote,
> The banknote begat the premium,
> The premium begat the ledger,
> The ledger begat the balance sheet,
> The balance sheet transferred the accounts,
> Until the accounts were all zero.[21]

Satoshi suspected what many economists were slow (or unwilling) to accept: Fiat currency is not a fundamental weakness if the underlying structure is strong and stable. The overall system is what breeds faith, and faith breeds stability, which breeds faith in ever-widening circles. There will always be gold bugs worried about the imminent collapse of the dollar, but these types (while loud) are so much in the minority they don't have an effect on the average American who likes dollars, earns them, spends them, and hoards them. Faith in the dollar is so deep and unthinking that many people don't really understand that the dollar is actually just a scrap of paper—there isn't any there there. What matters is that money works. Can you spend a dollar reliably? Yes. Okay, what's the problem? Move on.

How about Bitcoin? Can you spend a Bitcoin reliably? In general, yes, but the details have far more to do with distributed networks, mathematical hash functions, cryptographic public keys, and the development of entrepreneurial startups than any quasi-philosophical uncertainty about the physical existence of Bitcoin.

What Satoshi knew intuitively, and the market proved with the success of the short-lived alternative currency e-Gold in the first decade of the twenty-first century,[22] is that there existed a deep and as-yet-untapped need for a type of currency designed with the internet in mind. Credit cards were demonstrably a poor solution—sure they worked, but their circa-1950 technology made it easy to defraud the issuing companies, resulting in relatively high charges for every significant transaction and rendering small transactions impossible, as they cost more to process than they were worth. What the internet needed was Satoshi's boring grey currency solution, and since there wasn't anything capable of doing the job in 2009 Bitcoin swept the field. There were no "intrinsic objects" on the internet against which Bitcoin was competing, which like gold might prove more durable or easily divisible. It was the only game in town. If Bitcoin was easy to transmit and scarce (by design), that should be sufficient to get it going.

The problems troubling France during Law's banking reforms would be impossible to duplicate with Bitcoin. There's no Bitcoin King, able to tweak the servers and produce millions of bitcoins on a royal whim. There's no government in control of Bitcoin, either so strong (as in America) it moved off the gold standard with hardly a murmur, or astonishingly weak (as in eighteenth-century France) that it was unable to do anything to reverse looming disaster. Government oversight, once imagined to be a required and necessary attribute for a "real currency," might in fact be a weakness, and lack of such oversight one of Bitcoin's most underappreciated strengths.

At this point there's only one conclusion to draw: classic economic theories about what constitute a currency are wrong. Some economists[23] and pundits (such as Steve Forbes[24]) continue to fight a rearguard action, claiming Bitcoin isn't a real currency because Bitcoin fails to tick various boxes required by their theoretical understanding of currency (such as innate value). This objection is a lot like the one voiced by scientists who argued there must be ether in space because light has to propagate through a medium, and since light obviously strikes the earth ether must exist. What isn't admitted into this circular logic is the idea that light propagates fine in the absence of a medium, or that Bitcoin propagates smoothly in the absence of a physical "medium of exchange."

Give them Bitcoin, and they will come. And spend. And use. And keep. And after a few successful transactions, with everything working as expected, something else might arise: faith.

CHAPTER 2

SATOSHI NAKAMOTO: HOW BITCOIN WORKS

"JUST TELL ME, WHAT'S A BITCOIN?"

"**O**h my God, I get that all the time—*just tell me what's a bitcoin* . . . it's like they're really upset about it. They heard somebody talking about it on some garbage TV show and it looks like the big new thing and they have absolutely no clue. It eats at them; it's like not having the latest gadget or something, and they feel they should understand because they don't want to be left behind. The big fear is of being left behind. People fear that."[1]

The person I'm calling Bobby had written a few energetic and insightful articles about Bitcoin and I'd gotten in touch with him. He was a budding Bitcoin enthusiast doing Bitcoin on the side for local companies who want to "Bitcoin-enable" their businesses (his words, not mine). He didn't want his name used because he isn't always diplomatic about his clients. Bobby lives in California but not in any of the fun places because they cost way too much—again, his words, not mine.

"I had this crazy guy once—he was totally serious. I gave him the whole spiel, he seemed to be really getting it. Really deep. I was like, OK he *gets* it now. When I was done he looked happy and satisfied. But on the way outta the door he stopped and asked, 'So if I'm offline I can't receive any Bitcoins?' I almost lost it. Does that make *any* sense? Then two days later another customer asked the *exact same thing*. Where do these people come from? If you're offline do you suddenly lose the ability to get email? No. No. And no. It's not like your special Bitcoin box is sealed shut with cement until you get back online. How does anyone know you're online anyway? It makes no sense. That's what I'm dealing with. I'm not doing the exciting stuff in new markets, like crazy stuff in Singapore. I'm dealing with people on the ground. And a lot of the time Bitcoin just confuses them."

"How do you try to explain it to them?" I asked.

"I say it's like electronic money. You have an electronic wallet on your computer or phone and buy electronic money for it called bitcoins at Bitcoin exchanges. These you can spend using goofy long addresses. That's where it gets really hard."

"Yeah," I agreed, "That's not an elegant part of the system."

"And they usually want to know about mining. Some of them actually ask if they can mine and get bitcoins that way. I'm like, people, you are so behind the times, that's like four years ago. Maybe five. A generation or two. Why do people even want to know about mining? It's not something they'll ever do. It doesn't matter. It's out of their control. It's like interest rates. Somebody sets them in some way and it matters but you don't really have to know the details to live."

"Isn't it nice to know the details sometimes?"

"It depends on how nice the details are, doesn't it?"

The details matter because a lot of what makes Bitcoin new and interesting is rooted in the details. But it's also true that knowledge of the nitty-gritty isn't required to use or transmit bitcoins; in a similar way, almost nobody understands how the variable valve control system functions in a run-of-the-mill Honda, but it certainly works— letting you fly down the highway more efficiently than was possible twenty years ago. So, in order to simplify without dumbing down, I'll separate my description of Satoshi's invention into three tiers:

Tier 1: Just the basics. You can stop after this if you want, but I wouldn't.
Tier 2: Quite a few interesting details. If you stopped at 1) you'll miss out on the fun.
Tier 3: The whole shebang (within reason). Because you deserve the best.

Before describing these tiers, it's slightly redundant but worthwhile to think about how the world worked prior to Bitcoin, way back in 2009.

To buy something you had three major options:

- Pay in cash
- Pay with a credit card
- Pay with a check

Less frequent options included:

- Cashier's check/Money order
- Wire transfer
- PayPal
- Direct bank involvement for big purchases such as houses, involving loans, mortgages, etc.

Only two of these worked over the internet (PayPal and credit cards), and both required a centralized corporation taking a cut from all transactions. Particularly disturbing to the privacy lobby were corporate demands for personal data. Credit card companies know pretty much everything about their customers—phone numbers, home addresses, buying habits, traveling practices, the list is endless. They gather masses of data and keep it forever. PayPal is notorious for requiring reams of electronic and paper documentation prior to any large transaction, and if your PayPal account finds itself mysteriously frozen you must disgorge more mounds of paperwork to free it. There isn't much expectation of privacy, nor security, as hackers have targeted both PayPal and credit card companies extensively for current customer records and juicy historical data.

What about cash? It has one great advantage. When you pay in cash you don't have to divulge anything about yourself. You hand over the money and they hand you the widget and it's a done deal. Cash has problems though: it's relatively easy to steal, hard to transport in large amounts, dangerous to use (in some cases), and certainly annoying to keep replenished.

Bitcoin has been described as e-Cash because it attempts to replicate cash's best feature—its ability to pay for things anonymously without questions being asked or private data being revealed, making an end run around major privacy concerns regarding data mining, theft of customer data, etc.

With this in mind, let's begin.

TIER 1: MAKING IT WORK

Bitcoin uses e-wallets to store bitcoins. An e-wallet can be placed on your computer, phone, or other device; typically e-wallets are installed and run as small applications, secured by passwords or pass phrases of more than usual length and strength.

After an e-wallet has been installed, you are officially able to start receiving bitcoins.

Like normal cash, you can only do four things with bitcoins: keep them, receive them, spend them, or lose them (by forgetting your password or dropping your phone into a lake).

To spend bitcoins, you have to tell the Bitcoin system which user is going to receive your bitcoins. If you were paying in cash this would be the person on the other side of the sales counter, but in the world of Bitcoin there isn't any face-to-face. Instead of a direct physical transfer of cash, Bitcoin uses a long and ugly-looking string of numbers and letters, which acts as an address for Bitcoin users. You can't choose this value, picking something memorable such as MyBitcoinAddress4You2SendMoney2. Instead, it's generated by a mathematical function linked to your e-wallet, and since these sorts of functions don't care about aesthetics or the English language the results often look like this:

1Gpp38Da4kphbgsmMXbRaS95sSmytBeDYq.[2]

This sort of gobbledygook is unfortunately the norm. If you were purchasing a tin of biscuits from your friend Samantha for .001 BTC (BTC = bitcoin), you would go to your e-wallet, select the "send" function, and enter Samantha's bitcoin address. (Let's pretend it's

1Gpp38Da4kphbgsmMXbRaS95sSmytBeDYq.) You would also enter the amount of Bitcoin you wish to send (.001 BTC), and after that you hit SEND.

The transaction is transmitted over the Bitcoin network and all sorts of complicated things occur, including sending a notification to Samantha's e-wallet. The next time Samantha logs in she notices that .001 BTC has been added to her total. And the next time you visit her, she'll hand you the biscuit tin since you paid her .001 BTC as promised.

The simplest possible evolution from Bitcoin newbie to active user goes something like this:

- Desiree, who has never used Bitcoin before, installs a respected e-wallet (there are many). These wallets are generally free (see https://bitcoin.org/en/choose-your-wallet for a reasonable selection). When using a free wallet, Desiree is able to spend and receive bitcoins without cost; the wallet software does not take a "percentage" of every transaction. Many of the best and most secure Bitcoin wallets are both free and open source.
- Desiree hits INCOMING or REQUEST or a similar button in her e-wallet, and it generates a Bitcoin address specific to her e-wallet. This is how people send her bitcoins. She gives this long ugly address to her friend Igor.
- Igor, a longtime user of Bitcoin, sends .05 BTC to her address just for fun. If Desiree didn't have a friend like Igor gifting her bitcoins, she would have to go to a Bitcoin exchange and "purchase" bitcoins using real-world currency.[3]
- .05 BTC appears in Desiree's wallet.
- A few days later, Samantha gives Desiree her Bitcoin address.
- Desiree copies Samantha's Bitcoin address into her wallet's destination field, enters .001 BTC for the amount, and hits SEND.
- Desiree is now part of the Bitcoin community. She has received and sent bitcoins.

Desiree doesn't care about block chains, Bitcoin mining, hash functions, or other obscure details. A Bitcoin wallet can be thought of as a simplistic email program, sending bitcoins instead of messages.

When sending an email you enter an email address,[4] type a message, and hit send.

With a Bitcoin wallet you enter a Bitcoin address, how much you are sending, and hit send. That's it.

Most people don't know how email works, the incoming and outgoing protocols, the handshaking between servers and routers, the path the email travels across the network . . . but everyone uses email. Bitcoin wallets don't have to be treated differently—although if you keep large amounts of bitcoins in an e-wallet you should have a backup of the wallet (or two) kept in a safe location, such as a bank's safety deposit box, and strict security protocols, ensuring you can access your bitcoins even if your phone, computer, or whatever is lost or stolen.

The tricky part isn't setting up an e-wallet (no email or personal information is required), nor spending bitcoins once you have them. It's getting bitcoins in the first place. You can't, yet,[5] buy bitcoins using a credit card in the United States or Canada. You must use a Bitcoin exchange and a bank transfer, personal check, money order, or something else even more inconvenient. Whatever method you use, it usually takes a few days for the order to be processed, which means that the fastest and most technologically advanced method for instantly and securely sending money to anyone on Earth exemplifies—given the difficulty of purchasing bitcoins at an exchange— the reasons forcing it into existence. Why is it so hard, in this day and age, to extract your own money from a bank and have it transferred to another bank or merchant without a) paying high fees, b) visiting the bank in person, and c) waiting almost a week?[6]

Compare the difficulty of sending ten cents to a pal across town to the ease of emailing a friend in Berlin a PDF of all the religious writings of Leo Tolstoy. For the average consumer, working with small amounts of money, the banking system crawls along at a leisurely nineteenth-century pace.

TIER 2: DIGGING A LITTLE DEEPER

Tier 1 was essentially a functional description of how to use a Bitcoin e-wallet and didn't cover any of the exciting developments that went into making Bitcoin such an improbable success. Tier 2 fixes this.

Let's begin by reviewing how modern fiat currencies work: Paper currency is distributed by the government (let's not quibble about the semi-private Federal Reserve), and it's backed and guaranteed by the government. Legal and civil penalties for counterfeiting are unforgiving. The government prints the money, collects it, burns it when it's old and worn out, and ensures a consistent supply. The number printed on the paper currency indicates its value and that's that.

Bitcoin is far stranger. To see this starkly displayed, let's consider a thought experiment involving a small island nation consisting of ten energetic souls. Because they grew tired of carrying around hairy coconuts as currency, they decided to give another system a try. They set up a large chalkboard in the middle of their little village and balanced it on stilts so it could be seen from twenty or thirty feet away. The ten villagers' names are written on the chalkboard, along with a number next to each name. This number is the amount of virtual coconuts (VCNs) "owned" by each villager. When Judy goes fishing and afterward sells fish to Joe, she shouts out "Joe gave 1 VCN to Judy" and somebody hears, goes up to the board, and changes Judy's number from 11 to 12, and Joe's from 1 to 0. If Joe tries to buy something, people casually glance at the big board, notice Joe has no VCNs, and say, politely, *sorry, buddy.*

Look what's happening here. Coconuts have been replaced, entirely, by something that's "not real" (i.e., numbers on a board). And this doesn't bother anyone in the slightest because coconuts were themselves, clearly, just a way of keeping track of things, no different than a tally but much heavier. No government is involved in this new system. The chalkboard is visible to all and modified by all. Everyone is responsible for changing the values when somebody shouts a change should be made, and since it's in clear sight nobody can change values on the sly. If somebody were to sneak up with chalk in hand, ready to add 100 to their total, and nobody had shouted that such a change should be made . . . well, it would be noticed and stopped. Somebody in the village, somewhere, would see and complain.

What traditional economic textbooks rejected as an impossible concept, yet Satoshi believed, was that a currency consisting of corn is more inconvenient than a currency consisting of gold which is more inconvenient than a currency consisting of paper which is more inconvenient than a currency consisting of a small plastic card which is more inconvenient than a currency without any material component whatsoever. Because without something tangible to steal, it can't be stolen.[7] Without something tangible to lose, it can't be lost. Who likes the feeling of a wallet thick with icky, dirty stained one and ten dollar bills? Who enjoys jangling a pocketful of coins, throbbing with germs, to be thrown into a can and ignored until a poker game rolls around or a usurious change machine at the grocery store tempts or you happen to be someplace where the nuisance can be turned into something less annoying? Who likes giving their entire financial history to a credit card company and one's name / phone number/etc. to every inquiring merchant?

A "perfect" currency would do the following: magically keep track of how much currency everyone has, modify these amounts when things are bought or sold, and ensure nobody spends what's not rightfully theirs. Because magic isn't reliable, Satoshi came up with the next best thing: a public ledger. Nobody needs to carry around anything. Just look at the ledger to see if your customer has enough money to make a purchase, and if so alter the public ledger after something is bought or sold. Because everything is done in public, changes to the ledger are heavily scrutinized, and if a merchant tries to charge more than was agreed-upon, or a customer attempts to weasel out of paying, it will be noticed.

Let's return to our village's tall chalkboard. The system worked great when the village was small, but warm weather, nonexistent disease, and fruitful natives caused the island's population to explode. A single chalkboard no longer cut it. Soon there were twenty villages scattered across the island, and hundreds of villagers. How could they keep the VCN currency viable? Barring a vast overhead chalkboard floating in the sky, marked using mile-long sticks topped by neon-colored chalk, the present system couldn't possibly work.

Somebody proposed a slight variation to the system: Instead of one big chalkboard, everyone carries around a small personal chalkboard. Each time a villager passes another villager, they make sure to look at each other's personal chalkboards and ensure the two match. If one villager writes down a transaction ("Joe gives Mary 1 VCN") unrecorded by the other villager, the transaction is quickly added to the deficient chalkboard. The two villagers shake hands and continue on their merry way.

The island dwellers began each day with synchronized chalkboards. After they wake and start moving around and interacting with each other, purchases and sales (transactions) impact the villager's personal chalkboards in ripples. Imagine what happens when Bill, on the eastern end of the isle, buys a canoe from Bathsheba. ("Bill gives Bathsheba 100 VCNs" is written on his personal chalkboard in his own hand). Bathsheba writes the new message on her chalkboard as well, since Bill's chalkboard no longer matches hers. Initially, the transaction only exists on Bill and Bathsheba's chalkboards, but as they walk around they meet other villagers who add the transaction to their personal chalkboards, "rippling out" the news of Bill's big purchase. The transaction continues to spread as villagers talk and interact, and it passes, like a germ, through the population until even those living in the far western edge of the island record the news (through meetings at lunch, random encounters in the forest, etc.). At the end of the day the villagers come together for dinner and have a great reckoning, and everyone makes sure everyone's chalkboards match. The next day, they'll do it all over again.[8]

In a simplified form, this is how the Bitcoin network operates. Replace the island dwellers with computer servers, their personal chalkboards with ledgers, and instead of slowly walking and talking they are linked using the internet and communicating at a non-trivial fraction of the speed of light.

Bitcoin is based upon a public ledger, recording *all bitcoin transactions ever made from the first to the last.* It distributes this ledger to all the Bitcoin servers involved in processing transactions. When you send two cents' worth of Bitcoin to your pal, the transaction is recorded in the public ledger and it will be listed there forever—or at least until Bitcoin fails or we run out of electricity.[9] There might be, for example, one thousand Bitcoin ledgers residing in one thousand servers spread all over the globe; each ledger is 99.999999 percent the same, with the only differences occurring in the most recent entries. When somebody creates a bitcoin transaction, it's initially a single Bitcoin server (called a "node"), which adds the new transaction to its ledger. This node, Node 1, is in constant communication with a lot of other Bitcoin nodes, and quickly informs them that a new transaction has been added to its ledger. Node 2 looks at Node 1's ledger, sees the new transaction, and copies it because that's what nodes do. They compare ledgers and copy new transactions. Bitcoin transactions ripple across the network. Node 2 talks to Node 97 and Node 56 a few milliseconds later, and they see the new transaction on Node 2's ledger. They copy it as well. Pretty soon the new transaction has propagated through all the Bitcoin nodes, spreading like a wave, and within minutes all the servers in the world have a copy of the transaction on their ledgers.[10]

Before Node 1 even thinks about adding a new transaction to its public ledger, much less telling the world about it, Node 1 runs a few basic tests. First, every Bitcoin transaction must have an *input*, an *output*, and a *bitcoin amount*. The input proves that the transaction originator has bitcoins to spend. The output has to be a legal Bitcoin address. The bitcoin amount is the amount of bitcoin to be transferred.

Let's pretend Lester wants to send Miranda five bitcoins. He goes to his e-wallet, inputs the amount to send and Miranda's address, and hits "send." Lester's e-wallet creates a Bitcoin transaction with an input = 5.6 bitcoins, an output = Miranda's Bitcoin address, with the amount to be transferred = 5 bitcoins. (It's often the case that the input doesn't exactly match the amount to be transferred).[11]

Node 1 receives Lester's transaction, and the first thing it checks is whether Lester has five or more bitcoins to spend. How can it verify this? In the real world, the amount of currency somebody has is the amount they have on hand. We have to trust it isn't counterfeit, and we have to trust it wasn't used in a recent drug sale, resulting in it being (later) seized. It's not a great way to do things but it's what we're used to. Bitcoin solves the counterfeit/verification problem in an extremely elegant and foolproof manner.

Question: how many bitcoins does Lester have? Answer: Lester has exactly as many bitcoins as he ever received minus all the bitcoins he ever spent. Bitcoin (in effect) searches the entire transaction record from Day 1, from the so-called "Genesis" block to the most current record, and adds up Lester's incoming and outgoing expenses. Over the course of a lifetime Lester might have received 256 transactions totaling 500 BTC, and sent out 128 transactions, totaling 450 BTC. His current balance is therefore (500 BTC incoming – 450 BTC outgoing = 50 BTC). Yes, he can send 5 BTC to Miranda, since 5 < 50. He's got it. That part's legal.

Assuming Miranda has a valid Bitcoin address (and why would she lie about it?), the transaction proves to Node 1 that Lester has at least 5 BTC by pointing to some of Lester's unspent incoming transaction records on the public ledger totaling at least 5 BTC. This proof consists of three incoming transactions, such as 1.2 BTC incoming, 2.6 BTC incoming, and 1.8 BTC incoming (1.2 + 2.6 + 1.8 = 5.6). His e-wallet transaction wraps up this evidence of Lester's ability to pay and sends 5 BTC to Miranda, automatically remitting the remainder (5.6 – 5 =.6 BTC) back to Lester as a secondary Bitcoin transaction.

It seems obvious that any digital currency would be vulnerable to the sort of copy/paste piracy that occurred when file sharing was new and exciting and caused the music industry so much agony. If you have one bitcoin, why not copy it to create two bitcoins? Nothing could be easier! Satoshi got around the issue of "duplication" or "counterfeiting" of Bitcoin in a subtle way. Nobody is capable of copying bitcoins because nobody really *owns* bitcoins. Although Lester is allowed to send five bitcoins to Miranda, the five bitcoins he sent never truly resided in Lester's e-wallet, nor will the transmitted bitcoins ever get shoved in Miranda's e-wallet. Lester instead *transferred the right of ownership* of five bitcoins to Miranda via the public ledger. He essentially told the network, "I had a right to send five bitcoins, and I have proved it, and I now transfer their ownership rights to Miranda."

Bitcoin is, at base, a currency consisting of rights transferal. It's even more ethereal than most people realize: not only isn't Bitcoin a thing, it's not even a computerized duplication or translation or representation of a thing (such as an MP3 version of a song, or a JPEG of a photo). Bitcoin isn't a highly encoded, cryptographically secure, password-protected super cookie sitting on your hard drive ready to be spent; bitcoin ownership is nothing more or less than having the right to move numbers around in the Bitcoin public ledger and transferring that right to another party.

This might sound mysterious, but it's not much different from what we experience every day and accept without demurral. If you own a small company and hire a new employee, you grant the newcomer a large suite of "rights" not shared by members of the public at large. An employee can't be charged with trespassing for walking through property owned by the business during working hours; an employee has the right to a safe work environment and pay equal to or above the minimum wage; an employee has the right to work the cash register and handle money in the name of the business without fear of being charged with attempted robbery, etc. These rights are social and legal and, while real, are not something the employee can arbitrarily "duplicate" and transfer to a friend. These rights can be given up by leaving the job, or extended to other people by quitting and allowing the new person to take over the position, but in no meaningful way are these rights ever embodied in material form. Employment contracts can be burned or lost without suddenly destroying these rights; it's easy enough for an employee to prove he's an employee even in the absence of paperwork, given a suitable historical record.

Bitcoin works in much the same way. You prove you own ten bitcoins by pointing to the public record and showing where ten bitcoins were credited to your account in the past, while proving, at the same time, you haven't yet spent those ten bitcoins. This would be a daunting task for a human accountant but the sort of thing modern computers do so efficiently it's nearly instantaneous. It boils down to this: you can't counterfeit or copy what you never own. Lack of material substance is, occasionally, a positive benefit.

TIER 3: IS BITCOIN SECURE?

Leaving analogies behind, Bitcoin can be thought of as a distributed (peer-to-peer) public ledger leveraging block-chain technology to secure transactions and using public/private key cryptography to verify users (not, as you might think, to hide transmission information). In the world of Bitcoin the public ledger is called a "block chain" because one block of ledger transactions is linked to the next block of ledger transactions by means of rigorously one-way cryptographic hash functions featuring robust avalanche triggers. I'm not sure this description explains more than it obscures, but to supply every detail elided or omitted from the Tier 1 and Tier 2 discussions would be a book in itself; for an interesting Bitcoin overview, Satoshi's original white paper, "Bitcoin: A Peer-to-Peer Electronic Cash System," is an excellent starting point.[12]

I will, however, attempt to summarize the overall security scheme, which was one of Satoshi's crucial technological breakthroughs.

The most straightforward part of Bitcoin is the e-wallet security system. Most e-wallets are password or passcode protected, which not only stops an unauthorized intruder from opening the wallet but also encrypts the wallet data itself. If an encrypted wallet is stolen (a thief gets his grubby hands on your phone or computer), it won't do him any good because the wallet data is garbage without a valid password. It would take a hacker hundreds of years to crack the code. This is the first and most commonsensical way an e-wallet is secured and it's no different than the way you secure your online bank or email account. Pick a strong password and don't forget it![13]

The second security measure involves the strange, ugly, and impossible-to-remember Bitcoin address associated with the e-wallet (and created by the e-wallet), an alphanumeric string such as 1Gpp38Da4kphbgsmMXbRaS95sSmytBeDYq that is one half of a public/private key combination, the basic building block of internet security.

To explain public/private keys while avoiding unnecessary technological baggage, imagine hopping into a time machine and returning to 1790 and living the rollicking life of a wealthy London merchant. One morning you buy an iron-bound treasure chest with an amazingly intricate lock. Like the rest of the box, the lock mechanism is rectangular, wide, long, and utterly bullet-proof. The strangest feature of the lock is the fact that it has two escutcheons for two differently shaped keyholes. The seller hands you two extravagantly ornate keys and shows you how the lock works. He puts the first key into one of the holes and gives it a turn; turning it alters the tumblers of the second lock. He puts the second key in the keyhole and turns it; the lid pops open. To relock the box securely you must use both keys in any order, turning them in the opposite direction used for opening (functioning like a modern front door bolt lock, which requires a key to both open and secure).

One peculiar property of the chest is that you can give away one of the keys, even the chest itself, and not have to worry about somebody trying to ferret out the missing key shape. If a money-loving spy takes one of the keys and gets hold of the chest and inserts the key and turns it, he still has to figure out how the first key turn altered the tumblers of the second key, whose movement is wholly invisible from the outside. To pick a typical lock, a thief hears or senses when the internal mechanism slightly shifts as various options are tried and progress is slowly made. Because it's possible to tell when a lock pick attempt is closer or farther from successfully opening the lock, a solution is methodically approached through trial and error, eventually ferreting out the correct key shape. This isn't possible with a two-key lock given the complexity of the mechanism and a complete lack of feedback. This forces a putative thief to try every possible key shape for the second lock, and since this would require billions of keys and an endless amount of time the thief gives up.

Next, imagine the chest's owner had a functioning philosopher's stone and wishes to share its secret with a distant brother. To accomplish this, he mails his brother one of the two keys associated with the chest and informs him, in the accompanying letter, "I'm shipping a closed and locked double-key chest, and if this key opens the chest it's from me." He places the philosopher's stone in the treasure chest, closes it, locks it with both keys, and then (strangely) turns one key backward, unlocking the box halfway and removing the key. The other key, which hadn't been turned backward, is the one removed and mailed to his brother. After the chest is shipped and received, his brother can be confident in the chest's origins even if it gets mixed up with a hundred other chests during the long sea voyage. How is this possible?

It's time to limber up our logical muscles and figure out what's going on. It's not immediately obvious why a double-locked box is worth making a fuss about in the first place. Let's think about what happens when the chest owner's brother receives a key in the mail and is told when a ship will arrive with a matching chest. On the appointed day the brother wanders through the delivering ship's cargo bay and attempts to open, with the key his brother had mailed, each of the hundred chests he finds there. After sixty-one failures he suddenly hears a click and the chest, securely closed a moment before, opens under his hand.

Note that the double lock *isn't* a method to keep the philosopher's stone safe from thieves. A thief could have intercepted, duplicated, and forwarded the distant brother's key as it was sent through the public mail, hopped onto the cargo ship, and casually opened the chest mid-transit. Because the thief had the second key, and the first brother used his key on the chest already, the thief would be able to open the chest and steal the loot.

The possibly counterintuitive point of the two-key system isn't to keep the chest contents secure, but to ensure that if a *locked and unopened* chest arrives, and the delivered key opens the strange two-key lock, the contents *must have originated from his brother.*

Why is this true?

A thief might duplicate the mailed key and steal the contents of the chest in transit, in which case . . . well, that's too bad. The philosopher's stone goes missing. But there isn't any way for a thief to replace the philosopher's stone with a fake and relock the chest because *both keys* are required to lock the chest. The chest was half-unlocked before it was sent, and when it was initially locked the first brother had to use both keys. The only way for a thief to replace the contents of the chest and relock it and send it on its way, duping the sap on the other end, is to figure out the shape of the first key, have access to the second key, and use both to relock the chest (and afterward half-unlock it). This runs into the same problem as picking the lock; fabricating a key to lock the chest is equivalent to fabricating a key to unlock the chest, and both are impossible.

Thus, if you don't have both keys you can only *open the chest once.* If you open it and try to get it back into its half-unlocked state without using both keys, you're out of luck. This means, in effect, that any locked unopened chest opened using the mailed key *must* have come from the original sender. It's also true that an *opened* chest might have come from his brother, but we can't be sure the contents were left unaltered. And if the brother receives a chest that doesn't open at all: well, that's certainly been tampered with—either the lock's been broken or the mailed key mangled or something sneaky is going on. Much can go wrong, and only one thing can go right, but it's sufficient. We are guaranteed that a locked chest, opened using the mailed key, must have come from the person who initially locked the chest using both keys. It's not a great result, but it's enough.

This scheme is at the center of the security solution for the e-wallet problem. Let's imagine it in action: Alexander H. has a fresh e-wallet with a freshly generated Bitcoin address. His e-wallet is essentially a strong chest locked by two extremely long and involved keys. Alexander's first key (called a *private key*) is stored (in encrypted form) in the depths of the e-wallet, unseen by Alexander or anyone else (it's hoped). Only the e-wallet accesses and uses it. The second key (called the *public key*) is not a secret. It's extremely public; in fact it's essentially Alexander's Bitcoin address (the long string of letters and numbers used to send him bitcoins).

When Alexander sends George 10 BTC, his e-wallet uses something called a cryptographic hash function to take the transaction message, summarized below, and transform it into nonsensical code.

The simplified Bitcoin transaction message before being transformed (written in English):

Input: {Points to the Block Chain, which proves Alexander has bitcoins, whose sum is typically > 10BTC}
Destination: George's long Bitcoin Address
Amount: 10 BTC
Return transaction: Sends change back to Alexander

After going through a cryptographic hash function (a process called hashing), it looks like this:

3044022010336586f19b8e637ca7e81b86fa41495a419a8ad7f2dd
cf1adfce0a2ac4af3502206c2012195fe44dc8a54598e35fd1a47c94
10aa561f93a84aa143d4e4ff5f600501034d1e0b5eaf1e1b9be1cee
6a65f5155d97834a2112537496a6ce53b03abf19c2r

Bitcoin requires the transaction text and the values associated with it to be in English in order to process the transaction. The beauty of the cryptographic hash function used to encode transactions is that, like the duel-keyhole treasure chest, it accepts two keys (or function inputs). Either key can be applied to the locking function in any order, but they both must be known and used to encrypt and decrypt the message. Attempting to hack the keys would take, according to the most optimistic estimates, a few hundred years, and would require the entire planet's computing power working 24/7. It's the definition of not worth it.

Bitcoin receives Alexander's horrible-looking encoded sequence, which claims it's coming from the e-wallet associated with Alexander's Bitcoin address. Bitcoin says fine, let's check. It attempts to use the e-wallet's public address as a key to unlock the message. If Alexander's e-wallet used two keys to encrypt the message with a hash function, and partially unlocked the message using its private key prior to transmission, Alexander's second key (the public one) will successfully decrypt the transmitted mush into readable text.

If the public key transforms the code into a valid Bitcoin transaction message it must, therefore, be a valid message originating from Alexander's e-wallet. A hashed message is essentially equivalent to the double-locked treasure chest sent from brother to brother, the private key half-unlocking the chest before sending it, with the public key sent via mail and arriving well before the chest.

Wait a second. The public key is public, right? Yes. The transaction is going, half-encrypted, over the public internet, right? Yes. A nasty low-life thug of a thief could intercept the message, use the public key, decrypt the message, and see the transaction information, couldn't they? Yes.

It's naughty, but not that naughty. After all, the transaction is going to be posted on a public ledger and made visible to everyone for all eternity as soon as Bitcoin gets hold of it, so somebody reading it ahead of time is a bit pointless. If the transaction is intercepted and destroyed and never gets to the Bitcoin system at all, Alexander's e-wallet will soon realize it and try sending it again. Nothing too damaging has occurred.

What if the thief is smart? Instead of reading the transaction message and passing it along to the Bitcoin network, he alters it in precisely the spot he most cares about. He replaces "**Destination**: George's Bitcoin Address" with the obvious "**Destination**: Thief's Bitcoin Address."

Ha! The thief sends this clever message off to Bitcoin, which immediately rejects it. Why? Bitcoin attempts to use Alexander's e-wallet's public key on the now-unencrypted message, resulting in pure garbage. Before the thief got the message and decrypted it, it was encrypted. Messages going to Bitcoin should be encrypted. Any unencrypted messages are used as digital toilet paper.

What if the thief, thinking himself witty, re-encrypts the altered message before sending it off? That would be splendid. It's what the thief *should* do. But it's impossible; that's the whole point of the public/ private key combinations. To re-encrypt a message after changing the message (even a little bit) requires both of Alexander's public and private keys; attempts to brute-force a solution, generating coded output that will decrypt into a valid transaction message after applying the public key, is equivalent to discovering the private key, which is designed to be all-but-impossible to counterfeit. It's possible to get lucky and randomly produce such an encoding on the first try, but this is roughly equivalent to the chance that one individual will win every lottery in the world for ten years straight in an uninterrupted sequence. It's so unlikely it's mathematically equivalent to zero.

This public/private key system ensures that when Bitcoin receives a transaction from an e-wallet, and uses that e-wallet's public key to decrypt it, and thereafter gets a coherent message, Bitcoin *knows it originated from the e-wallet in question.* It's a valid transaction, not a thief trying some funny business. Bitcoin adds the transaction to the public ledger.[14]

The public/private key system ensures you can't counterfeit bitcoins; you can't force spurious transactions to be accepted; there isn't any way to hack or break the system once a message is sent from an e-wallet. The greatest point of vulnerability is the e-wallet itself—the obvious danger of having somebody use it in your place. If somebody steals your phone and wiggles it before the screen lock is activated, and if your bitcoin wallet isn't secured by a password, the thief can open your wallet application and send any bitcoins associated with it to whomever desired. There isn't anything anyone can do to reverse such transactions.

Buying something in the real world using cash involves a face-to-face interaction. Not Bitcoin. There aren't any after-the-fact memories of a purchaser from a seller unless a shipping address is involved. If there's a dispute after bitcoins have been transmitted, one of the party's out of luck. No force on earth, persuasive or threatening, backed by the plenipotentiary power of the world's governments with a papal bull in the back pocket (just to be sure), is able to wrest a spent bitcoin off the network and return it to an e-wallet. Similarly, bitcoins associated with a lost/corrupted/encrypted (using a forgotten password) e-wallet are forever lost to the system; these bitcoins, which exist on the public ledger, can't be spent because the e-wallet no longer exists that can prove it "owns the right" to them.

Unlike fiat currency, there's an upper limit to the number of new bitcoins that can be generated, as determined by Satoshi's code. Once that number is hit (21 million), it's over. Any bitcoins "lost" after this total is reached, due to e-wallet errors or failures, will forever reduce the amount of currency available in the system. It's the exact same thing that would occur should the government suddenly stop printing/replacing paper money. The overall total would suffer a steady decline as cash is accidently burned, spindled into unrecognizable form, obscured by fabric dye, lost in plane crashes, or drowned in salt water.[15]

The Block Chain, Mining, & Proof of Work

Years ago, when I was a Bitcoin newbie and web resources were still pretty sketchy, an enthusiastic gentleman I'm calling BC_Acolyte introduced me to the concept of the block chain.

BC_Acolyte: "The block chain's really what's important. All the other stuff is fluff. The block chain is the backbone. Bitcoin should be called the **B**lock**C**hain coin. The **B** and **C** that matter are the Block Chain. It's a solution to a problem. Real thinking went into it. The rest of Bitcoin is obvious."[16]

Me: "I think all of Bitcoin's pretty complicated."

BC_Acolyte: "The block chain's what's really cool. Nothing else matters. Who cares about wallets and transfers over the internet? People have been doing stuff like that for ages. What's new is the block chain."

Me: "I've not been doing it for ages."

BC_Acolyte: "You buy shit with credit cards and you buy shit with whatever. Every site on Earth has a stupid little icon of a shopping cart and you put icons of things in there and you pay for it and it's sent to a horrible hole in Texas where they wrap it up and mail it and then you have your new book or piece of fruit or whatever it was you bought."

Me: "I've never bought fruit over the internet."

BC_Acolyte: "That's not the *point*, the *point* is that that sort of thing is *boring*. Ever heard of E-gold? They did the same stuff for a decade before they were regulated out of business. It's not gold, it's E-gold. Go to a site and spend E-gold not dollars. It's been done. That's the boring part."

Me: "What's the non-boring part?"

BC_Acolyte: "The block chain. The block chain's going to be bigger than the internet."

Me: "C'mon. The internet changed everything. I read that in *Time* magazine at least ten years ago. It put the yellow pages out of business, as well as local newspapers and a lot of porn shops. And it let us see a lot of cat videos, right?"

BC_Acolyte: "Puh."

Me: "How can the block chain be bigger than the internet when the block chain requires the internet?"

BC_Acolyte: "How can a book be bigger than the invention of paper?"

Me: "The invention of paper allowed for the book."

BC_Acolyte: "True. Paper enabled further development. A book takes paper's world-wide transformative power and blows it sky-high. Paper's blank, dude. The internet's a bunch of wires and cables and routers and servers. Nothing there, really. The block chain's forever."

Me: "?"

BC_Acolyte: "The block chain is *real.*"

So I read up on the block chain and I read up on Bitcoin mining. The block chain is what locks up transactions, and the block chain is what miners secure when they are busy mining for bitcoins in modern Icelandic server farms, where hundreds of high-end computers fitted with the most efficient hardware work furiously to solve a difficult mathematical question: what number do you have to input into a randomizing cryptographic hash function in order to get a solution beginning with a certain number of zeroes, such as 00000000000000015ae8d6b73ea1f89241c90bb9bfe01de56397fa2c-7cd35c2?

The number of zeroes at the beginning of the solution is called the Bitcoin difficulty level, and back in the good old days it was a very small number, like one. Meaning that a solution such as 015ae8d-6b73ea1f89241c90bb9bfe01de56397fa2c7cd35c2c90bb9bfe01de5 would have qualified, since it starts with one zero. These days the difficulty level is sixteen zeroes, which takes not sixteen times as long to find one zero, but a period ramping up geometrically.

When Bitcoin was a baby, a few months old, the difficulty level was one because few people were trying to solve the hash problem, and there wasn't any specialized mining hardware around. If the problem was too difficult, nobody would ever find a solution, leaving the Bitcoin network completely stymied.

These days, Bitcoin miners, taken as a whole, represent the greatest concentration of computing power the world has ever seen. If the hash solution only required one zero, they would be solving the mining problem thousands of times a second. That's way too much. Bitcoin likes solutions, but not too many and not too fast, so it continually adjusts the rate of difficulty to ensure solutions are found at constant and relatively consistent intervals. If you decide to become a Bitcoin miner (which at this point requires millions of dollars of startup capital), you are not competing "against" the Bitcoin network to mine bitcoins. The number of bitcoins the network issues is stable.

You are instead competing against all the other miners out there because if any of them solve the mining problem before you do all your effort has been wasted. *They* get the bitcoin reward, and *you* have to start a new problem looking for a new solution.

What, exactly, is being "solved?" What does it mean to say somebody "mined a bitcoin"? What's the point of it? What does any of it have to do with digital currency?

The block chain is a fancy term for the public ledger previously discussed, which lists all the transactions Bitcoin ever made (Joe gives 1.04 bitcoins to Mary, etc.). Instead of putting these transactions into one big document, growing day-to-day as people send and receive bitcoins, it's broken up into a chain of transactions.

Transactions are chunked into blocks, varying in size but usually hovering around one thousand transactions, and a cryptographic hash function is applied to the transaction block. We've seen this function before, when e-wallets were secured using public and private keys. It's the same sort of function, but as input Bitcoin uses 1) the text of the block of transactions, and 2) another string of data, which is being "dug" out of the probabilistic soil by enterprising miners. After plugging these two keys into the hash function, a valid solution (hash result) is a number starting with a certain number of zeroes, currently set at sixteen.

Finding such a solution essentially secures a block of transactions. How? Let's imagine there are a hundred transactions in a given block ("Les gives .0034 bitcoins to Louis," "Bertie gives 1,004 bitcoins to Sally," etc.). The text of these transactions is fed into the hash function as an input—the entire block. The hash function needs two inputs in order to produce a result, so another string of text is created at random, used as the second input, and the hash function run. A number pops out. Most of the time this result will be a random number that, crucially, does not begin with a long sequence of zeroes, such as 000000000042809366. More likely, it will look like a typical randomized sequence: 943165027305916723 48. Now, it's possible to change the second input (keeping the transaction text input the same) and run the hash function again, generating a new result. This process can be repeated millions of times, with each unique second input giving rise to a unique hash result. If you happen to stumble upon a second input generating a solution starting with, say, sixteen zeroes… you've achieved something. Finding these types of solutions is what Bitcoin mining is all about.

The reason this secures the block is that the miner can publish to the world both the Bitcoin transaction block (used as input 1) and the solution string (used as input 2) and show, trivially, that the hashed result gives a number starting with sixteen zeroes. The solution string "locks" the transaction block, because any alteration to the transaction text, even changing one letter, will alter the hash output and ruin the sixteen-zero solution. If a thief wants to alter the transaction block and assign himself some bitcoins (illegally), the thief would also have to produce a solution to the altered transaction block that begins with sixteen zeroes. And that's really hard to do; Bitcoin miners the world over are working on the problem continuously, and it requires ten minutes (on average) of their combined effort to come up with a solution. A solitary thief hasn't got a chance. Because Bitcoin mining uses a well-designed and well-tested hash function, there simply isn't any way to "solve" the problem except by plugging in lots of numbers and seeing what works. This might not sound like much of an accomplishment, but if you manage the difficult task you are issued bitcoins by the network[17] worth a considerable sum. This not only rewards the miner for having solved the problem but adds new bitcoins into the economy, and it's the only way new bitcoins are "minted."

What's the point of all this? Satoshi was very clever in how he set up the system. The transaction block, used as one of the inputs for the hash function and consisting of a list of transactions, also contains a segment of data from the previous block in the transaction chain. When you "hash" a given block, you also "hash" a bit from the previous block. This links the blocks together and makes the block chain secure. Why can't somebody insert a transaction into the public ledger, pretending it took place on Jan. 1, 2010, which claims that e-wallet number one (under the thief's control) sent one thousand bitcoins to e-wallet number two (the thief controls it as well)? If the transaction goes through, the thief will be able to send one thousand bitcoins from e-wallet number two to a Bitcoin exchange and convert them into dollars—and profit.

The Bitcoin Block Chain

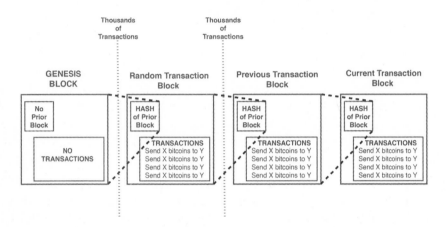

Clearly you can't let anyone write whatever they want in the public ledger, otherwise Bitcoin would be in chaos. Unscrupulous people would be gifting themselves bitcoins hand-over-fist.

The hash function ensures this doesn't happen. The hash function isn't applied to the entire transaction, turning it into cryptographic mush—instead, each transaction begins with something called a header, a block of text. The header contains a hash of all the transactions to follow, the special number used in the hash function to generate the multi-zero solution, the multi-zero solution itself, a hash of the previous header, and a few other details that serve to increase Bitcoin's security. Any change to any transaction—for example, a hacker inserting a bogus transaction sending 1000 BTC to wallet number two—won't match the hash value in the header because if you were to run the transactions through the hash function using the supplied solution you wouldn't get the desired result.

The hash function makes it computationally impossible for somebody to alter any of the transactions in a given block, because doing this would ruin the result generated by running the transactions through a hash function with the supplied solution.

A truly devious criminal could, of course, not only change the transactions in a given block but also come up with a new solution for the modified transactions and insert this changed value in the header. Bitcoin would be none the wiser. There isn't any difference between a valid block and a tampered block if they both have correct solutions in the headers. It sometimes happens that a "fork" occurs in the block chain, where two possible transaction blocks (slightly different in their contents) are both built on the previous block. The problem is that the criminal is solely responsible for solving the difficult hashing problem associated with his special customized and hacked transaction block, while everyone else in the world is busy solving the "valid" block. It's a race, and it's a race that any single individual or corporation will necessarily lose. The Bitcoin network is working twenty-four hours a day with massive computing power to solve these problems, and for any thief to go against it is computational suicide. It's also rather silly. If you have a computer fast enough to reliably calculate hash solutions, why not work as a miner and make your money legitimately?

The mathematical difficulty of solving the hashing problem is what keeps the block chain secure. Each block has undergone a "proof of work" exercise that is continually becoming more difficult. A well-funded computer hacker might tamper with a transaction block and find a solution relatively quickly, but . . .

A Forked Blockchain

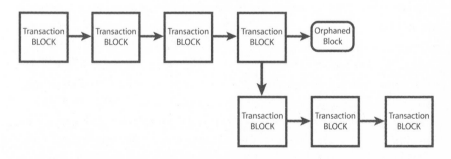

While he's busy churning away, other, more legitimate blocks will be solved and added to the previous block, and another block added on top of that. There isn't any way, given the size and scope of the Bitcoin computing network, to slip a bogus block into the block chain. Once a block is buried beneath, say, six blocks, the only way for somebody to tamper with it is to solve not only the block six levels deep but every block that follows (since they all depend on hash values altered by the thief). The hacker has to come up with six "proofs of work" before the global network has a chance to build more legitimate blocks on top of the current stack. He's got no chance.

The Byzantine Generals' Problem

With the introduction of Bitcoin, Satoshi solved a well-known problem in computer science called the "Byzantine Generals' Problem." This thought experiment imagines two or more people communicating over an untrusted network, attempting to organize a synchronized plan of action. Their decisions are made difficult because even when messages between the participants are received there's no guarantee they weren't tampered with and altered. But why is it called the Byzantine Generals' Problem? The best way to understand is to return to the past and discover what inspired its naming.

It's a curious fact that the Byzantine Empire was never called the Byzantine Empire during its heyday; it was a convenient label afterward applied, like "teenager" for those caught between childhood and adulthood, a term never used (nor the concept deemed useful) before 1920—which either meant teenagers didn't exist before 1920 or they did so under another name. "Byzantine Empire" is a useful term, though, designating the Eastern half of the Roman Empire after Emperor Diocletian's partition. The capital of the Roman Empire was moved from Rome to Byzantium (later Constantinople, later Istanbul); under Theodosius I, Christianity was the proscribed state religion, throwing away the Roman pantheon; and finally Heraclius changed the official language from Latin to Greek, completing a three-hundred-year transformation.[18] These changes were significant enough to radically distinguish the new empire from its ancient Roman origins and thus was born, over a long period of time, the Byzantine Empire.

While the Byzantine Empire retained the basic administrative bureaucracy of the Roman Empire, it slowly accreted a mass of new rules, regulations, strictures, customs, and ceremonies inherited or adopted from various kings and emperors, leading (in time) to elaborate and sometimes over-involved rituals (i.e., *byzantine*). Ambassadors and visitors from Europe were often at a loss to know how to behave or what was appropriate to discuss with whom; military leaders found the Byzantine army an unstable ally, capable of firm action working in close partnership but extremely sensitive to political entanglements at home or abroad. For reasons obscure to the uninitiated, the army might abruptly cease support or even turn traitor and supply crucial information to the enemy.

In 863 CE, the Arab army of Umar, king of Paphlagonia, invaded the Byzantine Empire, posing a serious threat to its continued existence. Emperor Michael III, who wasn't messing around, gathered forces from every far-flung province and split them into three armies—led by himself, his uncle Petronas, and a clever man named Nasar who had done good work a few years before beating back an attacking fleet from Africa. The three armies closed in from three different directions and attempted to surround Umar's army, which was holed up in a small town near the Lalakaon river, located in (what would later be called) northern Turkey. If they were able to coordinate their armies, they would have a good chance of defeating Umar, who had the smaller force but a better defensive position. If the Byzantine armies attacked one by one, in ragged and uncoordinated style, Umar would counterattack and destroy each individual army, or at worst slip back into Turkey. Communication was the key to Emperor Michael's plan.

Unfortunately, the Byzantine communication chain was as arcane as its seating arrangements during a royal feast. Runners were dispatched between the armies, carrying communications and proofs of legitimacy, but Umar's army (who had small forces posted all around the region) could 1) intercept and kill the messengers, 2) intercept and replace the messengers with messengers bearing counterfeit messages, 3) allow the messengers to pass unmolested, just to further confuse matters. The Byzantine army wasn't immune from tampering either; a general or a member of the general's staff might think it a fine thing for a rival general to arrive early and suffer defeat at the hands of Umar's army—allowing *their* general to arrive late and save the day, or at least gain political power from the first general's downfall. Generals had spies in each other's staffs; a messenger could be replaced by another messenger mid-route, or have the message subtly altered or made illegible by water—it was an absurd way to communicate. The big question arising from this mess: Was it possible for three generals to confidently synchronize their movements given a communication system riddled with error and doubt?

This difficult military situation embodied a long-standing computer science quandary and inspired its naming. It asserts that under these conditions there isn't any way for the three generals to arrive at a confident agreement about *when* to attack Umar's army. If the communication network is rife with slowdowns, contradictions, and failures, it's impossible to make progress. It looks as if Emperor Michael III is in a world of trouble, because if he can't communicate with his two generals a whole lot of nothing is going to occur. Luckily for the purposes of this book, Satoshi's writings had appeared to the emperor in a dream, giving him the solution to the problem.

The last time the emperor and his two generals were in the same room together, the emperor gave them both a special type of cypher and he explained how to use it to check the validity of future communications. The generals listened and nodded and wondered if the emperor had gone mad, but he hadn't. A month later, when they were closing in on Umar's army, the emperor was prepared.

The emperor created a short message using the cypher he had shared with his two generals. (The code might have been subsequently stolen by members of their staff and shared with the enemy; no matter.) It read:

At nine in the morning please attack the evil invader see you there

His cypher involved the following procedure: count the number of words in the message (thirteen), and convert every letter in every word into a number associated with its position in the alphabet (A = 1, B = 2, etc.). The number of words equals the numbers on the face of a fictional clock (again, thirteen). The typical clock we tell time with has twelve; this special clock, called a cypher clock, has thirteen since there are thirteen words in the message (it could have had seven or seventy-seven, depending on message length).

Once you know how many numbers are associated with your cypher clock (thirteen), it's possible to calculate what needs to be calculated. Take the first word of the message, "at." According to the alphanumerical scheme, "a" = 1 and "t" = 20. For each word, add together the values arising from rotating each letter in each word around the cypher clock—but this is too confusing to understand without an example.

First, let's remember what the cypher clock does. Imagine you are moving, clockwise, around the cypher clock (with thirteen digits). You go from one to two to three to four . . . all the way to thirteen. After you get to thirteen you have completed the circle and return to the number one. Applying cypher clock_13 to the number twenty gives a result of seven (the first thirteen steps take you back to the starting point, and there are seven left). Let's notate this as clock_13 (20) = 7. Notice that clock_13 (1) = 1 and clock_13 (2) = 2, since they have not "wrapped around" yet. But clock_13 (112) is harder to figure out. You have to go around the clock a bunch of times and see where you end up. It's a pain.

Cypher Clock

CypherClock_13(20) = 7
(Twenty steps around the
clock ends with 7)

The way the code works is this: you apply the clock_13 function to the initial letter in the word, and every subsequent letter picks up where the previous letter left off, even if it's the beginning of a new word. "A" equals clock_13 (1) = 1. After this you start at one (where the previous letter stopped) and for the next letter "t" (twenty steps) move around the clock until you get eight (try it and see). Since we have arrived at the end of a word ("at") add up the letter totals for each word and put it next to the word. Let's remember the message being transmitted:

At nine in the morning please attack the evil invader see you there

The word "At" = 1 + 8 = 9.

The next word is "nine." We have to start at the number eight, which is where the last letter of the previous word ended (the "t" of "at"). The value for "nine" is calculated like so: clock_13 ("letter **n**" = 14, starting at 8) = 9 + clock_13 (letter "**i**" = 9) [9 more starting at 9 = 5] + clock_13 (letter "**n**" = 14) [14 more starting at 5 = 6] + clock_13 (letter "**e**" = 5) [5 more starting at 6 = 11] for a total of 9 + 5 + 6 + 5 = 25.

And so on for the rest of the words in the message. You can add up the values for each word 9 ("at") + 25 ("nine") + rest of the eleven words and come up with a "message total," a single value that depends upon every letter of every word to be correctly calculated. If you append this value to a given message, it can be used to "prove" the message is legitimate—or at least a really good forgery involving a lot of math.

The following can be said about this cypher: 1) it's annoying to calculate, 2) changing the number of words in the message will necessarily change all the values (since the number of the clock function will change from 13 to something else), and 3) every letter in a given word affects every other letter. If a spy intercepts the message and substitutes "four" for "nine," the total value calculated over the entire message will be thrown off. If you change even one letter of "nine"—for example, the "i" into a "o"—this affects not only the number you calculated for that word but every number to follow, which started where "i" (before it was changed) left off.

Since the emperor has a large staff, he can send far more complicated messages than this single line example. If the emperor sends fifty copies of these long messages to each of his two generals, he knows at least a few of them will make it through by pure chance. His two generals, Petronas and Nasar, soon receive a flood of messages, about half of which will ripped or mangled, while the other twenty will be in various states of originality. A few will be doctored up fakes; others will be high-quality forgeries, with a cypher that looks correct but won't calculate to the right number, which was appended to the end of the message. What both generals do is have their cryptographic staff sit and work furiously fast, calculating the cypher for each incoming message and throwing away messages that are off. They will probably end up with one or two copies of Emperor Michael III's original message, as well as one very nice forgery that says the attack should occur at 3 p.m. not 9 a.m. and that also checks out according to the cypher. (The forgers had done a good job and calculated the correct value for the altered message.)

The important thing is that they all attack at the same time, not necessarily that they follow the initial plan.[19] If a general happens to pick the "wrong" of the two plausible messages, it isn't a disaster. He simply does what he was told to do: He puts his response first, the "original" messages from the emperor next, and then encodes the whole mess. He sends fifty copies of this off to the emperor and his fellow general. This makes the message even longer and harder to forge from a cryptographic standpoint.

When this message arrives at the emperor's camp he sees his general must have gotten tricked by a forgery (with a time of 3 p.m. instead of 9 a.m.), but he rolls with it and appends yet another message confirming the new time (3 p.m.) and wishing everyone a merry holiday. He dispatches fifty copies of this message to both generals. In this way a short message becomes long as it bounces between the two generals and the emperor and they continue to add to it/encode it. It takes a while, but by the end of a day or two everyone's extremely confident that the longest (valid) message getting bounced between them is from whom they say it is, since no forger would have a cryptographic staff big enough to alter it without ruining the cypher. It would consume too many resources for a single traitor, or even a traitor abetted by a small group of gifted mathematicians, to continually intercept and alter and fix the numbers for the very long messages being passed around.

In other words, it's possible to create messages that can't be altered without doing serious mathematical number crunching, and if you make this number crunching difficult enough it can essentially "guarantee" a given message came from whom it said it did—even if the communication pathway is highly unsecure.

In this way Satoshi, using "proof of work," solved a difficult and long-standing problem in computer science and also managed something rather magical: he allowed confirmed messages to be sent over an unsecure network. Unless the network is completely broken, barring all messages, there's always a way to get a message through and confirm it's from the person we think it's from. Thanks to Satoshi's revelation, all three of Emperor Michael III's armies converged on Umar's position at the same time the next day, and Umar found his defenses overthrown. The rout was on.

IS BITCOIN SAFE?

Ittay Eyal and Emin "Gun" Sirer are renowned cryptocurrency experts, interested in peer-to-peer systems, cryptology, and (after it arrived on the scene)—Bitcoin.[20] They work and teach at Cornell University, where Ittay is a post-doctoral student and Gun is an associate professor. I went to visit them one Monday in the middle of summer when the campus was relatively empty and the sky unparalleled in its purity.

Perched upon one of the four hills of Ithaca, much of Cornell University is built using an attractive grey-blue slate, locally available, which when cut into long lengths three or four inches high and stacked in staggered rows creates sturdy walls or foundations, and when slimmed and narrowed is suitable for more delicate tasks, such as the curving arch above a bay window. The slate's million-year age and implacable resistance to weather is inspiring; staring at a building's bulging corner quoin it's impossible to imagine the stone ever decaying—there it will sit for the next millennia or two, handsomely resisting snow, sleet, and sun.

In shocking contrast is Gates Hall, fruit of Bill and Melinda Gate's twenty-five-million-dollar donation to Cornell's Computing and Information Science department, an aggressively modern building with a gleaming façade of stainless steel panels that march in unison from one end of the building to the other . . . but they're not following the expected military plan. Halfway across the building they start to diverge, dipping below the horizontal before drifting back up, a nervous few pulling away from the building entirely, as if they no longer want to be associated with the aggressively *au courant* design. By the time they reach the far end they're closer to chaos than order, a silver wave breaking against the corner of the building. But this imaginative fancy's only skin deep (literally); beneath the flowing panels is a recognizable rectangle, and inside the building is an open architectural plan; our spirits plummet as we stare down at polished concrete. Whimsy is banished; if there's fun it's of the rebar variety.[21]

I tramped up to the fourth floor and walked down a hall and took a right and there they were, already talking, comparing notes, waiting. Ittay was younger than I expected, Gun far more charismatic than your average CompSci professor, the sun an unexpected enemy, flooding through the wall of windows at the back of the office. It might have been nice in the winter but right now the light, bouncing off steel panels and reflecting through acres of glass, was bright enough to blind.

These two are experienced hands when it comes to peer-to-peer networks such as well-known file-sharing implementations like Napster, Kazaa, and LimeWire, or more recent versions such as Tor or Bitcoin. A peer-to-peer network consists of many small servers (nodes), typically hosted by members of the public and by definition *not* under the control of a central authority. It's hard to shut down a peer-to-peer network because if you shut down one node, well, that's no big deal. There are still a thousand nodes out there, scattered across the globe, ready to pick up the slack. To completely shut down a well-designed peer-to-peer network requires an inordinate amount of work; even the US government, whose dislike of Tor is well-attested, isn't able to knock it offline.[22]

Is the Bitcoin network safe? Broadly speaking, Gun and Ittay both agreed: *yes.*[23] The details remain muddy, but Ittay is reasonably confident:

The Block chain . . . is here to stay. This is an algorithm that has survived field testing in extreme conditions . . . an attacker could have
made immediate earnings by targeting the system. Nevertheless, the
core algorithm remained stable, as the only attack publicly known,
selfish mining, requires significant resources to be executed with
guaranteed success. The peer-to-peer network used to distribute
transactions and blocks, on the other hand, is much more vulnerable. The designers of this network have made some accurate
design choices, but with the diverse environment in which it operates, there seems to be no silver bullet. . . . The infrastructure facilitating block chains in five to ten years may be quite different from
the existing one.

In general, Bitcoin's a robust and well-tested network reasonably
resistant to standard attacks. But as with any new technology, problems
are going to crop up that have to be identified and patched. And this
is where it gets bizarre.

The point of greatest weakness is local: e-wallets. It's relatively
easy to forget or lose a password or have an e-wallet become corrupted. It's also possible to have an e-wallet targeted and stolen,
which is more than a little terrifying.

Gun explained such a theft in this way:

"You can't trust servers. . . . On the other hand, you can't trust
your local machines either. . . . People come in and break into your
machine and empty out e-wallets. For example, Christian Decker,
he's a graduate student in Switzerland [ETH Zurich—Distributed
Computing Group] . . . he's a great guy . . . but he lost ten thousand
bitcoins. He was one of the early miners. . . . Let's see, that's about
three million dollars that was stolen? That's a lot . . . particularly for
a graduate student!"

[We laugh.]

"Was his computer stolen?"

"No, they broke in. The machine was connected to the network;
look at this [grabs Ethernet cord connected to his own computer].
He was just connected."

"Somebody hacked the machine and stole the wallet?"

"Yes."

"They knew what they were doing and they targeted him?"

"I think so; he's rather well-known and famous.[24] . . . But this has absolutely nothing to do with Bitcoin. The infrastructure we have is horrible for maintaining the security of Bitcoin assets. It's always been bad and now with Bitcoin there is more incentive to break in."

This was disturbing but a bit too specific to cause me much general worry. Most people are not well-known Bitcoin researchers with piles of bitcoins sitting on our local machines, ergo we won't be the target of this sort of advanced hacking often (if ever). But more devious attacks can take place.

Ittay started talking about random number generators:

"Random numbers . . . you don't really get random numbers using a random number generator on a computer. You get pseudorandom numbers instead, and they often fail, and when people find the failure they can guess the initial seeds and recreate the cold wallet [private key] that's been carefully constructed and safely hidden away under an Egyptian pyramid somewhere."

Gun broke in:

"Blockchain.info lost some money this way. They were getting their seed value from random.org, and random.org[25] changed their URL structure. Usually you contact random.org and it returns 200-OK ("The request has succeeded") and it gives you a random number. The random.org guys changed their URL structure so instead of 200-OK it responded with 301 ('The URL Moved to a new address'). This is a typical redirect. But the blockchain.info code was written badly. It started to treat the 301 error code as the *seed value* for new e-wallets. Suddenly everyone is getting the same seed. They are all creating the same address. That's pretty terrible."

Gun went on, "The other story I have in this vein that I think is hilarious is outlined in my colleague Nadia Heninger's paper.[26] They looked at this issue: if you pick bad random numbers, you will pick bad private keys that other people can predict. Also if you misuse something when you are signing transactions, there is a little field value called a nonce. . . . you are never supposed to reuse a nonce. . . . Well, some implementations will reuse a nonce and if you do the private key is immediately obvious. So they wondered if this ever happened before. They go through the block chain and identify 320 affected accounts, and the grad student who did it is like 'Great we got rich!'"[27]

"Could they really take the money from these e-wallets?"

"Yes, it's easy," Ittay said.

"It's trivially easy!" Gun shouted, "They could sweep these accounts and collect the money from all 320 accounts!"

I asked, "So they would gain ten bitcoins or something?"

"No, no, how much do you think was there?"

"Uh. Ten bitcoins," I repeated.

"Nope. It used to be much more than that. But they sweep the accounts and they realize it's almost zero. Why? Because somebody else came before them and swept it all away. All the proceeds went into one address.[28] So there is somebody out there who is smarter than Nadia—who I have infinite respect for—her colleagues at Michigan—who I also have infinite respect for—some of the best cryptographers in the world plus their graduate students . . . that guy or girl is better than this collection of people and they are keeping it quiet."

"How much was swept out?"

"I don't know, but it's in the paper. [It turned out to be $12,000 worth of bitcoins.] This is all teenage stuff. This is the network growing up."

That's what it felt like to me as well—growing pains. These are interesting academic questions, but they depend upon edge-case failures so rare that they can be essentially ignored. As time passes companies will be more strict and sensible in their use of truly random seeds. People, including successful Bitcoin miners, won't leave their bitcoins in an open wallet on their work PC. There's always going to be theft and robbery, whether of gold, dollars, or bitcoins; the question should be, "Does Bitcoin make this sort of theft more or less difficult?"

Bitcoin is experiencing the same growing pains as cash. Back in the day, people really did stuff their mattress with money, or hide it in an iron chest buried in the back field. Before banks were widely available (and trusted) these alternatives weren't viewed as crazy—it was a whole lot better than carrying wads of cash around. In 2012, before people understood how valuable bitcoins were, owners were often reckless in their security measures (or lack thereof); leaving an unencrypted bitcoin wallet on a computer or phone, assuming nobody will steal it, is exactly the same as leaving bags of money in the living room assuming nobody will break into your house.

While Bitcoin theft is a real concern, widely publicized Bitcoin losses educate the public more than they generate panic. Extremely secure hardware e-wallets have been introduced, allowing users to plug them into a computer's USB port when bitcoins are to be received or spent. These types of hardware wallets are impregnable to viruses, generally hack-proof, and because they can be removed from the internet and put into a safe deposit box (or other secure location), they represent the first step on what will surely be a long road to increased Bitcoin security. As with any valuable item, be it a painting, bar of gold, or suitcase full of rubber-banded cash, security depends upon the user. Since Bitcoin comes with a built-in locking mechanism (a password/passcode), it's fundamentally more secure than many other valuables—after all, you have to buy a safe to secure gold, while a long and involved Bitcoin password is far stronger than any safe ever invented.

CHAPTER 3

SATOSHI NAKAMOTO: A ROCKET-POWERED LAUNCH

WHY NOW?

Satoshi created Bitcoin because he was convinced a purely digital form of currency was both theoretically possible and computationally feasible. It turned out he was right, and now that we know a little about how Bitcoin works—e-wallets and the block chain and mining and all the rest—it's time to ask why Bitcoin appeared when it did and why it was such a spectacular success. What inspired Satoshi to start work on Bitcoin in 2007 and release it in 2009? After its release, why was Bitcoin adopted by a group of enthusiastic supporters numerous enough to drive growth and network stability?

Was it nothing more than a freakish coincidence? A result of perfect timing? Or were there other motivating factors, lurking beneath the surface, which helped make Bitcoin the success it was?

Satoshi directly revealed a few of his reasons for creating Bitcoin in a message board post from late 2008:

[We will not find a solution to political problems in cryptography] . . . but we can win a major battle in the arms race and gain a new territory of freedom for several years. Governments are good at cutting off the heads of a centrally controlled network like Napster, but pure P2P networks like Gnutella and Tor seem to be holding their own.[1]

Satoshi wanted to carve out a "new territory of freedom." This is the language of resistance, asserting the primacy of "freedom" in a landscape dominated by, apparently, a severe *lack* of freedom. Satoshi's adversarial understanding of government's attitude toward centralized networks is also noteworthy, likening it to "cutting off . . . heads"—both violent and fatal. This didn't make a whole lot of sense until a week later (November 14, 2008) when Satoshi wrote: "[Bitcoin] is very attractive to the libertarian viewpoint if we can explain it properly. I'm better with code than with words though."[2]

The puzzle pieces begin to slide into place.

The banner of the American Libertarian Party, "Minimum Government, Maximum Freedom,"[3] takes it for granted that government—any form of it—impinges upon personal freedoms, ergo reducing government increases personal freedom. There are many ways to shrink the government's footprint, and regulation reduction is one of the most popular with big corporations, as regulations are thought to be nothing more than governmental interference in an otherwise efficient "free market."[4] Another method is privatization, such as efforts to turn Social Security into an individually controlled and wholly optional retirement savings scheme, thereby increasing everyone's "freedom to choose" by opening up the possibility for speculative and ill-informed investments,[5] as well as sober and inspired choices.

Another slightly more subtle way to reduce the role of government in our lives is by moving away from government-sponsored and government-managed currency. Doing so *en masse* functions as a thermonuclear missile aimed directly at the fiduciary base of a government. If ten percent of a population stops using the national currency the inflow of taxes is hampered but the government limps along. If fifty percent of a population stops using the national currency it's in danger of becoming worthless—removing nearly all economic levers from government control. Forget twiddling with interest rates; at that point the government would be happy with a functioning economy.

Satoshi was not the first to make digital currency a priority and a goal; the Cypherpunk[6] movement, begun in the late 1980s and formalized in 1992 with the Cypherpunks mailing list, discussed digital currencies extensively, used various short-lived implementations, investigated their limitations, and promoted their possibilities. Cypherpunks (named in joking imitation of *Cyberpunks*) had a relatively clear and well-defined set of beliefs, extensively discussed in Eric Hughes' famous "A Cypherpunk's Manifesto" (1993).[7] It boils down to a vigorous defense of privacy and the necessary use of cryptography to this end:

> Privacy is necessary for an open society in the electronic age. . . . Privacy is the power to selectively reveal oneself to the world. . . . Privacy in an open society requires anonymous transaction systems. . . . Privacy in an open society also requires cryptography. . . . We cannot expect governments, corporations, or other large, faceless organizations to grant us privacy out of their beneficence. We must defend our own privacy if we expect to have any. We must come together and create systems which allow anonymous transactions to take place. . . . The technologies of the past did not allow for strong privacy, but electronic technologies do. We the Cypherpunks are dedicated to building anonymous systems. We are defending our privacy with cryptography, with anonymous mail forwarding systems, with digital signatures, and with electronic money.[8]

This looks amazingly prescient. Fifteen years before Bitcoin, people were talking about and hoping to create an "anonymous transaction system" using cryptography and digital signatures, which would function, in part, as "electronic money." This is a perfectly valid and no-nonsense description of the current Bitcoin network. It doesn't include some important Bitcoin features, such as its distributed nature or "proof of work" mining scheme, but the idea was already there. The Cypherpunks were way ahead of the curve when it came to their understanding of governmental control and/ or interest in communication, either phone or computer based. Privacy laws were not sufficient. Noted Cypherpunk legend John Gilmore put it this way:

> I want a guarantee—with physics and mathematics, not with laws— that we can give ourselves things like real privacy of personal communications. Encryption strong enough that even the NSA can't break it.[9]

The Cypherpunks were in an antagonistic battle against what they felt were governmental operatives constantly working to undermine privacy and restrict cryptographic research and its dissemination. Occasionally, as with the Clipper chip,[10] law enforcement went to shameless extremes, placing "backdoor" access directly into cryptographic hardware, explicitly allowing government taps on demand. For the Cypherpunks it amounted to a cold war: "We are literally in a race between our ability to build and deploy technology, and their ability to build and deploy laws and treaties. Neither side is likely to back down or wise up until it has definitively lost the race."[11]

To get a sense of how paranoid some of the government activity was, let's turn our attention to the so-called Hacker Crackdown of the early 1990s, when the US government launched Operation Sundevil,[12] a widely publicized Secret Service raid of sites in fifteen different cities, resulting in three arrests and the confiscation of lots of expensive computers. Triggered by telecom discomfort with "phone phreaks" who were illegally tapping and using phone lines for (mostly) harmless pranks,[13] it was thought time for the feds to *get serious*.

In their desire to get to the rid of the new and confusing "hacker subculture," the Secret Service were too greedy—and tone-deaf—to limit themselves to valid targets. In 1990, the Austin, Texas, headquarters of Steve Jackson Games (SJG)[14] was raided by the US Secret Service and all copies of the still-in-development role playing game *GURPS Cyberpunk*[15] were seized by the authorities. Steve Jackson Games, to the uninitiated, is a well-respected game company famous in the gaming community for its varied offerings. Founded in 1980, SJG has released a broad range of games over the years: *OGRE* (a strategic board game), *Car Wars* (combat simulation using cars, trucks, and motorcycles), *Chez Geek* (a tongue-in-cheek "geek culture" card game), and *Munchkin* (a tongue-in-cheek "role-playing" card game). The company grossed over eight million dollars in 2013, and employs forty-three people full time. Casual gamers might have played a Steve Jackson Game before, serious gamers probably have, and hard-core gamers—*no doubt*.

In 1990 Steve Jackson Games was developing *GURPS Cyberpunk* as a futuristic science fiction role-playing game and had hired Loyd Blankenship, aka "The Mentor" (a well-known computer hacker) to write it, assuming he would add a bit of insider knowledge and flair. A day after the Secret Service seized every computer they found at SJG, Steve Jackson (armed with a lawyer and tape recorder) marched into Secret Service headquarters demanding an explanation. That's when the affair descended into parody, as described by Bruce Sterling in "Gurps' Labour Lost":

> There was trouble over GURPS Cyberpunk, which had been discovered on the hard-disk of a seized machine [from SJG]. GURPS Cyberpunk, alleged a Secret Service agent to astonished businessman Steve Jackson, was "a manual for computer crime."
>
> "It's science fiction," Jackson said.
>
> "No, this is real." This statement was repeated several times, by several agents. This is not a fantasy, no, this is real. Jackson's ominously accurate game had passed from pure, obscure, small-scale fantasy into the impure, highly publicized, large-scale fantasy of the hacker crackdown.[16]

The end result of this raid was *Steve Jackson Games, Inc. v. United States Secret Service*, which came to trial in 1993 and resulted in Steve Jackson Games receiving $50,000 in damages and $250,000 in attorney fees. The trial was widely reported, and the Cypherpunks were publicly horrified but privately emboldened. This was war, if any further proof was needed. What's remarkable is that, in the long run, the Cypherpunks won. We have Bitcoin; we have Tor[17]; we have encrypted email and encrypted chat and encrypted everything (including laptops and systems). The government had it both right and wrong; from their point of view, they were right to attempt to stem the tide but wrong to imagine they would succeed.

While a stable and secure digital currency was desperately desired, it wasn't thought to be computationally feasible. Cypherpunks were forced to wait, but when E-Gold, a non-cryptographic alternative currency appeared in 1996, legions of libertarians flocked to it. Libertarians viewed E-Gold as a way (at long last) to escape the national currency and make financial transactions without burdensome governmental interference though the purchase and online transfer of "real" gold.

According to E-Gold's wildly optimistic founder, Douglas Jackson (no relation to Steve Jackson), "E-Gold is a private, international currency that would circulate independent of government controls, and stands impervious to the market's highs and lows. . . . [E-Gold is] a cure for the modern monetary system's ills. . . . E-Gold is a Libertarian dream . . . [spurring an] epochal change in human destiny . . . probably the greatest benefit to humanity that's ever been thought of."[18]

E-gold had significant limitations. First, it was centralized, not decentralized. All transactions went through E-Gold's servers and were logged, recorded, and saved for posterity. From a privacy standpoint this was significantly worse than using cash. Second, in 2001 the USA PATRIOT Act redefined what constituted a "money transmitter," and suddenly E-Gold was an illegal business operation, unlicensed in any state. Despite attempts to fulfill relevant requirements, by 2007 E-Gold was effectively shut down due to money-laundering issues stemming from lack of FinCEN (Financial Crimes Enforcement Network) regulatory compliance, and the libertarian movement was left without any alternatives. It was galling: Libertarians had access to a safe and stable alternative currency until it was torn out of their hands by the (hated) government and its (hated) financial regulations.

Suddenly it was quiet in the world of digital currency. Many gave up on the concept as either technologically impossible or as something the government would immediately regulate out of existence. Dark days. Unhappy days. Not desperate days, simply long, hot, steady, boring days. Then Satoshi came along and chucked a grenade in the window.

An anonymous currency *was* technologically possible. A peer-to-peer, difficult-to-eradicate network *could* support it. The block chain *would* secure it. Proof of work *expanded* and *protected* it. It was anonymous, safe, and could be encrypted for privacy. Cypherpunks and libertarians could join forces, hold hands, and jump up and down in excitement.

The stage was set: costumes designed and produced, supporting actors waiting in the wings, the audience fidgeting in front, a full orchestra well-tuned with the conductor's baton raised and on the verge of dropping. Silence filled the auditorium as the seconds passed and the audience, eager for the production to start, groaned and glanced at their watches and wondered *What's taking so long?* Suddenly Bitcoin entered stage right, picked out by an overwhelmingly bright spotlight. The audience, at long last, began to clap.

The world had been waiting.

THE ACHE OF THE LIBERTARIANS

> I have always found it quaint and rather touching
> that there is a movement [libertarianism] in the US
> that thinks Americans are not yet selfish enough.[19]
> —Christopher Hitchens

Libertarianism boggles the mind with its structural variety and in the stridency of its supporters and defenders. Even lifelong libertarians are sometimes surprised by what other libertarians assert as dogma. When you think you have dug into a rabbit hole as deeply as possibly there's always something beneath the surface capable of shocking— including the assertion that American libertarianism is in fact a complete perversion of true libertarianism, and that the word "libertarian" has no real meaning in the United States.[20]

Because of libertarianism's fundamental importance to the development and popularizing of Bitcoin, and its role in the development on online "drug stores" hosted on the Dark Web (the focus of the next two chapters), it's crucially important to look a bit more closely at libertarian beliefs, particularly how they've been incorporated into mainstream American politics.

To illustrate the varieties of American libertarianism, I introduce a choose-your-flavor system with some popular options already laid out.[21] While all libertarians agree on maximizing individual freedom, it's not always clear how to achieve this goal. Common points of difference include:

- Foreign Intervention
- National Currency

- Government size
- War on Drugs
- Private Resource ownership (of natural resources)
- Capitalism
- Patriot Act

For example:

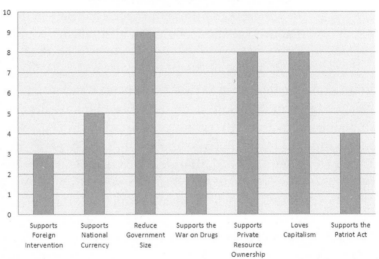

Mainstream American Libertarianism

Mainstream American libertarians feel strongly about reducing the government's size, but from that point on they are hard to pin down. Some care about currency, others don't. Most support capitalism and strong private mineral/resource rights, but it's not at the top of their concerns. Foreign intervention isn't completely out of the question, just looked down upon.

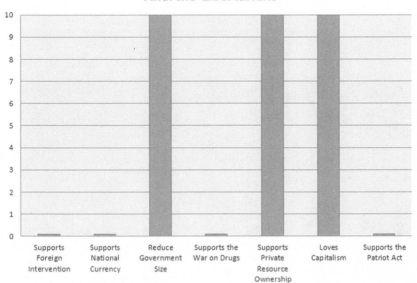

Anarcho-Libertarians

Anarcho-libertarians want the government entirely removed. Gone. They would like to sweep away the national currency and live in a "free market paradise" without any regulations whatsoever. This desire goes hand in hand with intense support of capitalism and private resource ownership (of oil, coal, and other natural resources). No government means no foreign interventions.

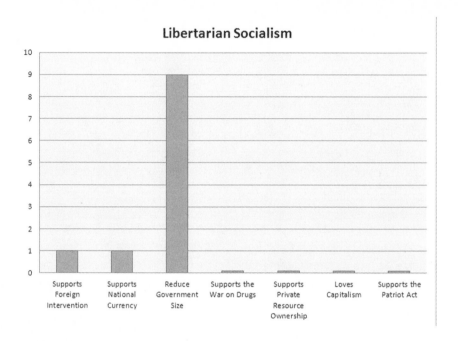

Libertarian Socialism

Social libertarians want the government dismantled and re-placed by voluntary associations. Natural resources should be equally divided among all citizens, and capitalism isn't viewed as the preferred method to achieve maximal personal freedom. There isn't any room here for foreign interventions, wars on drugs, or an out-of-control national currency.

Mainstream American libertarianism is currently associated with the Republican party and with former congressman Ron Paul and his son, the current Senator of Kentucky, Rand Paul. Ron Paul claims it's merely a coincidence that Rand's first name matches Ayn Rand's last—Ayn Rand, the author of hugely bestselling books such as *Atlas Shrugged*,[22] who through her fictional characters and public lectures and private harangues and endless nonfiction writings, with titles such as *The Virtue of Selfishness*, espoused what became known as "Objectivist Philosophy," asserting that the only rational goal of life is pursuit of self-interest, which necessarily leads to happiness. Central to her theory is the primacy of individual rights, which no society or government should limit in any way. When *Atlas Shrugged* first appeared in 1957 it was a sensation, arriving at the perfect moment for an audience hungry for what she was saying.

American libertarians often laud Ayn Rand as their saint despite Rand's loathing not only the term "libertarian" but their gleeful appropriation of her novels and other writings. Rand likened libertarians to a worthless and plagiarizing band of "hippies of the right," accomplishing little except taking her philosophy and twisting it to their own political ends. In her own words, "[Libertarians] sell out our fundamental principles for the sake of some superficial political action."[23] She wasn't a fan.

Under the broad banner of libertarianism, Ron Paul ran a moderately successful but ultimately doomed 2012 presidential campaign, and his son took up the mantle for the 2016 contest. The growing libertarian presence in the Republican party nearly matches the power of the diminishing Evangelical wing, and Rand's philosophy, married to modern American *laissez faire* capitalism, has proven to be an attractive concept for those looking for a place in the Republican party but unwilling to toe the line on so-called "social issues." These often include liberty-quashing causes such as opposition to gay marriage (limiting one's freedom to marry whom one likes), deeply invasive legislative restrictions on contraception and abortion (limiting one's freedom to make these types of fundamental decisions), and the "War on Drugs" (limiting one's freedom to control one's body by taking or not taking whatever substance is desired).

These long-standing Republican positions are more-or-less repellent to libertarians who are all about liberty, freedom of choice, and the holy status of uncoerced individual decisions, mixed with a profound skepticism regarding political and social institutions that inevitably attempt—even if unintentionally—to impinge upon the pure freedom with which humans are blessed at birth.

This is an overgeneralization of contemporary American libertarianism, but it's not far off the mark—a core libertarian belief is the assertion that individual freedom should never be violated. Most American libertarians would also agree with the following two principles:

1. Limited, minimally invasive government, and
2. Limited *mandatory* engagement in various parts of society, including the mainstream economic system (i.e., people should have the freedom to choose otherwise).

The first is a long-standing Republican mantra, made famous by Reagan's assertion, "The nine most terrifying words in the English language are: *I'm from the government and I'm here to help.*"[24] This statement was sharpened into legislative action by the infamous and ultimately ill-fated "starve the beast"[25] plan to shrink the government by reducing taxes, cutting income, and forcing budgets to contract by necessity. It sounded good but didn't work. Former vice president Cheney, along with other high-level Republican officials, were of the opinion that Reagan had proved that "deficits don't matter,"[26] leading to a topsy-turvy economic scheme whereby lower taxes fueled an *expanding* government, slowing an economy burdened by ever-rising deficits. Still, most Republicans support limited, minimally invasive government, and "starving the beast" was broadly acceptable if the beast being starved didn't include various sacred cows, such as military spending, law enforcement budgets, and social security (given the strength of the elderly voting block).

The second point ("Limited mandatory engagement in various parts of society") helps separate extreme libertarians, both left- and right-wing versions, from their mainstream Republican brethren. What does it mean to have the "freedom" to liberate oneself from the current economic system? What is the current economic system? How and why would one choose to live without it?

From a libertarian, freedom-loving, privacy-loving, suspicious-of-large-entities point of view, you could reasonably expect to do the following in America without much trouble: buy most of your necessities using cash, go on short trips using cash, make local purchases using cash, pay for local services with cash . . . but that's where it ends. If you want to purchase a plot of land in a forest you might be able to do it without a bank or lawyers being involved, but it's unlikely. For bigger purchases, such as a house, cash doesn't work. Traveling overseas, or something as simple as catching a plane, requires a mountain of "invasive" paperwork: not only passports or driver's licenses but a credit card for the plane ticket, hotel reservations, and purchases abroad or in an unfamiliar state. . . . It would be nice to travel in a private manner without being forced to jump through such hoops, but in today's world it's nearly impossible.

For libertarians, lack of choice infests everyone's working life. Suppose you choose to work as an architect but wish to opt out of the national currency (no cash, no banks, no loans). You'll be hard-pressed to find people willing pay using anything but dollars. The ways you are paid, checks and balance transfers and other messy means of moving money around, force you to either stop working as an architect (restricting your freedom to do what you really love) or require you to plug yourself into the modern economic marketplace—use cash, get a bank account, take out a mortgage or at least rent an office, purchase a smart phone. It might feel like you have a choice but if you want to have a mainstream career you don't: you *must* become involved with large financial entities, and support the national currency, in order to achieve your dream. The only alternative is frittering away your life doing an end-run around what the rest of us easily and conveniently accomplish on a daily basis—pull out the plastic, swipe the machine, and disgorge a social security number on request.

In 1845, Henry David Thoreau famously retired to Walden Pond with the following goal:

> I went to the woods because I wished to live deliberately, to front only the essential facts of life, and see if I could not learn what it had to teach, and not, when I came to die, discover that I had not lived. I did not wish to live what was not life, living is so dear; nor did I wish to practise resignation, unless it was quite necessary. I wanted to live deep and suck out all the marrow of life.[27]

Thoreau became an inspiration for legions of libertarians,[28] particularly with his essay "Resistance to Civil Government," (1849) which features language much-quoted to this day:

> I heartily accept the motto, "That Government is best which governs least"; and I should like to see it acted up to more rapidly and systematically. Carried out, it finally amounts to this, which I also believe—"That government is best which governs not at all."

Thoreau's attempt to remove himself from society and live a life aligned with his belief in transcendentalism and self-reliance proved far more difficult than he originally imagined. After moving to Walden Pond, Thoreau was arrested by a wandering tax inspector[29] and jailed as a tax delinquent for failure to pay poll taxes over his objections to the Mexican–American War. (He was bailed out by a forgiving aunt after one night in the slammer.) To be fair, Thoreau's goal wasn't to live a fully independent and hermit-like existence—or else he wouldn't have had his clothes regularly washed by his mother nor purchased various foodstuffs from the center of Concord, a short one-mile walk from his cabin. His aim was to remove himself from the hustle-bustle of society, to simplify his life, and to concentrate on writing a book. Yet even in his seclusion Thoreau could not escape economic activity; not only did he do odd jobs around town to earn additional money, paid in cash, but his agreement with Emerson was predicated on paying "rent" on the land in exchange for clearing scrub and brush—thus improving its value.

Thoreau wasn't able to fully disengage in 1845 when the economy was far less complicated and entrenched than it is now. It appears that modern American capitalism won't allow an individual to opt out with any degree of grace; it's an all-or-nothing proposition. Either you live in a tent, getting by with cash however you can, or you are associated with tens (hundreds) of organizations that take your money, process it, track it, and tax it. Is there no escape for a freedom-loving libertarian?

"What Is to Be Done?"—Experiment.

Ross Ulbricht, libertarian *par excellence*, creator of the Dark Web drug superstore Silk Road, and star of the next section of this book, speaks for a large contingent of like-minded believers when he says, "*This* is the beauty of Libertarianism. The people are free to *choose* what [monetary] system they want. No need for one-size-fits-all government solutions. If you want to use a debt-based inflationary monetary system [US dollars], go right ahead, it doesn't affect me so long as you don't try to force me to use it as well."[30]

How realistic is this "choice" to accept or reject the US dollar, or any national currency for that matter? Doesn't it require a community of like-minded individuals, working together off the grid in what appears to be a new version of an old idea: a commune?

Back in the day, communes were, necessarily, physically communal. You went some place with a bunch of dissenters and there you were: a clearing in a forest or a jungle or a prairie or a small town in America circa 1820. Joining a commune was an all-or-nothing proposition, involving separation from the rest of the world, both socially and economically. Nobody joined because they believed deeply in one or two vague claims; such an important undertaking required full faith in the creed being professed. Most of the time it required quitting a job, moving away from home, and leaving friends and (sometimes) family behind. Entering a commune was the choice of a true believer, striving for an earthly utopia.

No longer must a commune imply proximity: the internet has forever altered this dynamic. New communication tools have made it possible to actively participate in a global drive toward a theoretical, rather than physical, utopia: a utopia of belief, airy and philosophical but nevertheless generating on-the-ground change. Many libertarian arguments are based on thought experiments involving a fictional preindustrial community and how they might organize their behavior along libertarian lines for maximum freedom; this type of thing is called "State of Nature Theory" and it is used as a test bed, both informing and generating results. Fictional characters participate in a "real" commune to generate data. Why couldn't nonfictional characters, otherwise known as human beings, participate in a dispersed (though vibrant) theoretical commune to generate "real" action?

Was the goal maximum freedom? It's now possible to join a commune without committing the body. While the internet opened the door to dabblers and half-hearted adherents, it also vastly expanded the audience, a net gain by any measure.

The desire for a new type of currency, facilitating escape from traditional economic systems, was central to many communes that sprang up in the nineteenth and twentieth century. Satoshi, perhaps unwittingly, tapped into a long American tradition of utopian belief and experimentation. It's important to locate Bitcoin in this historical movement, which starts with Charles Fourier, a globally influential "socialist utopian," who inspired Josiah Warren's 1827 experiment in a time-based currency with the Cincinnati Time Store, leading directly to Ithaca Hours, a modern implementation of the same idea. From Thoreau's singular sequestration at Walden Pond (a protocommune of one) to modern examples such as the Free State Project (a dispersed commune attempting to become local), Bitcoin is part of a long history of experimentation and contrarian pushback against the status quo. A look at Bitcoin's ancestry helps to illuminate where it stands in the current ideological landscape.

Charles Fourier (1772–1837)

Charles Fourier, an extremely imaginative French philosopher, was the inspiration for many nineteenth-century utopias. Considered the first "utopian socialist," Fourier attempted to put his idealistic visions and dreams of new (and better) type of society into practice through well-received speeches and copious publications.

Fourier was interested in constructing utopian communities with specific architectural and economic systems, in which the strife- and conflict-based paradigm of his contemporaries would be replaced by a more communal, cooperative scheme. Reasonable criticisms of French culture and economy were mixed with heady theorizing about sexuality, a rejection of the industrial revolution, and the role of women in society (he's credited with coining the word *feminism*).[31] Included in his mix of ideas was a far more sympathetic understanding of children and their needs—Fourier viewed them not as small, lazy adults requiring constant punishment but as active and energetic learners, always busy doing something (even if it's not often what most adults want). Readers were left with two impressions, neither moderate: either they found Fourier's radical writings inspiring and visionary, spawning utopian experiments all over the globe, or he was regarded as a crackpot and actively disparaged.

Fourier explained his discomfort with the mercantile system in his essay *On Trade*, translated in 1845 by Friedrich Engels (of Engels & Marx fame):

Trade becomes pernicious from the moment the go-betweens, due to their excessive number, become parasites [on the social body] and are ready to conceal goods, to let them rise in price under the pretext of an artificially produced scarcity, in brief, to rob simultaneously the producer and the consumer through speculation tricks instead of serving both as simple, open go-betweens. . . . [T]his is no longer simple commerce, open offering of commodities free from any intrigue, it is compound commerce, whose endlessly changing tricks give birth to the thirty-six typical vices of our trade system and are tantamount to a legal monopoly. When one lays hands on the total product by ruse in order to make it dearer, that is robbing more by means of intrigues than the monopoly does by armed force.[32]

Fourier's take on money, currency, and economics is difficult to summarize, but shares with many of his contemporaries broad criticisms of the unregulated capitalist system. He thought middlemen, standing between producers and consumers, often acted as swindlers who artificially increased prices simply because they could get away with it. One of the big problems for Fourier was, not surprisingly, money, particularly in the form of paper currency— evil enough in itself but also enabling a variety of bad behavior on the part of corporations and governments. Again from *On Trade*:

Meanwhile, for a century a new science called Economics has been exalting hucksters, stockjobbers, corner-men, usurers, bankrupts, monopolisers and commercial parasites to the peak of honours. . . . [O]ur trade systems, which are now gaped at with stupid veneration, are the antipodes of truth, of justice, and therefore also of unity. It is difficult to make clear to a century that precisely that operation which it considers to be the masterpiece of all wisdom is nothing but the seal of ignorance stamped on its entire policy. Let us but look at the already known results: maritime monopoly, fiscal monopoly, growing national debts, bankruptcies in unbroken succession resulting from paper money, increasing villainy in all business relations. Already now we can stigmatise the mechanism of free trade, i.e., of free lying, that veritable industrial anarchy, that monstrous power in society.[33]

In Fourier's view, paper money no longer functioned to smoothly accelerate the transfer of goods from seller to buyer. Once the "middlemen" stepped into the system (i.e., the "stockjobbers, corner-men, usurers, etc."), money stopped behaving as a neutral means of payment; its value was constantly manipulated by private interests and governmental whim. Paper currency held in a safe might fluctuate by 10 percent or more every week; it could be worthless at the end of the year or have doubled in value, despite sitting in a dusty safe doing nothing. Currency was just another means of speculation, driving "an unbroken succession [of bankruptcies]." In response, many Fourierist communes—for example, the North American Phalanx (1843–1856) in Colts Neck Township, New Jersey—rejected US currency and issued their own, which was dollar-sized[34] and made of paper but had a bust of Charles Fourier prominently displayed in the center. "Fourier dollars" were used internally to keep track of accounts between commune members, and no outside observers were given access to the currency, making it function purely as a means of exchange, not a speculative instrument.

Cincinnati Time Store (1827–1830)

Fourier's writing inspired an experiment by the early American anarchist Josiah Warren, who was devoted to overthrowing hierarchical organizations wherever he found them, starting with but certainly not limited to local, state, and federal governments. To this end Josiah created the Cincinnati Time Store in 1827, founded upon the principle that an object is worth exactly as much as the labor and time it took to create it, and to charge more is manifestly unethical—this being in firm contrast to the capitalistic assertion that something is worth precisely what somebody else is willing to pay. To better explain this principle Josiah coined the term "Cost the limit of price," which pointed toward this equivalence of cost (what you pay) and price (the required labor).

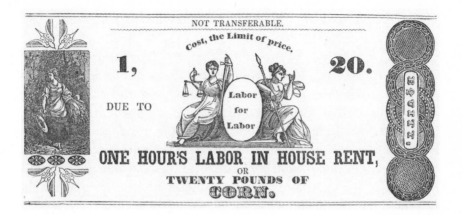

Josiah Warren's book *Equitable Commerce* includes a descriptive subtitle that pretty much lays it all out: *A new DEVELOPMENT OF PRINCIPLES for the HARMONEOUS ADJUSTMENT AND REGULATION of the PECUNIARY, INTELLECTUAL, AND MORAL INTERCOURSE OF MANKIND, PROPOSED AS ELEMENTS OF NEW SOCIETY.* The book was published in 1849 in Utopia, Ohio, a town founded a few years before by a group under the sway of Charles Fourier. After a two-year struggle to maintain their colony, the Fourierists sold the colony to a band of roving spiritualists called the Brotherhood, who believed all government should be abolished and people should organize in accordance with "God's will." Things didn't work out well for the Brotherhood.[35]

On the other hand, the Cincinnati Time Store was wildly successful, with Josiah Warren often doing more business in an hour than conventional stores managed in a day due to the comparative cheapness of the goods being sold. How was this possible? Imagine the following scenario: a corn farmer, busy farming and with a great store of corn in his barn, calculated it had taken him an hour to produce a certain amount of corn (it was roughly twelve pounds in Josiah's time). The farmer, instead of converting this corn into dollars, went to the Time Store and turned sixty pounds of corn into Time Store script worth five hours. With this script he "paid" four hours to a carpenter for four hours of work, with an additional hour of script spent at the bakery for five loaves of bread. The farmer's net gain from sixty pounds of corn was greater than it would have been if he had converted corn into dollars and paid the carpenter and baker separately in cash.

On the other side of the transaction, the Time Store script paid to the carpenter was worth more than four hours of labor paid in dollars, and the same could be said for the baker who ended up with what was essentially twelve pounds of corn for five loaves of bread. This win/win situation is possible because the middlemen and overhead costs have been excised from the system; there's no corn broker buying up large amounts of corn and dividing it into smaller amounts and taking a cut from the proceeds; no carpentry shop to maintain, just the carpenter doing the work; no sales lady manning the bakery counter, just the baker amongst the ovens producing bread. As proprietor of the store, Josiah Warren took as salary a fraction of the total daily script exchange total, a percentage so small it was invisible to most customers, and far less than even a fair-minded middleman's typical fee.

As long as there were enough people using the system, and everyone got what they needed on a regular basis, the Time Store script worked fine—in fact, it worked to mutually benefit everyone involved. Unfortunately for his customers, Josiah Warren was a dreamer and a radical, and he was unwilling to spend the rest of his life sitting behind the counter of an unusual though increasingly successful store. Tempted by a utopian communist society being set up by the former industrialist Robert Owen in New Harmony, Indiana, Josiah abruptly closed up shop, unable to resist the tempting opportunity. The New Harmony collective failed after two years, but it did manage to bring together a collection of scientists and philosophers who made lasting contributions to science long after the utopia had been converted into a standard American town. Robert Owen, son of the founder, blamed the utopia's failure on the wild mix of settlers, "A heterogeneous collection of radicals, enthusiastic devotees to principle, honest latitudinarians, and lazy theorists, with a sprinkling of unprincipled sharpers thrown in."[36]

Josiah Warren founded the Cincinnati Time Store to solve ongoing problems the current economic system was uninterested in addressing, which he outlined at the start of *Equitable Commerce*, here quoted in full (the numbering scheme is original to the text):

Problems to be solved:

1. The proper, legitimate, and just reward of labor.
2. Security of person and property.
3. The greatest practicable amount of freedom to each individual.
4. Economy in the production and uses of wealth.
5. To open the way for each individual to the possession of land, and all other natural wealth.
6. To make the interests of all, to co-operate with and assist each other, instead of clashing with and counteracting each other.
7. To withdraw the elements of discord, of war, of distrust and repulsion, and to establish a prevailing spirit of peace, order, and social sympathy.[37]

It's curious to see how closely these "problems" align with standard libertarian objections to modern America, particularly, "The greatest practicable amount of freedom to each individual," as well as Josiah's focus on voluntary cooperation instead of coercive inclusion in an economy where such choices can't be made. The libertarian dream is far from new; it's been modified over the years but ultimately has its origins in a long line of freedom-loving idealists.

Ithaca Hours (1991–Present)

Following Josiah Warren's lead,[38] in 1991 Paul Glover introduced the Ithaca Hours currency to Ithaca, New York (best known as the home of Cornell University and Ithaca College). Paul is a community activist, teacher, economic maverick, and contrarian rebel against "mainstream corporate culture."[39] His take on the national currency of the United States is refreshingly frank, and looks with intense suspicion to Nixon's gold standard shock: "Dollars enter circulation through forces beyond our control, such as multinational corporations, foreign investors and large banks. . . . The dollar's value has fallen because it is backed by nothing but federal debt ($14 million million) that can never be repaid. . . . [It's] funny money."[40] In comparison, Paul's home-grown currency, Ithaca Hours, is based on nothing less than "the real skills and time of local people, which represent our real productive capacity."[41]

This is an interesting example of left- and right-leaning libertarian convergence. Paul Glover, in many ways a traditional "far left" liberal, highly suspicious of capitalism and corporate power in general, shares a disdain for the US currency equally with those on the far right, the so-called anarcho-capitalists, who hold the "free market" to be utterly sacrosanct. No force, governmental or otherwise, should distort the market's operation, including any dependence upon a national currency that fluctuates every time politicians (or the federal reserve) change their mind or a foreign country purchases or dumps dollars. Anarcho-capitalists would love to have a nongovernmental currency available; in many of their idealistic thought experiments, anarcho-capitalists trade with each other using gold (by weight), which while pleasantly old-fashioned has obvious limitations.

Paul Glover intended one Ithaca Hour to be a measure of productivity over an hour of time—exactly the same scheme used by the Cincinnati Time Store. If it takes ten minutes of work to collect sufficient flour, yeast, and fresh water for a loaf of bread, and another fifty minutes to make it and bake it, the resulting loaf of bread is worth, by definition, one Ithaca Hour. One of the founding principles of Ithaca Hours is that Hours cannot be invested nor can interest ever be paid on them. They are not a medium for speculation, nor should they be stored or banked.[42] Because they represent work, they will resist inflation and swings in value: "Ithaca Hours are as steady as the clock, because minutes neither expand nor contract. Ithaca Hours, when properly issued, represent basic labor that produces real goods and services."[43] They are, in other words, as anticapitalist as a currency can possibly be while still functioning as a currency.

Ithaca Hours are local, while the modern economy is relentlessly global, seeking lower prices and lower salaries wherever they can be found. Ithaca Hours stay in the community, while dollars flow to the ends of the Earth. Ithaca Hours require face-to-face interactions and place responsibility for the currency in the hands of the users, while most "normal" economic activity occurs between strangers, or by flipping bits in computer ledgers. There is no bank or central reserve for Ithaca Hours, merely a board of directors, meeting in public, whose members can be elected or replaced as the community sees fit.

Other Currency Alternatives

As he grew older, Ezra Pound spent more time reading and writing about economics than composing poetry, and the poetry he did compose was often stuffed to bursting with explicit economic themes.[44] Like Fourier and his followers, Pound believed currency interfered with transactions rather than facilitating them and "international finance" was little better than a parasite leeching off the economic activity of those who created real goods (the "producers"): "History, as seen by a Monetary Economist [Pound himself], is a continuous struggle between producers and non-producers, and those who try to make a living by inserting a false system of book-keeping between the producers and their just recompense."[45]

Pound was shocked to discover that most currency isn't actually circulated; a very small fraction, sometimes less than 10 percent, is actually used for everyday transactions, with the rest stored in banks or purchased by foreign entities of various types. The majority of currency is simply sitting around acting as a "store of value" and growing dusty in safes all over the globe. One of the more imaginative ways of punishing currency hoarders (known as "banks" in other contexts) is to create a demurrage currency,[46] which has a very interesting feature: it quickly depreciates, thus must be quickly spent.

The canonical currency experiment of this type occurred in the Austrian town of Wörgl, nestled in the mountains in the Tyrol region. In 1932, Austria was undergoing a severe national depression, and Wörgl was getting crushed by a combination of high debt and high unemployment. The burgomaster of Wörgl, Michael Unterguggenberger, thought things dire enough to try something new: he created "Certified Compensation Bills," an alternative (local) form of currency, which devalued at a rate of 1 percent per month. In other words if you held on to Certified Compensation Bills for a year they would depreciate 12 percent (losing 1 percent per month). This effectively forced the circulation of these bills to skyrocket, as users attempted to spend them before the end of each month, avoiding a 1 percent devaluation, a small but significant loss. The "currency velocity"—how often a currency is actually used over a period of time—greatly increased, which theory claimed would spur growth.[47] Did it really function this way?

Yes. It's been called "The Miracle of Wörgl," and the effect of the currency was astonishing: "Wörgl was the first town in Austria which effectively managed to redress the extreme levels of unemployment. They not only re-paved the streets and rebuilt the water system and all of the other projects on Mayor Unterguggenberger's long list, they even built new houses, a ski jump and a bridge with a plaque proudly reminding us that 'This bridge was built with our own Free Money.' . . . The French Prime Minister, Édouard Dalladier, even made a special visit to see first hand."[48]

In 1933 the Austrian National Bank issued an injunction barring the currency; when the town continued to use it, the army was called in to enforce the ruling.[49] Moneyed interests were openly hostile to the idea and cracked down hard; by September 1933, Wörgl was forced to capitulate, and that was the end of the Certified Compensation Bills.

Since then, many alternative currencies have been proposed and realized, testing aspects of currency other than velocity. Notable in this regard is the Community Currencies in Action (CCIA) collaboration project,[50] active from 2012 to 2015, which conducted experiments with a broad range of currencies across Europe. "Time credit" currencies (similar to Ithaca Hours) were introduced in Amsterdam and the United Kingdom; a "business currency" SoNantes (Nantes, France) facilitated business-to-business trades and enhanced the regional economy; a Belgian e-wallet, E-portemonnee, rewarded environmentally friendly behavior (waste reduction) with credits able to be spent on sustainable products or services.[51] All the alternative currency experiments achieved sustained local use, with generally favorable results for everyone involved.

Ithaca is home not just to Paul Glover's Ithaca Hours but a new combination paper/digital currency alternative: Ithacash.[52] Ithacash is a "social currency" created by alternative-currency enthusiast Scott Morris, aimed at improving childcare and elderly care, spurring volunteering, expanding education, and increasing regional food security. Ithacash has a minor demurrage feature, much lower than Wörgl's 1 percent per month devaluation, which is only applied to the digital form of the currency and acts a minor impetus for generating higher currency velocity. Rather than replacing Ithaca Hours, Ithacash works side-by-side with the older currency, and Paul Glover (consulted during the development of Ithacash) is fully supportive of Ithacash's social focus and move into the digital realm.

The Free State Project (2001–Present)

An online libertarian organization called "The Free State Project" advocates something similar to a commune, if not as extreme; in 2003 it selected New Hampshire as the state of choice for motivated libertarians, urging twenty-thousand freedom-loving citizens to move to New Hampshire for the goal of "Liberty in our Lifetime." Once in New Hampshire, the idea is to reform local government into something far closer to a libertarian paradise than is currently found anywhere else in the country. Their pledge reads, "I hereby state my solemn intent to move to the State of New Hampshire. Once there, I will exert the fullest practical effort toward the creation of a society in which the maximum role of government is the protection of individuals' rights to life, liberty, and property. Anyone who promotes violence, racial hatred, or bigotry is not welcome."[53]

The Free State Project claims to have over fifteen-thousand validated moves so far, and they expect to reach their ultimate goal in late 2016. In recent polling, somewhere around 22 percent of all Americans consider themselves libertarian,[54] a number which skews young and is slowly increasing. This comes to tens of millions of people, who as a group attend college more frequently than any other demographic and are far more internet-friendly than your average American.[55] There seems to be a vast hunger in the country for an alternative to the modern financial system, and the Free State Project is extremely open to currencies of any type: "New Hampshire has a very active cryptocurrency economy and has the longest running Bitcoin meetup group. Many legendary Bitcoiners are FSP [Free State Project] supporters or participants, and the inventors of the first Bitcoin ATM—Lamassu—are participants of the FSP. The Free State Project community is also gold/silver currency-friendly."[56]

That some of the earliest Free State Project advocates were enthusiastic Bitcoin supporters should not be surprising; what is unusual from a historical perspective is that instead of the crumbling of its real and metaphorical foundations—nineteenth-century American communes typically lasted less than two years—a few far-sighted Free State libertarians became Bitcoin millionaires due to their deep suspicion of the dollar's debt-encumbered value.

WHAT DOES SATOSHI THINK?

The author of *The Book of Satoshi*,[57] aptly named Phil Champagne, is bubbly and enthusiastic yet sounds older than he looks. Phil spent a few months collecting all known message board posts, emails, and other digital evidence of Satoshi's existence, and organizing them chronologically (by theme) to better indicate what the man was thinking and why he made the choices he did.

The major drawback of *The Book of Satoshi* is that much of it involves back-and-forth conversations between Satoshi and fellow Bitcoin developers, supporters, and early critics. A high percentage, certainly above 90 percent, concerns dry technological issues, as in this example:

If SHA-256 became completely broken, I think we could come to some agreement about what the honest block chain was before the trouble started, lock that in and continue from there with a new hash function. If the hash breakdown came gradually, we could transition to a new hash in an orderly way. The software would be programmed to start using a new hash after a certain block number. Everyone would have to upgrade by that time. The software could save the new hash of all the old blocks to make sure a different block with the same old hash can't be used.[58]

It's impossible to parse this sort of thing for information about its author; even a lively postmodern literary critic, experienced in making hay with little or no grass, would have great difficulty "interpreting" the real Satoshi from these sorts of gnostic utterances. Any time Satoshi writes a few lines about a nontechnical subject it's a big deal, and I've included these rare quotes directly in this book (sometimes more than once).

Reconstructing Satoshi's inner life, his personal beliefs and goals, is like the task faced by archeologists when confronted by burned and buried figures from Pompeii. The blackened objects were once alive—they have the general contour of humans—but digging beneath the surface reveals emptiness. Nothing remains except a hollow shell. Similarly we know Satoshi's general outline—programmer and contrarian—but further details are difficult to discover. It was my hope that Phil Champagne, who has read all Satoshi ever wrote multiple times, might function as an interpreter, revealing something far more interesting than concerns about SHA-256 hashing.

Phil's a true believer and wants to be well ahead of the curve. He believes Bitcoin is going to be around for a long time and that even if it's eventually supplanted by a cryptocurrency underpinned by a better system, or with more attractive features, Bitcoin's nevertheless what started the revolution.

Yet during our interview Phil was forced to admit there's a lot we still don't know.

Q: Do you know who Satoshi is?
A: No.

Q: What about that guy in California the papers were all excited about?

A: No. Almost certainly not him. People have moved past that.

Q: Do you think it's a problem that the creator isn't around, to stick up for his creation? Doesn't it make Bitcoin seem a bit sketchy, like a not-quite-respectable uncle the family tries to ignore?[59]

Phil's answer was a somewhat wandering yes-and-no agreement; it would be better, of course, if Satoshi had emulated Linus Torvalds, the famous programmer of a home-brew replacement for Windows which, somehow, took off and now claims a significant portion of the market.[60] But it's not true that Satoshi's anonymity necessarily reflects badly upon Bitcoin; it could be nothing more than a matter of choice. Linus Torvalds created an open-source alternative to Windows and after two years slowed his coding involvement, choosing instead to step back and monitor progress. Satoshi essentially did the same thing, except instead of monitoring he disappeared. He put his open-source currency out there and once it was stable faded away.

Q: Was Satoshi afraid of something? He left just a day after WikiLeaks talked about accepting Bitcoin, which was Bitcoin's first major splash in the global media.

A: I think Satoshi knew there would be important code fixes to come. I don't think he thought the network was ready for all the traffic. You know what he posted when he heard about it? "WikiLeaks has kicked the hornet's nest, and the swarm is headed towards us." Other people in the Bitcoin forum were pushing for letting WikiLeaks accept Bitcoin, saying *Let's do it, bring it on.* But Satoshi was against it.

[Satoshi's exact post ran: "No, don't 'bring it on.' The project needs to grow gradually so the software can be strengthened along the way. I make this appeal to WikiLeaks not to try to use Bitcoin. Bitcoin is a small beta community in its infancy. You would not stand to get more than pocket change, and the heat you would bring would likely destroy us at this stage."[61] Satoshi was concerned that a sudden influx of global attention would flood, cripple, and possibly destroy the still-fragile Bitcoin network.]

Q: If he was worried about the network don't you think he would have wanted to stay on and see what happened, and try to fix things if they broke?

A: I don't know. That's a big mystery. Nobody knows why he left.

Q: Do you think Satoshi was a libertarian or a rebel? An anarchist? Or just a person who loved the idea of cryptocurrency?

A: Nobody knows for sure. He did talk about how libertarians would appreciate and support Bitcoin. He knew about the libertarian take on things and what they were going for.

Q: Do you think Satoshi holds a lot of libertarian views?

A: I know a lot of people who support Bitcoin are either libertarians or very unhappy with the financial system. . . . I know that what happened in 2008 [the global banking crisis] is not an unrelated or unique event. I think that next time it's going to be worse, and there *will be* a next time . . . and I think at that point people will begin to see Bitcoin as having a lot of value. . . . If there is a big crash and these fiat currencies start to print a lot more money, and inflation happens, Bitcoin might get a big boost. Because you *can't just print more Bitcoin.* Scarcity is at the root of the system. If the dollar spirals out of control and we start using wheelbarrows of it to buy bread, Bitcoin isn't going to change. . . . It's still going to be limited.

Q: After doing all this research, and writing your book, do you have a special sense of who Satoshi really is? Either something concrete you discovered, or an overall impression? Is Satoshi a he, a she, a group of people . . . ?

A: I go to a lot of Bitcoin conferences, and I talk to a lot of people, and they all have so many strong opinions. I talked to this one guy who was really into cryptocurrencies; he really liked the idea of them, and he was even somewhat supportive of Bitcoin. But he was sure Satoshi was an NSA plant, the whole thing was an inside job. And this didn't make much sense to me. I couldn't figure out why the NSA or the CIA would want to give this new sort of technology to the world. It's all open source, so it's not like they can hide anything in there. It's like they just said, here is a great new thing, enjoy. Why would they do that?

Q: Do you think Satoshi's a group of people?

A: I don't think so. I think he's a native English speaker, or at least really proficient. His messages all seem to come from the same individual. They don't *feel* like they were constructed by committee or by people taking turns. He's really consistent in the way he writes. He even apologized to people in the Bitcoin forums when he felt he was being rude or dismissive of an idea. Satoshi feels like a person, and that usually can't be faked. Especially when some of the messages were coming at a fast pace, one after another.

Q: Man or woman?

A: We might as well be calling Satoshi a she. It's impossible to know. But from Satoshi's background in cryptology and his programming abilities it's more than likely that Satoshi's a he. Just because of who is into that stuff. 90 percent or more guys usually. But I'd like Satoshi to be a she, sure. It's more interesting that way.

Q: Do you know why Satoshi invented Bitcoin when he did?

A: Do you know about the secret message hidden in the genesis block?

The genesis block? No, I didn't, but I certainly was going to find out.

THE GENESIS BLOCK

The Banking Debacle of 2008

The genesis block: it's the first Bitcoin block even mined, and because Bitcoin had to start somewhere people call it the *genesis block* since it generated the first bitcoins. Let's remember though . . . in order for bitcoins to be created, somebody has to a) have them and b) send them to somebody. This transaction is added to a transaction block and mined and a bitcoin reward is generated, adding bitcoins to the system. But this leads to a paradox. Bitcoins are created by mining a block of transactions, and a block of transactions implies bitcoins have moved from wallet A to wallet B. If there are no bitcoins to move from wallet A to wallet B there can't be any transactions, and without transactions to be mined no bitcoins can be awarded.[62] You need bitcoins in order to mine bitcoins, but the only way to create bitcoins is to mine. If you start at zero, it looks like Bitcoin can't get off the ground.

Satoshi was forced to make the genesis block a unique block, which didn't process any transactions (there were none to process) nor did it point to a previous block in the chain (there wasn't one). Instead Satoshi artificially generated a small number of bitcoins using this block and assigned them to e-wallets under his control. Satoshi was then able to send these bitcoins to a tiny group of curious insiders and volunteers who had signed up to test the new currency. As soon as the first transactions were posted, the transactions could be bundled into blocks and the blocks mined, creating new bitcoins and adding to the preexisting block chain. It was a tentative and slow liftoff.

The genesis block looks like this, when viewed in raw hexadecimal:[63]

```
00000000    01 00 00 00 00 00 00 00   00 00 00 00 00 00 00 00    ................
00000010    00 00 00 00 00 00 00 00   00 00 00 00 00 00 00 00    ................
00000020    00 00 00 00 3B A3 ED FD   7A 7B 12 B2 7A C7 2C 3E    ....;£íÿz{.²zÇ,>
00000030    67 76 8F 61 7F C8 1B C3   88 8A 51 32 3A 9F B8 AA    gv.a.È.Ã^ŠQ2:Ÿ.ª
00000040    4B 1E 5E 4A 29 AB 5F 49   FF FF 00 1D 1D AC 2B 7C    K.^J)«_Iÿÿ...¬+|
00000050    01 01 00 00 00 01 00 00   00 00 00 00 00 00 00 00    ................
00000060    00 00 00 00 00 00 00 00   00 00 00 00 00 00 00 00    ................
00000070    00 00 00 00 00 00 FF FF   FF FF 4D 04 FF FF 00 1D    ......ÿÿÿÿM.ÿÿ..
00000080    01 04 45 54 68 65 20 54   69 6D 65 73 20 30 33 2F    ..EThe Times 03/
00000090    4A 61 6E 2F 32 30 30 39   20 43 68 61 6E 63 65 6C    Jan/2009 Chancel
000000A0    6C 6F 72 20 6F 6E 20 62   72 69 6E 6B 20 6F 66 20    lor on brink of
000000B0    73 65 63 6F 6E 64 20 62   61 69 6C 6F 75 74 20 66    second bailout f
000000C0    6F 72 20 62 61 6E 6B 73   FF FF FF FF 01 00 F2 05    or banksÿÿÿÿ..ò.
000000D0    2A 01 00 00 00 43 41 04   67 8A FD B0 FE 55 48 27    *....CA.gŠý°þUH'
000000E0    19 67 F1 A6 71 30 B7 10   5C D6 A8 28 E0 39 09 A6    .gñ¦q0·.\Ö¨(à9.¦
000000F0    79 62 E0 EA 1F 61 DE B6   49 F6 BC 3F 4C EF 38 C4    ybàê.aÞ¶Iö¼?Lï8Ä
00000100    F3 55 04 E5 1E C1 12 DE   5C 38 4D F7 BA 0B 8D 57    óU.å.Á.Þ\8M÷°..W
00000110       8A 4C 70 2B 6B F1 1D 5F   AC 00 00 00 00          ŠLp+kñ._
```

Most of the data has meaning only to the Bitcoin network, but if you look carefully on the right you'll see something strange. Instead of a random sequence of characters, periods, and a scatter of punctuation marks, we find the following message, written in perfectly plain and legible English: "The Times 03/Jan/2009 Chancellor on brink of second bailout for banks."

This text does two things: it defines the lower limit of Bitcoin's birthday. The genesis block could have been created after this headline was published, but certainly not before. Second, it refers us to a *The Times of London* article published January 3, 2009, where the

Chancellor referred to is The Right Honourable Alistair Darling, Chancellor of the Exchequer,[64] and the action under debate is, "[the decision] within weeks whether to pump billions more into the economy as evidence mounts that the £37 billion part-nationalisation last year has failed to keep credit flowing. Options include cash injections, offering banks cheaper state guarantees to raise money privately or buying up 'toxic assets.'"[65] It was part of the freak-out associated with the 2008 global financial crisis.

That Satoshi included this message in Bitcoin's genesis block—literally the root of the currency—is key. In order to understand how this event triggered the development of a new currency, it's important to step back for a moment and review what caused the world to convulse in 2008. What was Satoshi—and many others—so upset about, and why had he included bank bailouts in the genesis block?

Wall Street Acting Badly, and the Failure of Trust

First, a brief history of modern financial malfeasance. It's been over eight years since the start of the banking crisis, and while everyone knows, broadly speaking, what happened and who's to blame, recent evidence has surfaced that more clearly indicates the root causes. It's finally possible to stand back and dispassionately determine what caused the crisis and forced an unpopular bailout, uniting Far-Left Democrats with Republican libertarians in loud disapprobation for rescuing banks either "unjustly" or "against the will of the marketplace," which otherwise would have resulted in widespread Wall Street bankruptcies.

It's difficult to overstate the effect of the 2008 bailout on libertarians or those leaning that way (many were converted in its wake). In their view, the bailout created perverse incentives and moral hazards, setting a dangerous precedent—concisely formulated by libertarian Harvard economist Jeffrey Miron:

> The obvious alternative to a bailout is letting troubled financial institutions declare bankruptcy. Bankruptcy means that shareholders typically get wiped out and the creditors own the company. Bankruptcy does not mean the company disappears; it is just owned

by someone new (as has occurred with several airlines). Bankruptcy punishes those who took excessive risks while preserving those aspects of a businesses [*sic*] that remain profitable. In contrast, a bailout transfers enormous wealth from taxpayers to those who knowingly engaged in risky subprime lending. Thus, the bailout encourages companies to take large, imprudent risks and count on getting bailed out by government. This "moral hazard" generates enormous distortions in an economy's allocation of its financial resources.[66]

The problem wasn't only government interference; one of Satoshi's central projects in developing Bitcoin was to remove the need for a "trusted third-party" to verify transactions. The banking crisis was caused by lack of transparency and (far too much) blind trust. Investors trusted banks (blindly) to invest conservatively and wisely—as they claimed to be doing. Banks trusted mortgage brokers (blindly) to sell them honest and viable mortgages. Everyone trusted the ratings agencies to do what they were supposed to do when asked to rate the new securities honestly and wisely.

The financial system is opaque by design, and it was impossible for even the most well-informed investor to know exactly where his or her money was going and what risks were associated with these investments. Satoshi, as well as the Cypherpunk movement more generally, objected to *trust without verification*. Early 2008 Wall Street was a bastion of unverified trust; by comparison, Bitcoin was designed to be private and anonymous but *verifiable*. You can *prove* you sent ten bitcoins to Sue down the hall; it's listed on the public ledger. Very little about how a bank functions is visible to the public—trust is required without proof being offered.

Let's remember what Satoshi had to say about currency, banks, and trust:

> The root problem with conventional currency is all the trust that's required to make it work. The central bank must be trusted not to debase the currency, but the history of fiat currencies is full of breaches of that trust. Banks must be trusted to hold our money and transfer it electronically, but they lend it out in waves of credit

bubbles with barely a fraction in reserve. We have to trust them with our privacy, trust them not to let identity thieves drain our accounts.

[When] strong encryption become available to the masses . . . trust was no longer required. Data could be secured in a way that was physically impossible for others to access, no matter for what reason, no matter how good the excuse, no matter what. It's time we had the same thing for money. With e-currency based on crypto-graphic proof, without the need to trust a third party middleman, money can be secure and transactions effortless.[67]

The banking crisis of 2008 forced these issues of trust into the limelight.

In 1998, the Glass-Steagall banking legislation was repealed, removing stringent limitations on banking options related to FDIC deposits.[68] While the power of Glass-Steagall had been waning for decades, its final repeal explicitly allowed investment banks to accept deposits, and permitted deposit-taking banks to invest funds as they saw fit. In 2000, following the dot-bomb crash of high-tech stocks, Federal interest rates plunged to 1 percent or lower and stayed there for years. Banks and individuals could no longer purchase bonds and achieve any sort of decent return, resulting in a surge of money flowing into other investments.

The advent of mortgage-backed securities (where mortgages were purchased, bundled together, tranched into various risk cat-egories, and sold), along with extremely naive or collusive ratings by major ratings agencies (triple-A assessments were routinely given to dubious securities), led to a huge new securities market. It threw open the door to the greatest repository of wealth in the country: houses, buildings, and the land they sit upon. A bank was offered one thousand mortgages from a holding company, and if each mortgage was worth on average $250,000, that's suddenly a pool of 250 million dollars to be organized, sorted, and sold as a security, which, because it was "backed" by actual land and homes, was deemed secure. The mortgages had, on average, an interest rate of 9 percent, while most bonds were paying less than 5 percent, and the 4 percent spread (difference) was vastly appealing to investors. Even if the banks took

1 percent as their payment for doing all the paperwork, it netted 3 percent more profit over many other investments. Since real estate mortgage defaults rates in American were, traditionally, extremely low, this looked like free money. You would be crazy not to grab 3 percent extra on the slight risk that, somehow, a bunch of mortgages would, all at once, fail catastrophically. It had never happened before. Even the most conservative banks were seduced.

What could possibly go wrong?

A lot. Once Wall Street saw how much money was involved in bundling mortgages to create mortgage-backed securities, and how much profit could be made from skimming away a percentage of the total, vast quantities of bad behavior occurred. Banks chased ever-higher margins and aggressively overlooked the possibility of mortgage defaults. Soon so many banks were chasing so many mortgages that the mortgage market began to dry up. Mortgages were becoming hard to find. What was the solution?

Increase home ownership, which had willing supporters at the highest levels of the federal government. George W. Bush believed home ownership drove economic prosperity. In 2002 Bush gave a spur-of-the-moment speech entitled "White House Conference on Increasing Minority Homeownership." Bush delivered it without teleprompters, from a text so heavily peppered with awkward Bushisms it must have been his own, as evidenced by the following: "You see, we want everybody in America to own their own home. That's what we want. This is—an ownership society is a compassionate society."[69]

In the speech Bush stated that his goal for the year was to "use the mighty muscle of the federal government" to spur housing growth, and he promptly matched words with deeds. Bush introduced affordable housing tax incentives and forced Fannie Mae and Freddie Mac to loosen their standards for low-income lending. Bush also proposed significant changes to mortgage regulations, allowing first-time buyers to qualify for government-insured mortgages with *no money down* (today, this looks absolutely insane). Bush concluded his speech with a stern message to mortgage lenders: "Corporate America has a responsibility to work to make America a compassionate place [by loosening mortgage standards to allow low-income accessibility to home ownership]."[70]

Corporate America listened, grateful. They got to work and undertook what they understood (and were told) was nothing less than their noble and patriotic duty. They promptly issued a huge batch of new mortgages, some at subprime rates of interest, some structured in ways previously illegal, with catastrophic balloon payments that would surely never be made. Many of these new types of mortgages were issued by companies that made money by quickly reselling their mortgages, not from any expectation of long-term mortgage repayment.

In other words, since mortgages were almost immediately "flipped" to banks who securitized them, it became not only possible but profitable (in a too-good-to-be-true story that actually occurred) to issue a $500,000 mortgage to a California farm worker whom the issuer knew would not be able to pay more than a month of the mortgage. How was this rational? Follow the money: after default, the sleazy mortgage issuer isn't affected, since they already sold the bad mortgage to a bank; the bank doesn't care, since they already securitized the mortgages and sold them to investors, for example a German investment group; and initially the Germans didn't care, as failure of a mortgage in the securitized bundle had little impact on the overall rate of return. It all held together and everyone made money except the farm worker, whose credit was destroyed for the pleasure of living in a mansion for a few months.

The rating agencies, looking at historical data of mortgage defaults, and unaware how much the rules had changed regarding "on the ground" mortgage issuance, gave everything a cheerful green light. A local bank, issuing a local mortgage, had to be vigilant against home buyers likely to default on their mortgage, due in part to the legal and administrative expense of foreclosure and eviction. Because of securitization, the thread of responsibility was severed. No longer did the mortgage issuer suffer if the mortgage failed in five years or five months. The incentives had changed, leading to all sorts of perverse results.

Not only were mortgage-backed securities diluted by hastily issued and often doomed mortgages, a new type of security suddenly arrived on the scene: unregulated derivatives, based on collateralized debt obligations (CDOs) applied to mortgage-backed securities.

They were the final product of what had become an unstable house of cards. These CDOs took a mortgage pool and sliced it up into tranches, which were bundles of higher- or lower-defaulting mortgages (at least from a historical perspective). Higher-risk defaults gave a higher return, and lower-risk default gave a lower return. Another type of investment instrument spawned by these CDOs, Credit Default Swaps (CDS), were essentially bets placed on the mortgage-based CDOs, either that the mortgages would continue to be paid as normal, or that mortgages would default in such numbers as to depress the CDOs' returns. Banks and institutions were able to create and sell these types of derivatives in an unregulated fashion, and it soon became apparent that the booming market for CDOs and CDSs (as well as the mortgage-backed security underpinning the entire system) had become both huge and massively complicated. It was often unclear which banks held derivatives on what security—or if an issuer would be able to pay if a derivative, structured to grow if mortgage default rates skyrocketed, suddenly increased in value a hundredfold.

From Fourier's point of view these developments were little better than "stockjobbers" gone wild: middlemen pulling so much value from both sellers and buyers that it was impossible to imagine the system remaining stable for long. Surely somebody was going to catch on to the fact that massive amounts of money were being funneled into private accounts without any redeeming social value or (much) labor being involved . . . weren't they?

If housing prices continued to rise and defaults remained comparatively low everything would be fine, but due to the rot created by the banking industry's insatiable demands, enabling subprime mortgages and the businesses that pushed them, a reckoning had to come. The real estate bubble inflated faster and faster and the number of suspect or outright fraudulent mortgages continued to increase until a tipping point was reached. In early 2008, for the first time ever, a mortgage-backed security contained so many mortgage defaults that it wasn't able to pay interest to its owners. Derivatives based on the security's failure were triggered, causing more money to be paid by the issuing bank. The entire financial market took note and held its collective breath.

If one mortgage-backed security could fail was another soon to follow? Was it a fluke? No fluke; another security soon failed, triggering a massive sell-off of any lingering mortgage-backed securities before investors realized how worthless they were—banks were desperate to get out before the bottom dropped out of the market. Some managed the trick; others didn't. But even after unloading their mortgage-backed securities, many banks were still in trouble. They had issued derivatives based on these bundled CDOs, most of which assumed housing prices would continue to rise. But not all of the derivatives. A few were structured so that the bank would lose an almost infinite amount of money should total default occur. Banks with the foresight to insure against this eventuality put almost impossible pressure on their insurers, who also began to fail. Everything collapsed at once: Wall Street, bank insurers, European banks, the rest of the world. When the real estate market imploded so did the economy.

The global recession of 2008–2012 was the direct result of Wall Street's greed, lack of oversight, and audacity (fueled by other people's money). Alan Greenspan, tireless opponent of financial regulation for derivatives, and indefatigable proselytizer about the efficiency of the unfettered free market, was finally forced to admit the inescapable truth: "Those of us who have looked to the self-interest of lending institutions to protect shareholders' equity, myself included, are in a state of shocked disbelief."[71] It was a face-saving way for Greenspan to admit that markets don't always "self-regulate," since short-term profits for everyone associated with mortgage-backed securities were so large and easy to come by that long-term objectives, and unease over the long-term safety of investors, were distinctly secondary considerations. In 2006, Merrill Lynch's mortgage division distributed bonuses worth, in aggregate, between five and six billion dollars; Dow Kim, the head of operations, took home $35 million all by himself.[72] With this much money flying around it would be an act of madness to suggest slowing down or double-checking the books or worrying about a mortgage issuance company. Wall Street was whizzing around at a few hundred rotations per second, and rational actors held onto the carousel and grabbed as many brass rings as they could get their hands on.

The result of the 2008 collapse? Banks largely to blame for the debacle were saved using public money, including the English bailout Satoshi chronicled in the genesis block.[73] In the United States, where there are no rules in place to limit executive pay, bank executives were rewarded with million-dollar bonuses in the midst of their firm's technical "bankruptcy." Public outrage was immediate, the Occupy Wall Street movement was born, and libertarians clicked their tongues with disapproval: the free market had, again, suffered terrible interference. Banks should have been allowed to fail, regardless of short- or long-term economic damage to the economy. A "moral hazard"[74] had been established, incentivizing perverse banking behavior. If disaster struck, the public paid the price. Libertarians chanted "privatize profits, and socialize losses"[75] to whomever was listening.

By 2009 faith in those running the banks plunged, and over 40 percent of the public claimed they had no confidence in Wall Street whatsoever.

Recession—mistrust in banks and financial institutions—anger toward Wall Street—unstable economies all over the globe. It was, looking back on it, the perfect time to introduce a new type of currency that calmly avoided every institution responsible for the disaster of 2008: banks, governments, and Wall Street itself.

A Leap of Faith

Seen in the light of the 2008 subprime mortgage crisis and broad disapproval of Wall Street, Bitcoin is a revolt against the status quo. By 2010 there existed a disgruntled public relatively open to the idea of a new currency that could serve as an end-run around many of the fees and inconveniences associated with modern banking as well as the systematic dangers inherent in Wall Street financial institutions. Bitcoin's timing was excellent, and surely not coincidental, but it takes a lot more than vague unease and good timing to get a currency up and running.

Imagine walking into a store and asking if they'll accept a new type of currency as payment for goods. After determining you are indeed serious, and not a gold-standard freak of one of the expected varieties, they might listen and think it over. It comes down to faith. Why would anyone believe a new currency won't become valueless in the next second, minute, or hour? Common or preferred stock represent a real-world investment, a percentage of a material company, and even stocks (as we all know) are a risk and capable of becoming worthless. What chance had a bit of paper without similar backing? It's a guarantee of loss. Even worse is a currency without a tangible symbol of worth in paper or specie, existing only as a sequence of electrons flowing through a computer system running open-source code. It sounds closer to a scheme cooked up by a con-man than anything vaguely respectable.

Who would accept such an insane proposition?

Not a brick-and-mortar store of the standard variety, which requires stable and expected cash flow. Not a white-collar professional, who doesn't need to take any risk at all. You would be hard pressed to find anyone willing to accept bitcoins beyond Bitcoin enthusiasts. What was needed was somebody, or something, desperate and without a reasonable alternative. Enter OkCupid.com.

Online dating sites have been around for over a decade and are full of honest lonely people searching for serious long-term relationships, as well as scammers and horndogs of the filthiest variety. Many sites require payment to access all their features, and many users (mostly men) would like to have such access but are not able to obtain it easily. Credit cards reveal actual names, and billing records live forever and might have to be explained to spouses, partners, etc. It's awkward.

A need existed (anonymous payment to a dating site) without a solution. Bitcoin stepped into the void. Nobody desperate enough to use bitcoins was ever going to pay using more traditional methods. It was a perfect combination from a business perspective: a slight increase in profit with little downside. It allowed the dating site to seize a market that could not be otherwise captured; typical users, who paid in typical ways, were not going to use bitcoins, which came with slight but real risks. Even if bitcoins lost value rapidly after being accepted, or were valueless after a few months, the dating site had plenty of time to convert them into dollars, typically the same day they were accepted. In 2013 OkCupid became the first "well-known" site, with a user base of millions, to accept bitcoins—another advance in the currency's steady drive toward respectability.[76]

Moving away from a national currency demands a leap of faith, a leap greatly hindered by the possibility of something truly frightening: partial or complete monetary loss. Many idealists will work for a cause and gather petitions and organize workers and talk the talk, but as experienced fundraisers will tell you parting people from their money—even hard-working idealists—is an art as much as a science. Having a good argument, promoting a worthwhile cause, and presenting a proven track record isn't enough. This was Bitcoin's early obstacle. No matter how strongly sympathetic many were to the cause, even true-believers opted to spend more time than money on the project. It was unlikely that Bitcoin would have gotten off the ground were it not for two fundamental drives: sex (fueling OkCupid) and drugs. In many ways the development of Satoshi's Bitcoin parallels that of a wayward teenager: after an inauspicious birth, and childhood's slow development, comes an explosive and unpleasant puberty. The second stage of Bitcoin's development occurred on the Dark Web, and its most famous enabler was Ross Ulbricht, aka the Dread Pirate Roberts.

CHAPTER 4

ROSS ULBRICHT: INTO THE DARK

It is VERY IMPORTANT to remember that animals raised for slaughter are kept in tightly controlled environments. . . . Humans are not. . . . [P]eople are also subject to an enormous range of diseases, infections, chemical imbalances, and poisonous bad habits. . . . You will obviously want a youthful but mature physically fit human in apparently good health. A certain amount of fat is desirable as marbling to add a juicy, flavorful quality to the meat. We personally prefer firm Caucasian females in their early twenties. These are ripe. But tastes vary, and it is a very large herd.

—"Butchering the Human Carcass
for Human Consumption"
(a presumably parodic essay
hosted on the Dark Web)[1]

A BRIEF SEMI-AUTOBIOGRAPHY

Ross Ulbricht was a member of the OkCupid online dating site and surely paid for upgraded membership using bitcoins—as we will soon discover, he had lots and lots of them. His profile is still online (http://www.okcupid.com/profile/ross-0), and what follows is data supplied by Ross himself, so take it with a grain of salt.

Height: 6′2″, weight: 165 pounds.

Straight/White/Does not smoke, but /Does drugs "sometimes," and /Eats anything, plus he /Likes dogs AND cats.

Worships the self-help classic *The Power of Now: A Guide to Spiritual Enlightenment.* [Ross is all about living in the moment].

Favorite song: "I'm Alive" by the Electric Light Orchestra, from the *Xanadu* soundtrack.

Favorite movies: *Best in Show* and *The Lord of the Rings.*

His automated OkCupid personality profile pumps out the following not-very-specific indicators: More optimistic/More drugs/More kinky. He's got a picture posted with the caption, "A shrine of dildos in thailand, no joke!"[2] and in it he's mugging for the camera with both hands pushing on his cheeks, making his lips a perfect circle—an ironic visual simulation of Betty Boop's shocked helium squeak.

What else? The internet is like a "second brain." His family is his "rock." He's agnostic, "but not too serious about it." "Many think I look like Robert Pattinson[3] at first." Please drop him a message if you are, "Bright, honest, curious, patient, happy, and well-adjusted."

A brief summary of Ross's life, according to Ross:

"I'm a scientist turned entrepreneur. I started out experimenting with organic solar tech and thin-film crystals. I've also built several businesses over the years in investment management, software, and books. Now I am an independent investor and plotting my next venture. So, if you have any great startup ideas, let me know!"

What's he do well? "Solving problems, giving advice, maintaining an infectious happiness despite my circumstances, standing up for what's right, and ping pong."

["Standing up for what's right"—this will be severely tested as Ross's site, Silk Road, grew into a monster.]

Ross spends a lot of time thinking about "Economics, politics, business, markets and the future." Under "Yearly Income" he coyly writes "Rather not say," because entering thirty million dollars[4] would have attracted too much attention.

As dating profiles go it's not that embarrassing. Profiles can't handle much scrutiny and were never intended to. They're supposed to supply a reasonably honest sketch, with enough detail for prospective matches to decide *yea* or *nay* or *hmmm, let's see* and strike up a conversation.

Ross comes across as a slightly druggy, moderately spiritual, and reasonably well-off scientist turned something else: businessman or entrepreneur. He's a happy guy able to remain happy regardless of circumstance, and unless you are virulently anti-drug or opposed to meat-eaters (he's a big fan of BBQ) there isn't any real reason to run away screaming. His photos are appealing or at least assertively bland. Ross seems like a normal guy. He's hugging a black puppy. He's upside-down doing a water skiing trick. Ross is single and straight and living in San Francisco, and when he made this OkCupid profile he was a little more than a year removed from life in prison.

In May 2015, Ross Ulbricht was convicted of running Silk Road, the first large-scale internet drug warehouse. When asked to describe Ross, friends often used words such as "quiet" and "thoughtful." His family found the police's initial round of accusations almost incomprehensible; there was no way Ross could be the Dread Pirate Roberts (the screen name for Silk Road's lead developer), who oversaw a vast empire of drugs, hacking services, illegal weaponry, and for-hire hit men. It made no sense at the time—and for many, it still doesn't.[5]

Born March 24, 1984, to Lyn and Kirk Ulbricht, Ross attended middle and high school in Austin, Texas, and experienced a relatively typical upper-middle-class existence. According to those around him, Ross was polite and a good student. With a deep love for the outdoors, Ross rose through the Boy Scout ranks, and on the strength of charity work (eagerly undertaken and seriously pursued) ultimately become an Eagle Scout. He sailed through high school without much trouble, graduated from the University of Texas at Dallas with enough academic acclaim to earn a full scholarship to Penn State, and by 2006 was pursuing a graduate degree in materials science. He told people he was happy. Ross looked happy, most of the time— but in quiet moments Ross doubted both himself and his academic endeavors. After earning his master's degree, Ross abandoned his science career, started a company or two, and when they failed (or he lost interest) Ross didn't know where to turn. That's when he read about Bitcoin and imagined how it might help newly minted libertarians, like himself, escape the straitjacket of governmental (or bank) supervision and control. He was immediately hooked.

Upon hearing the charges leveled against him, Ross's half-brother Travis Ulbricht confessed to being baffled, "He's an exceptionally bright and smart kid. . . . He's always been upstanding and never had any trouble with the law that I knew of."[6] His mother, staunchly defending him against all charges, attempted to make sense of the idea of her son as criminal mastermind, "Who he's been portrayed as is so not him, it's absurd. . . . He's one of the best people I know . . . my son as a child was so calm and peaceful he was like a little Buddha."[7]

While publicly proclaiming his innocence after being arrested, Ross filed a legal petition for return of 29,000 bitcoins (worth $14.5 million), which the government seized from a single e-wallet on his confiscated laptop. If you are wondering how Ross accumulated such a quantity of bitcoins while living in a small, unobtrusive one-bedroom apartment in San Francisco, his lawyer has a simple nonanswer: "It's not illegal to have bitcoins."[8]

The existence of a site like Silk Road prompts a series of important questions: what if everything, regardless of legality, was available for sale on the internet? What types of objects and services would appear? Would the site descend into chaos, or would it achieve a level of respectable stability?

Silk Road wasn't created in a vacuum. Ross leveraged the opportunity presented by two new technological developments, Bitcoin and the Dark Web—a secure, encrypted, and mostly secretive "parallel internet" where peer-to-peer communication is safe and generally untraceable. Add to this volatile mix Ross's increasing interest in libertarian economics and the freedom-at-all-cost philosophy underpinning much of what he read and the result was an economic experiment he called Silk Road.

Is the Dark Web truly secure? Was libertarianism really a major factor in Silk Road's development? Does it make sense to describe Silk Road as a libertarian utopia enabled by the Dark Web?

Yes to all. Libertarianism as a philosophical and economic theory was as necessary to Silk Road as any cryptographic or technological development. As Silk Road grew and prospered, Ross become increasingly confident in the rightness of his cause. Ross ultimately imagined Silk Road capable of nothing less than saving the world. His libertarian experiment was going to defeat the War on Drugs, recapture lost personal liberties, and reshape the economic landscape. After Silk Road *everything* would be different.

First, let's look at the Dark Web, and figure out how it functions—without it, Silk Road couldn't have existed. Once the Dark Web makes a little more sense, it's time to turn to the confusing intersection of libertarianism and what I am calling "nerd culture," which (when combined with the Dark Web) ultimately spawned the Dread Pirate Roberts and everything that was to come: millions of dollars of profit, worldwide notoriety, and an FBI sting operation years long in planning and execution.

THE DARK WEB

Once upon a time the internet was known as the "Information Superhighway," which like all propaganda past its expiration date now sounds slightly ridiculous, but it's still useful as a metaphor. The interstate highway system and its lauded superhighways form the unglamorous backbone of our economy; if all asphalt suddenly melted, leaving behind pebbles and filler, our highly efficient transportation system would be left in ruins and everything would stop: food left in fields, steel girders on eighteen-wheelers, employees stranded in suburbs. We depend upon the internet in a similar if not so extreme degree; nobody will starve[9] should our T1 cables become waterlogged, but life as we know it would certainly end.

We give thanks for this dazzling technological achievement about as often as we recognize the magic of turning on a light—infrequently. At least with electricity the story is somewhat familiar. Most of the time it begins in a dark mine as strips of coal are extracted from between layers of sedimentary rock by a longwall shearer. The strips are bundled and sent to a coal preparation plant where they are fed into the maw of an electrical generation station. The resulting electrical power is transported over transmission lines for hundreds (sometimes thousands) of miles before funneling into smaller neighborhood grids, at which point the current runs through a step-down transformer to reduce the voltage to a more manageable level, saving you from incineration should you accidentally close a circuit with your thumb and finger. Electricity runs through wires hidden in walls and buried in floors and laced through ceilings and eventually supplies power to the kitchen light fixture. A switch is flipped and electricity flows across a tungsten filament surrounded by inert gas (sealed in an elegant glass bubble)—producing hot bright light. We turn on lights automatically, unthinkingly, but it's the fruit of over two hundred years of innovation and unending maintenance of all the relevant systems.

The internet's communication network's not as extensive as the electrical grid but it's far more complex, since information travels in both directions. Electricity flows from generators to houses; except when solar panels are involved, houses rarely send any back. The internet depends upon give-and-take, uploading and downloading. How does this work on a mechanical level?

Imagine sitting at your home computer. To run a simple search (using the "Information Superhighway" metaphor) it's time to start driving down I-80 toward Google's servers. In essence, the computer dispatches the equivalent of a bike messenger, capable of riding close to the speed of light, who is tasked with carrying a message to Google and returning with a response. Before leaving, the messenger notes the computer's address, a long sequence that reliably identifies it— in this example, let's pretend it's been boiled down to the following string: "Upstairs_Computer." The bike messenger shoots out of the computer loaded with our search term, "cheese fermentation," and his first stop is the local modem. This is either a cable modem, a DSL modem, or another modem linked to our local provider (usually we pay this company for internet access; sometimes it's hosted by a school or business).

Our bike messenger makes a note of the modem's address so he can later retrace his steps, and hits the onramp to the public internet. This is the true superhighway; extremely fat fiber-optic trunk lines offer our messenger maximum speed. He shoots toward California, making it there in less than a second, and pulls up to Google. The

Google server takes our search term—"cheese fermentation"—and notes the computer it came from ("Upstairs_Computer") as well as any other details embedded in the message. After running a search, Google hands our messenger a pile of data and tells him to go back home. The messenger turns around and travels the path in reverse, since he recorded the addresses of the major modems and routers along the way. Before long the bike messenger has returned to the local internet provider, and speeds over to the local modem, and from there it's a leisurely drive down a wooded lane ending at the "Upstairs_Computer." The messenger dumps Google's data and stands around, waiting.

A browser interprets the pile of received data and displays it in human-readable form. Search complete.

Reviewing the round trip, it's easy to understand why experts confidently assert that the internet isn't anonymous. In order to receive data, a computer must have a fixed address (like "Upstairs_Computer") and it, in turn, is associated with a local modem connected to the computer via an Ethernet cord or within easy Wi-Fi distance. Most of the time the data we send over the internet isn't encrypted; anyone listening to internet traffic or monitoring the fiber-optic cables could read not only the search term, "cheese fermentation," but also the sequence of stops the search made on its way to Google, as well as the fixed address where it originated and to which it will eventually return. In theory, and in real life, it's possible to read the search message, subpoena the entity linked to the modem used to transmit it, determine the street address/customer name associated with the account, and determine exactly which computer in the house sent it. The actual person pushing the buttons might be unknown—it could have been a burglar typing, after all—but that's relatively minor. A single message out of the blizzard of internet data is tracked to its origin: a specific computer in a specific house at a specific time.

This isn't a flaw; it's a necessary condition of the system. In order to receive messages, you must indicate where to send the return data. It's possible to send Google a query stripped of any return address. The confused Google server will bundle up its data and dispatch it into the void, but obfuscating the return path is useless as a privacy ploy. Gaining anonymity by making it impossible to receive data is the same as not using the internet at all.

In 2015, computer networks don't promise much privacy and likely deliver far less than most user's minimal expectations. Given enough time, money, and manpower, anything you do on the web can be traced back to your computer: a chunk of data sent at this time to this location, another packet received a few seconds later. Ease of tracking creates a massive number of problems. It's dangerous for dissidents in oppressive regimes to use the internet for fear of being traced directly, or of compromising friends and allies by using their computers and resources. After being made aware of increasingly sophisticated global corporate espionage techniques, many businesses have become wary of using something as basic as email. Lack of anonymity impacts a researcher's ability to dig into obscure topics without (possibly) revealing his or her identity, or at least the rough location of the inquiries. A typical internet user, busy shopping or tweaking his fantasy football team, doesn't much care if somebody goes through a lot of trouble to read his communications; for others it's a matter of life, death, or economic blackmail.

Edward Snowden's leaks of classified United States government documents have conclusively proven that the radical privacy advocates' criticisms were not only true but mild in their overall scope.[10] The National Security Agency (NSA) has been collecting Short Message Service (SMS) messages from phones and other devices for the last ten years. Internet data is copied continuously in its entirety from router taps placed on major US and foreign providers, either with their knowledge and complicity or not[11]. Underwater fiber-optic cables have been compromised. Phones calls are recorded—not only the numbers dialed but the actual conversations. Location-tracking data for users of cell phones is logged and stored. Emails and phone calls from the president of Brazil and the German chancellor Angela Merkel have been intercepted, read, and filed away. There is no reason to believe that anything you do over the internet, or anything however remotely connected with your phone, is going unrecorded.

The highly unsecure, easily tapped internet inspired the creation, in 1995, of more reliable ways to communicate. It was, paradoxically, produced by employees of the United States Naval Research

Laboratory, who had been tasked with protecting online US intelligence communications. The secure network they came up with was further refined by the Defense Advanced Research Projects Agency (DARPA) in 1997 and finally released to the public in 2002 as The Onion Router (Tor). The US government was deeply involved with funding, research, and development of technologies leading to Tor, which quickly turned into one of the most powerful weapons available to the public against governmental overreach and spying. In other words, the government developed and made public the system they are now desperately trying to hack. It wasn't clear, back in the late 1990s, that privacy would be an issue for citizens as well as spooks, the eavesdropping enemy not external but our own internal surveillance programs. The government should have read the Cypherpunk manifesto!

Tor introduced the idea of a free and anonymous online network using something called onion routing. Imagine repeatedly peeling the skin off an encrypted onion in order to get to an unencrypted core—that's the eponymous inspiration for Tor. The overall concept is simple, even if its implementation is complex.

First of all, all Tor transmissions are encrypted. A Google search sent using Tor is encrypted up to the moment it reaches Google; anyone intercepting it midstream gets gibberish unless they manage to break the encryption (almost impossible). That's an excellent start. More important is what happens during the transmission itself. In our previous example, using standard internet connections, the search-bearing bike messenger went from Point A (a home computer) to Point B (a local modem) to Point C (the public internet) to Point D (Google) and back again. Every step of the way, the message being sent was appended with a history of where it had been and where it was going, making it trivially easy to track to its source.

Tor changes all this. The Tor network uses servers (called nodes) linked together in a random sequence to obfuscate the origin and destination of any given transmission. Instead of sending a Google search message from Point A (home computer) to Point B (modem) to Point C (the wild, open internet), Tor wraps the message in various encrypted skins, layered five or ten deep. The Tor-encrypted search message, ultimately destined for Google, initially reveals nothing to the world except the command "Go to Tor node 1,405." Everything else is encrypted, and the actual message is buried deep within the encrypted layers. Only Tor node 1,405 has the special key enabling it to decrypt the next part of the message, which says "Go to Tor node 531." The message gets shunted to Tor node 531 which decrypts it, and this time it says "Go to Tor node 42." Each node is being run by a different Tor server linked to the internet; the message might travel halfway across the world as it bounces from node to node. The message keeps getting forwarded until its inmost core is exposed by a lucky node, which finally decrypts and reads the real purpose of the message: "Go to Google.com and run a search for 'cheese fermentation.'"

All this bouncing around makes it impossible to track the path of a given message. If a Tor transmission is intercepted by the government or foreign agents or curious aliens, they will end up with a message plucked from between Tor nodes, whose contents is encrypted and unreadable and whose origin in similarly obscure. Where did it come from? Another Tor node, and that's very uninformative, because thousands of messages are bouncing from node to node every second. Since Tor nodes can't be forced to divulge what previous node a message has come from, all that can be learned from an interception is, "This message came from Tor node 513." Asking Tor node 513 for more information about its transactions is impossible. Not only won't it tell if it could, it physically can't. After a Tor node forwards a message to another Tor node that forwarding event is erased from memory and isn't stored on any hard drive. Unless there are extremely few messages flowing through Tor nodes, the origin of any given message is necessarily lost in a data blizzard— and there are always lots of messages moving through Tor, with more arriving every day.

When the Tor node that decrypted the core message sends it off to Google and receives a reply, the node immediately wraps the message in new layers of encrypted skins and forwards it to a different Tor node. What happens next is the same process in reverse. After bouncing around a while, becoming progressively unwrapped by ten or more Tor nodes, one of them again reaches the core, which consists of Google search data and, crucially, the address of the home computer it was originally sent from. The Tor node reencrypts this and sends it to the Tor client running on the home computer, which handles the final decryption. After long travels and countless encryption/decryption cycles, the Google search is finally sitting on the hard drive, and it's almost impossible to imagine how anyone could ever trace it back to its source.

Imagine a spy intercepting the message between Tor nodes. Who cares? It's encrypted and only tells the spy that an unknown message was sent from one node to another. What about intercepting it before it hits Google? All that can be determined is the search term and the Tor node it was sent from, not the originating computer, for that information remains on the Tor network, safely encrypted. What about before the message returns to the home computer? It's encrypted, and the exposed part only says it was delivered from a Tor node. All external links between the home computer and the eventual Google search have been broken. There isn't any way to trace a message once it enters the Tor nodes where it is randomly batted around.

Does this really work? Yes. The combination of strong encryption and message path mixing between Tor nodes makes for a relatively secure network. Has the NSA broken it? Likely no. There were indications[12] that the NSA had *possibly* tracked one or two messages on the Tor network back to their source, but this involved rare conditions (very few Tor nodes in a remote location) that are unlikely to be duplicated with the robust Tor network available in the United States and most of the world.

What is the result of this anonymous, encrypted, free network? Sites such as WikiLeaks, where people are able to upload and download content without fear of reprisals, giving whistleblowers invaluable assistance in their drive to expose governmental or corporate malfeasance . . . as well as sites advertising the following:

High quality counterfeits USD/EUR!
   High quality counterfeits, Our money, is almost perfect, can be passed at most retailers easily. Sometimes the colouring in certain batches might be a little off, , but to most cashiers it's all the same and we're always working to improve it. Shipping from France.

Or:

GRAND OPENING SPECIAL
    Methaqualone(Quaaludes) Capsule- 300mg -2 MAX PER ORDER-12 USD = 0.018 BTC

Or:

> I will "neutralize" the ex you hate, your bully, a policeman that you have been in trouble with, a lawyer, a small politician. . . . I do not care what the cause is. I will solve the problem for you. Internationaly [*sic*], cheap and 100% anonymously.
>
> Doing this over the Tor network is probably the safest way to do it at all. I do not know anything about you, you do not know anything about me. The desired victim will pass away. No one will ever know why or who did this. On top of that I always give my best to make it look like an accident or suicide.

When the Tor network became available in 2004, new business opportunities opened up. Counterfeiters produced high-quality copies without running the risk of actually using the money themselves—instead they mailed out hundred-dollar bills for one tenth of the printed value. In this way counterfeiters are able to perfect their art, receive and fill anonymous orders online, and carefully (I assume they are wearing gloves in a clean room and no fingerprints are transferred) stuff envelopes for distribution into mailboxes at random and scattered intervals around a nameless city. Tor and a home computer makes it impossible to trace the origin of the counterfeiter's advertisement, any incoming orders, or the flow of bitcoins from customer to merchant. If the cops get involved it's likely due to a slip-up on the part of the counterfeiter: somebody randomly stumbled across their setup or they attempted to mail a thousand packages at the same time, were caught on camera, and the police put two and two together.

This is what is meant by the Dark Web: a free network created by Tor nodes and funneling data anonymously and safely from computers to servers and back again.[13] Anything done on the Dark Web can't be traced to a geographical location, even a country, much less a specific computer. Using the Dark Web, people can communicate safely and securely; Tor-based email and messaging (functioning much like Gmail and entirely free) allows security-conscious businesses to safely transfer data; and everywhere the powerless and the fearful, the vulnerable and the marginalized, have a safe and secure method to expose the truth wherever it is found, whomever it might upset, no matter how much money or political power is arrayed against them. And lots and lots of drugs can be sold.

Drug sales predominate Dark Web stores. Sites are in vigorous competition over heroin, fighting over both quality and price, although pharmaceutical drugs are also quite popular. Quaalude and its close cousins from various families (barbiturates, benzodiazepines, nonbenzodiazepines) are widely featured, and given their laboratory origins and guarantee of relative purity are brisk sellers. Much more disturbing than the ubiquitous drug stores are the "service provided" advertisements, featuring claims I hope are either parody or scams or something lodged between the two. Hit men are strangely numerous and claim to be more than willing to "off" somebody for as little as "100 bitcoins." Other services are less extreme, thus more likely. Hackers peddle their wares, promising to break into your enemy's, or boyfriend's, Gmail account within hours, fully guaranteed. Others sell viruses or malware or spyware of the most intrusive nature; the most disturbing spyware is engineered to control webcams or phone cams remotely without activating the webcam "in use" light, allowing a voyeur to watch and record the ongoing stream. Potential customers are assured there is no way the subject being filmed on the other end will ever know their webcam or phone camera is transmitting a recording over the internet, opening the door to a spectacular number of horrifying abuses.

Trust Me, OK?

In the early days of the Dark Web the major problem with these types of service ads, and even professional-looking sites, was trust. Sure, a hit man says he can make it look like an accident, but he won't meet any client in person and he won't give his real name (of course) and he suggests forwarding fifty bitcoins into an e-wallet and asks potential customers to wait for an encrypted email with further details. It might work, and it might not. There just isn't any way to tell. And if it doesn't work there's absolutely no recourse. That's the problem with anonymity. It cuts both ways. Sure, you are safe from the police, and protected from snoops and spies, but in achieving this security you are forced to relinquish your real identity and the protections commonly associated with it.

On the Tor network you are who other people believe you are, no more and no less. If you don't come across as a legitimate hit man (and I can't possibly imagine how a legitimate hit man ad reads), you won't get any business even if you have worked for the Sicilian mob for the last fifty years and can point to a long trail of bodies in your bloody wake. A Dark Web drugstore *might* mail a pack of Quaaludes for twenty dollars, as advertised, but if the site is new it's a risk, no doubt. Then again, how can you tell how new a site is, or how respectable? Ask around, look for reviews, try the messages boards . . . but who says the reviews aren't written and posted by the drugstore owners themselves? And so it goes, tempting things—arguably juicy things—are offered and the price seem reasonable . . . but is it genuine? How can anyone trust what's being said? Con artists love the Dark Web. They are able to perfect their art in complete anonymous safety. If somebody falls for their scam and sends the con artist bitcoins it's all over—the con artist wins, there simply isn't any way to track him down. Who is to say the Dark Web, as a whole, isn't an elaborate fraud?

For online products, there's a way to get around this issue. Imagine setting up a Dark Web poker site called Dark Poker, allowing those in the United States (for whom online poker is still illegal) to play real poker for real money. New users could post on a secure Tor-powered message board their desire to join the site, and include the following information: a secure Tor-based email address, a link to a Bitcoin transaction that proves they sent (say) five bitcoins to the Dark Poker bitcoin address, and their requested poker name.

The Dark Poker site monitors the message board thread, notes five bitcoins added to its e-wallet, links this deposit to the secure email listed in the post, and creates a new user with the suggested name. Dark Poker credits the user five bitcoins and a site password is emailed to their secure email site. The user can then log on and play to his heart's content. If Dark Poker wants to be transparent and make it clear they are not going to abscond with everyone's bitcoins, a different thread can be used for bitcoin withdrawals. A user posts that they want a certain amount withdrawn and the bitcoin address to send it to. The Dark Poker site sends them bitcoins, and proves it by linking to the public bitcoin transaction. If Dark Poker suddenly stops sending bitcoins after requests have been made it will be clear almost immediately and everyone will stop sending Dark Poker bitcoins until they explain what's going on.

As long as users don't keep too many bitcoins at the Dark Poker site, and they withdraw them regularly if they win big, it's fairly safe. Sure, the site could abruptly pack up and leave, but careful users wouldn't lose much. If Dark Poker has a relatively high "rake" (the commission they receive from any pot) it might be more profitable to stay in business and make an semi-honest living (as far as US laws are concerned). This sort of input and output transparency is possible with Bitcoin, even if it's rarely implemented.

The real problem occurs when you use Bitcoin to pay for material things. It's one thing to sell cocaine on the Dark Web a handful of times, but it's another to do it for years, mailing packages all over the world without getting caught. The danger involved in procuring and handling drugs is significant, making retirement a tempting option. Instead of mailing packages to the next five hundred customers, why not keep their bitcoins as well as the product? Leave the drug-dealing site open as long as possible—until word gets out that merchandise isn't getting mailed anymore—by which time you might have cleared twenty or thirty thousand dollars, and possibly more. Unlike drug shipments, Bitcoin theft is impossible to trace. The bitcoins were taken and that's all that's known. The thief retreats into the shadows.

Why would anyone run a drug superstore for very long, given the dangers of running it and the lovely untraceable joy of stealing everyone's bitcoins after initially proving the store's legitimate?

There's only one way to get around the issue of trust. First, create a stable drug marketplace hosted on a server with a solid and anonymous connection to the Tor network. Second, allow drug merchants to sign up with the site and, eBay-style, become sellers. The host site isn't touching any of the drugs; in theory, it will remain above the fray and out of reach of the cops. This greatly reduces the temptation to cut-and-run; if you are making plenty of money in a safe way, buffered from real-world illegal activities, why bother stealing it in a safe way?

Third, include a mechanism for customer feedback. Allow customers to rate the site, rate different merchants hosted on the site, and air complaints as well as praise. Customers will be able to warn other (potential) customers of bad merchants and guide them toward good ones. Feedback is the first line of defense for shoddy or nonexistent service. As on eBay, highly rated merchants, trustworthy and prompt in their shipments, will find their business booming. New merchants could be forced to keep a certain number of bitcoins in escrow, controlled by the site, until they had proven themselves to be legitimate traders. Once they built up a positive reputation the escrowed funds would be released and the merchants, now legitimate partners, would be allowed to proceed with a greater volume of sales.

This was Ross Ulbricht's vision for Silk Road, and he incorporated all of these sensible trust-building mechanisms. It was an immediate success. Customers browsing the Dark Web craved the legitimacy Silk Road provided; at long last there was a site with standards, actively trying to corral and contain chaos. Absolute freedom to say whatever you want and make any claim under the sun is fine in theory, but as a social experiment the Dark Web showed that policing is always necessary, even if it's self-policing. Because of Ross's careful management of vendors, implemented via rules and regulations,[14] Silk Road became a trusted site for many, the go-to destination and warehouse for mostly illegal merchandise, including but not limited to: LSD, cocaine energy six-packs, vaporizers, suboxone, MDMA crystals larger than a child's fist, Adderall, Grade AAA kiwi hash, psilocybin in dizzying fungal varieties, chloroform, fake Ray Ban sunglasses, dense nugs,[15] neon-colored vibrators of shocking Japanese design, counterfeit Chanel dresses, White Widow marijuana seeds, and a large lemon butter cookie. The latter, no doubt, heavily doped.

It was all too good to be true.

Enter Bitcoin

The idea of an internet drug marketplace has a long and sordid history. There currently exist many quasi-legitimate drug stores on the normal unencrypted internet where people can buy Vicodin or codeine from online sites hosted in countries where such purchases are legal, and customers can feel reasonably confident about the purchase. Given the small amount of money changing hands, and the minor drug violations involved, most of these businesses fly under the radar. It is asymptotically unlikely (approaching zero) that local or federal law enforcement is tracking such shipments, or would take much interest in somebody's twenty-dollar purchase of painkillers, much less waste their time arresting and prosecuting the victimless white-collar (and often white) criminals. These sorts of drug stores operate in a grey area, selling genuine drugs and supplements alongside mild narcotics that are illegal in some but not all countries without a prescription. As a rule they don't sell universally illegal (schedule one) substances: hallucinogens, heroin, cocaine, or any of the stronger opiates—such products would fatally undermine any argument that the drug store in question is legitimate if perhaps a little loose in their prescription requirements (or lack thereof).

Such stores were a baby step toward the ultimate goal—a website openly selling any drug under the sun, choice and availability only a click away. Not only the expected home-grown or -brewed options (crack, marijuana, magic mushrooms, meth), but high-end laboratory pharmaceuticals as well (such as Dilaudid, medical-grade cocaine).

The government would be extremely interested in all purchases from such a site and likely would be tracking every transaction. In order to make a purchase from such a site, a prospective buyer would have to a) send money and b) supply a mailing address. Sending money requires paperwork, forms, and identification given to an independent financial entity (postal order, Western Union, bank balance transfer, etc.). None of these are private nor claim to be; in fact large money transfers must, by law, be transparent and reported. If somebody transmits money for a drug, a shipping address must be included, which is (at best) a PO box and (at worst) a home address.

Given a bit of snooping, the authorities would have everything needed to prosecute: a name, a record of money changing hands, the delivery destination, and ultimately the (intercepted) drugs. This makes for an extremely poor business model, as the dangers are two-fold: the money is perilous to send, and the product is risky to receive. A rudimentary sting operation might result in felony charges and multiyear prison sentences. Only the most desperate (or stupid) customers would dare to use such a site.

Perhaps inadvertently, Bitcoin solved both of these problems.[16] Anyone in the world can anonymously send bitcoins to an electronic wallet, which can be accessed by the anonymous owner of the wallet and the bitcoins eventually converted into cash. A Bitcoin user on a secure network (such as Tor) can safely transfer bitcoins to another e-wallet without the possibility of anyone tracking the transaction. This takes care of problem one, how to send money: Bitcoin is the anonymous solution to the problem of traceable paperwork and third-party involvement. As for the second problem, a shipping address, sufficiently secure and encrypted communication networks guarantee that only the drug site will have access to this information. As long as the drug seller wasn't informing the DEA about shipments,[17] a drug marketplace was fully feasible, the shipping address being the only point of customer contact. From the point of view of entrepreneurs without respect for local, national, or international law, an opportunity had suddenly opened up. Sites rushed to fill the void.

Silk Road was the most successful of the early adopters. It wasn't perfect, but it was good enough, and it was soon doing over $3 million a month in sales. Consumers in Australia could order high-quality opium balls from Thailand and have them mailed directly to their homes. Without leaving the couch or negotiating in dangerous back alleys with dubious dealers, customers could get their fix safely, affordably, and (a good percentage of the time) as agreed upon.[18] Since Bitcoin was the engine driving the enterprise, demand for bitcoins skyrocketed. The new currency had found a thriving user base.

THE DREAD PIRATE ROBERTS
AND LIBERTARIANISM, AGAIN

The Dread Pirate Roberts is a character in the cult book and movie *The Princess Bride*, a fact incredibly obvious to those of a certain age and inclination who lump it together with Monty Python movies[19] and *This Is Spinal Tap* and *Office Space* and *Best in Show* and other well-written, generally funny movies of the type often shown on college campuses and known for their broad quotability in many situations (though fewer than imagined). *The Princess Bride* screen adaptation features a young Robin Wright as the princess bride; the scene-stealing Andre the Giant and his impossibly annoying partner-in-crime played by Wallace Shawn, whose death by overthinking is one of the best scenes of the movie; Inigo Montoya as an expert fencer who famously stops using his off-hand when the going gets tough—an almost endless series of iconic scenes and characters. ·

The Dread Pirate Roberts is a swashbuckler caught between two warring nation-states and feared by everyone for his ruthlessness and fencing skill. He wears a mask at all times, obscuring his true identity, and it's eventually revealed that the Dread Pirate Roberts isn't an individual but a title: the name given to the current captain of a mighty pirate ship, retained through the ages for its fear-provoking and surrender-inducing power. It's not possible to kill the Dread Pirate Roberts; as soon as you whack one another pops up.[20] It's a label that can be passed down from an aging pirate to a young buck, which is exactly what happens in the novel: Westley, a farm-boy-turned-pirate, greatly impresses the current (and bloodthirsty) incarnation of the Dread Pirate Roberts, and Westley is thereafter groomed as his replacement.[21]

That the Dread Pirate Roberts, a name broadly acknowledged as ridiculous even by characters in the tongue-and-cheek world of *The Princess Bride*, inspired the administrator of Silk Road isn't as strange or unusual as it might seem. If Silk Road had been run by Green_Bay_Packers_Rule, or Brittany4eva . . . *that* would have qualified as unusual. But the Dread Pirate Roberts fits in quite comfortably with a certain slice of the population, loosely but not exclusively termed "nerds."[22]

American culture, never shy of stereotypes, knows nerds when it sees nerds and doesn't mind pointing them out. But what began as a pejorative term for the intelligent but socially inept has changed over time, and it's not unusual these days to overhear a beautiful ingénue in dark-rimmed glasses call herself, with pride, a "nerd." Pinning down the confusing characteristics of nerdiness is tricky, but there's something culturally significant embedded in the old stereotype, shedding light on the conjunction of the Dark Web and a harmless pirate from a children's book.

Socially speaking, nerds are at the bottom of the totem pole; a nerd is either unable to climb any higher or uninterested in something as shallow as social status. A nerd is shy and romantically challenged, physically uninspiring, and indifferent to sports. Solving problems with logic and close argumentation is vastly preferred over fisticuffs. Most are male, some are female, most are white, some are Asian, and a tiny sliver are African-American or other mixed race blends.[23] Many have a higher-than-average level of education compared to the average American. Nerds are more-or-less optimistic, happier than the average American, not prone to irony, and though shy capable of the most amazing displays of unselfconscious exhibitionism (ComicCon, Cosplay festivals, etc.).[24]

Claims that "nerds" are the "new mainstream"[25] are hard to justify, at least if shows such as *The Big Bang Theory* are used as evidence (and they often are). Broadcast TV generally thins unusual elements into a bland dilution, little differentiated from the norm. It's not that we're all becoming geeks and nerd culture is a juggernaut crushing everyone beneath its weight. . . . The truth is much more plausible and far more boring: the superficial indicators of nerdiness are appropriated and grafted upon an otherwise humdrum situation comedy.

Yet there is such a thing as nerd culture, a diffuse, hard to define but you-know-it-when-you-see-it quality often distilled and hardened by college into lifelong form. Nerds are often, but not exclusively and certainly not all-inclusively, interested in the following: video games, anime, and Star Wars; Renaissance Fairs, the Far Side, and D&D (Dungeons and Dragons). They are generally antisport, intellectual, and obsessive. Nerds are socially nervous and reliant on communal jokes in order to remove stress from social interactions with a ready bag of references and quotes. A nerd is the opposite of the wit: the wit sparks the moment while the nerd returns, again and again, to past laughs, to the safety of communal humor. Thus the heavy quotability of the most beloved nerd movies: they are an endless source of social lubrication for those who share their sense of humor, and require little more than a good memory to exploit. Delighting in puns and verbal absurdities, nerds are both self-aware and unapologetic in their love of highbrow (or at least higher-brow) art and entertainment. Nerds know they are nerds and that non-nerds look down on them. It's just that they profess not to care (and, to their credit, they often don't).[26]

Nerd humor in that most canonical nerd field, computer programming, illustrates the nerd mindset very clearly. A long line of programmers have been having fun with their coded creations from the start of compiled executables. What came to be known as "Easter eggs," features or messages made visible after entering elaborate and often impossible-to-stumble-upon-by-chance keyboard input, reveal a playful instead of idealized sense of creativity. Unlike a painter who, after finishing a painting, is loath to touch the canvas again, and would certainly resist adding a small visual joke in one corner for those observant enough to notice, programmers have no problem goofing around with their code. It's not unusual to find light humor even in a software's most sensitive features. The Linux kernel, one of the most important and deeply buried processes of the free, open-source, Windows-replacing system Linux, has an extremely powerful reboot() function that requires the user to enter one of three so-called "magic numbers" in order to be activated. These numbers happen to be Linus Torvalds's children's three birthdays, apparent after you convert the number's decimal values into hexadecimal (a base 16 numbering scheme). Ponder that: a child's date of birth is the key to a system reboot.

Programmers at MIT in 1963 (which shows how far back this sort of thing goes) named a UNIX process a daemon, inspired by Maxwell's Demon, a well-known thought experiment featuring a molecule-sorting demon.[27] To this day the UNIX and LINUX systems feature daemons of all kinds, from the mail daemon to the telnet daemon to hundreds of other daemons, giving a distinctly medieval flavor to the computer's most fundamental processes. Easter eggs have become extremely common, with examples such as *The Book of Mozilla* hiding in the Firefox browser, a video game accessible from any YouTube video, and a psychoanalysis program (ELIZA) buried in the Macintosh OS.[28]

Apparently nothing's too big or important to exclude messing around with, a notion made concrete by the video game industry's sudden success four decades ago, which essentially kicked off and defined what it means to be a computer-obsessed nerd.

Nerd Origins with Atari

Imagine the time and place: 1972, the sunny vales of Sunnyvale, California, in the early days of what later became known as Silicon Valley. A small company called Atari had created an arcade version of *Pong*, an extremely basic computer game that, in retrospect, looks like virtual tennis played using huge square pixels. Two players control two separate white rectangles that can be moved vertically; a white square representing the "ball" bounces between them, if both players manage to intercept the ping-ponging ball with their virtual "racket." What people responded to, and what made the Atari home version of *Pong* such a huge hit, was 1) it was an entirely new type of game, and 2) for the first time in their lives, television wasn't a passive medium. People weren't able to do much but they could at least do something: move a white rectangle up and down and have their television respond to their input. For a generation trained to sit for hours, motionless, in front of a screen, this qualified as a revolution. What had been static was now dynamic.

The key to Atari's early success was management's broad-minded understanding that lack of software development tools and easy graphical interfaces and plug-in modules and shared code meant that game programming was both difficult and demanding. Code modifications had to be assembled in binary, burned into a cartridge, shoved into an Atari 2600 game console, and loaded on screen to see what changes, if any, were visible in the output. Programming was done in assembly, which if you have never seen it looks a lot like random input:

```
;  -----------------------------------
processor 6502
VSYNC = $00
VBLANK = $01
WSYNC = $02
NUSIZ0 = $04
NUSIZ1 = $05
COLUPF = $08
COLUBK = $09
PF0 = $0D
PF1 = $0E
PF2 = $0F
SWCHA = $280
INTIM = $284
TIM64T = $296
```

Early Atari 2600 programmers typed in thousands of lines like this, relatively blind, hoping when he (it was almost always a he) got a chance to see it on screen the results weren't too far from what he imagined he was doing.

Given these requirements, and a tiny pool of qualified software developers, Atari was forced to do what was best for it despite internal qualms. Programmers were treated as crucial employees and had *carte blanche* to eat what they wanted, wear what they wanted, drink what they wanted, and smoke what they wanted.[29] As long as they met their programming quotas (*this* amount of work done in *that* amount of time), management was content not simply to step back but to enable what became an early crucible of programming culture.[30] Atari spawned not only the most famous video games in history, but originated much of what later became crystalized as "nerd" values. Roughly speaking, it didn't matter what you wore or what you looked like; it didn't matter if you had five martinis for lunch or smoked weed in the courtyard from a purple bong; it didn't matter if you enjoyed working after midnight and could be found napping at your desk from eight a.m. till noon. What mattered was, in this order, 1) having fun, and 2) working hard on a job you loved, which lead to 1), which led to 2), and so on in a delirious closed loop.

Early Atari programmers were, as a group, amazingly talented, highly creative, open-minded, and overwhelmingly productive. It is said that each programmer was responsible, in a single year, for generating over 10 million dollars in profit. As Atari became more popular the programmer's profitability increased, and management would have been crazy to change anything. Instead, they installed a hot tub on the premises (". . . with the Atari Fuji symbol on the back wall in orange and blue tile"[31]), enabling a series of world-class coed hot tub parties. They brought in kegs when milestones were reached, and in general everyone rode the wave for as long as they could.

The overriding philosophy, if something so straightforward can be said to define a philosophy, could be summed up with this phrase: *if it causes no harm, don't worry about it.* Atari worried if a programmer missed a deadline or produced shoddy work. That was a problem. If a programmer produced good work and wasn't actively bothering anyone else—no worries. Drug use and abuse was rampant.[32] Potential hires were taken into interview rooms and causally handed lit joints to see how they would react. (If you wanted the job you partook, or at least declined without making a fuss). Yes, these things were technically illegal, but the defining spirit of the company and the nascent Silicon Valley culture overrode such details. Rules were silly if they stopped people from behavior that clearly didn't harm anyone except (possibly) themselves. Rules were even more silly if they got in the way of a programmer's enjoyment, his ability to produce a game, and deep immersion in a job well-loved.

For many of these early Atari game designers, primitive graphics and an unforgiving programming language weren't enough to stop them from looking back on the period with longing: regardless of later successes with other companies, producing vastly more sophisticated games, many view their time at Atari as the highlight of their working life. They worked with friends and partied with friends and sometimes didn't leave the office for a week, and what they produced was lauded and praised and played the world over. Wasn't it the perfect storm? Wasn't it the best of all possible worlds?

Atari supplied the map not only for how nerds worked and played but also with their casual view of drug use and the respect they afforded restrictive drug laws (not much). This hard-working, hard-playing, extremely productive group of people spawned an industry, and for many it wasn't coincidence—they were given broad latitude and freedom to work and conduct business as they saw fit. Would a stringently top-down management style have succeeded half as well? Would a drug-free environment have helped or hindered overall efficiency? It's impossible to know for certain, but it seems unlikely.

Atari functioned as a minor libertarian experiment; while most participants didn't consider themselves libertarians, Atari nevertheless allowed them the freedom to do what they thought best. They were treated as adults, and if they failed to achieve their goals, or got out of hand, or stole from the company they accepted the consequences (often immediate firing). A Dark Web drug site such as Silk Road took what began at Atari and pushed it to the limit.

The penalty for operating Silk Road, which the government considered a "Continuing Criminal Enterprise" (running afoul of the dreaded Kingpin Statute[33]) carries a mandatory minimum of twenty years' imprisonment. Since this is applied on top of any other penalties, the net result is often life in prison. This is pretty far away from Atari employees bringing kegs of beer to work or alternating weed with small energizing bursts of cocaine. Involvement in large-scale drug trafficking requires interactions with people you wouldn't want to anger nor trust. It looks, on the face of it, like an enterprise as distant from a humorous children's book as you could get, and choosing a name such as Dread Pirate Roberts is unlikely to inspire a drug-dealing or -buying stranger's confidence in an upstart venture. But that's missing the point.

Yes, Silk Road was illegal and was surely going to cause trouble for somebody, somewhere, but the fact that it was illegal didn't imply, *ipso facto*, it was immoral. Or even something to take that seriously. It's famously illegal to remove a mattress tag in a store display, but is doing so necessarily immoral, or a light-hearted act of civil disobedience by somebody who sees this extension of the legal system into bed tagging as absurd and essentially asking to be laughed at?

What's broadly called nerd culture has contrarian views lodged deep in its DNA. The status quo isn't something to be coddled and blindly respected. If certain drug laws are silly, ignore them. If broadly accepted cultural values based on sports or fashion or ironic detachment seem pointless—ignore them. Don't be content letting bad solutions dominate. A better way should be found, no matter how challenging the task.

Consider the primacy of Microsoft Windows in 1991. It was pretty much the only operating system being used on non-Macintosh home computers, and it was owned by a patent-happy, litigious, and immensely powerful corporation that often revised applications or changed code in ways that did not improve the product or code but rather improved the company's bottom line. Code idealists, who constitute the majority of high-end programmers, find this offensive: code should be improved at all times, and extended, and made more stable, and fixed. Code should not suffer the whims of marketing, nor require a massive expenditure on the part of an independent programmer in order to purchase Windows-licensed programming tools. The current situation was thought to be a problem, and Microsoft's near monopoly wasn't inspiring anyone with confidence. What was to be done? Linus Torvalds, a one-man Windows demolition team, picked up the gauntlet.

In 1991 Linus Torvalds announced Linux. It was an alternative to Windows and had a few extremely unusual features: 1) it was free, and 2) it was open source. Open source means the code used to create the product can be viewed, downloaded, and modified by anyone with access to the internet. These changes could be submitted to the Linux design team, and if they like what they see, and it's a solid stable improvement, the change will be added to the latest Linux code. *But wait*, says the stolid businessman, *you can't do that. . . . Give away code for free? Give away a system for free?* Wasn't the point of doing this sort of thing to get very rich very quickly, or at least get reasonably rich over the course of a few years? What was Linus thinking?

He was changing the way the world works. Open source has serious limitations, of course. Nobody was being paid to improve Linux, support it, maintain it, or debug it. Who would do this sort of work for free? Well, if the project was one that many thought was needed (or long overdue), and it was professionally done from the start in the "right way" . . . lots of people. Since its introduction, thousands have contributed to the code, and Linux is now considered to be the most stable, most virus-resistant, most reliable system available. People from all over the world saw Linux's value and worked to improve it. Linux led the way, and it's how a lot of later coding occurred. Including, famously, Bitcoin.

This is how change happens, the process, the method. Something's wrong, a huge entity stands in the way of obvious progress, and programmers figure a way around the problem.

Thieving Murderous Mitts

Ross Ulbricht is a direct inheritor of this contrarian programming spirit. He's also a card-carrying Libertarian, and much more forthright about its influence on his life than the more reticent Satoshi. Ross proudly proclaims:

> Silk Road was founded on libertarian principles and continues to be operated on them. It is a great idea and a great practical system, but it is not a utopia. It is regulated by market forces, not a central power (even I am subject to market forces by my competition. No one is forced to be here). The same principles that have allowed Silk Road to flourish can and do work anywhere human beings come together. The only difference is that the State is unable to get its thieving murderous mitts on it.[34]

From a libertarian point of view, the War on Drugs[35] is indefensible, and libertarians have worked for years to limit or end the government's gradual expansion of power and the corroding of individual civil rights, justified in the name of this "war." According to 2011 Libertarian Party Chair Mark Hinkle, the War on Drugs has resulted in, "A relentless violation of the lives and property of Americans, including many who have never taken illegal drugs."[36] To put it bluntly, a penal solution is far worse than the problem, and it's not the first time banning drugs was attempted. Prohibition (1920–1933), the nationwide ban on alcohol sale and consumption, is the canonical counterexample, and a particular favorite of libertarians due to its inarguable status as a historical fiasco. It's worth briefly looking back on why Prohibition came to be, and what lessons—if any—it teaches.

In 1919 those pushing for Prohibition, from both the Left and Right, were spearheaded by suffragists (and the women's movement more generally), who pointed toward alcohol's deleterious effects on the health of the nation. They cited religious injunctions against drunkenness and (not far behind) debauchery, invoked economic arguments concerning the damage caused by lost productivity and industrial accidents, and claimed that sites of drinking (bars, saloons, etc.) fostered moral and spiritual decay. Not to mention the obvious links that existed between alcohol and prostitution, alcohol and violence, and alcohol and any number of wicked things. Alcohol was *bad*, and banning it would necessarily result in *good*. This was the basic argument, which was easy to state, hard to refute, and seemed to align with common sense. Before long the eighteenth amendment of the US Constitution was ratified, despite howls from alcohol producers and moderate tipplers all over the land.

By the time of its repeal, Prohibition's effects had been, indisputably and with universal historical and academic agreement, disastrous. According to the best and most accurate statistics, Prohibition failed in even its most basic goal to stop or at least inhibit drinking: by 1933 more Americans were drinking more alcohol than ever before. Prohibition had also generated a massive number of fairly hideous unintended consequences, including the obvious one—a thriving black market for alcohol so lucrative that criminals, for the first time in America, organized themselves into bloody fiefdoms and made massive piles of cash. The subsequent flow of illegal money crippled and corrupted the police and legal system; it increased crime as gangs skirmished for territory with powerful new guns funded by bootlegging; it destroyed the US revenue stream when the country needed it most (from the disappearance of alcohol taxes); and it caused a vast increase of alcohol-related deaths due to poisoned or poorly distilled liquor—the list of negative consequences is impressively long. One of its most pernicious effects, singled out as having the greatest and most damaging long-term effect upon America and its citizens, was philosophical.

In 1922, a short two years after Prohibition had begun and before many of its worst effects were seen, Fabian Franklin, a teetotaler and former editor of the *New York Evening Post*, explained the harm being done in *What Prohibition Has Done to America*:

The prime reason why the Prohibition law is so light-heartedly violated by all sorts and conditions of men, why it is held in contempt by hundreds of thousands of our best and most respected citizens, is that the law is a gross outrage upon personal liberty. Many, indeed, would commit the violation as a mere matter of self-indulgence; but it is absurd to suppose that this would be done, as it is done, by thousands of persons of the highest type of character and citizenship. These people are sustained by the consciousness that, though their conduct may be open to criticism, it at least has the justification of being a revolt against a law—a law unrepealable by any ordinary process—that strikes at the foundations of liberty.[37]

What Prohibition Has Done to America was written by a man who voluntarily stopped drinking for health and spiritual reasons, and who had sympathized with and supported the initial push for Prohibition. It didn't take him long to see how muddle-headed it was.

Prohibition made criminals of a large swath of the population, and did so by direct infringement of citizen's freedoms—an attack that, even if Prohibition had been wildly successful from a health and human happiness standpoint, would still be unacceptable to libertarians. That Prohibition failed so spectacularly was proof, if proof is still needed, that the only way to safeguard against a repetition of this legislative boondoggle was to firmly, loudly, and actively oppose all such government interference in the future.

Ross Ulbricht, born in 1984, grew up in the middle of what was the most rapid expansion of federal drug control spending in the history of the United States. From roughly $33 billion in 1985 to $128 Billion in 1992,[38] Ross's childhood was bracketed by draconian Public Service Announcements ("This is your brain on drugs") about the horrifying results of a single puff of marijuana, as well as the famously ineffective D.A.R.E (Drug Abuse Resistance Education) program that preached a "zero-tolerance" message that ultimately failed to live up to its increasingly modest goals. The American prison population more than tripled, with the majority of new incarcerations being drug-related offenses. It's no wonder Ross Ulbricht decided to take a stand against what he viewed as an immoral, illogical, unscientific and essentially un-American War on Drugs. Ross wasn't satisfied with the typical libertarian position, which would have happily accepted drug legalization and taxation as a way to dig out of Prohibition-style injunctions and legal penalties for smoking plant X or taking pill Y. In Ulbricht's own words, posted on the Silk Road forum:

> I keep hearing this argument come up when people talk about drug prohibition: legalize, regulate and tax it. On the surface it sounds like a good idea. No more drug war, more tax revenue, government regulators can make sure it is safe. Makes sense, right?
>
> I can't help but think something is wrong though. Feels like the bastards that have been screwing everyone over all this time still win in this scenario. Now all that money can go to the state and to their cronies, right?
>
> Here's the rub: the drug war is an acute symptom of a deeper problem, and that problem is the state. If they "legalize, regulate and tax" it, it's just one more part of society under their thumb, another productive sector that they can leech off of.
>
> If prohibition is lifted, most people here will go away. You'll go back to your lives and get your drugs from whatever state certified dispensaries are properly licensed to sell to you. Drug use will be as interesting as smoking and drinking.
>
> Here's my point: Silk Road is about something much bigger than thumbing your nose at the man and getting your drugs anyway. It's about taking back our liberty and our dignity and demanding justice. If prohibition is lifted, and the drug industry is placed under the yoke of the state, then we won in a small way, but lost in a big way. Right now, drugs are ours. They aren't tainted by the government. We the people control their manufacture, distribution and consumption. We should be looking to expand that control, taking back our power, no giving what is ours to the very people that have been our enemies all along.
>
> It's easy to justify though. Think of all the horrors the war on drugs has caused that will be gone, almost instantly. That pain could stop![39]

Ross's goal wasn't simply to reclaim individual liberties by exposing the War on Drugs and stopping its corrosive effects, but to inhibit all drug-related revenue streams from attaching themselves to the government in the first place. As any libertarian will tell you, if you give money to the government the government will spend that money and grow.

Ulbricht wanted the government to legalize everything and afterward keep out the way. Once free of stringent laws, citizens will start businesses selling cocaine or marijuana, or importing opium and heroin, and the free market will sort out which stores are too expensive, which have poor or adulterated product, and which can't be counted on to retain sufficient inventory. In the long run the result will be much like the market we have for, say, coffee: slowly increasing quality, an almost overwhelming abundance of choice, and a wide range of options from cheap to absurdly expensive. Sure, there will be growing pains and people will be hurt and users will take too much or become addicted and have it ruin their lives, but Ross's answer to this is simple: it's happening already in great numbers, whether by incarceration or via drug-related violence and lack of quality control. The current system isn't working, and we know from Prohibition version 1.0 that it can't work and never will work. The solution? Stop throwing bad money after good.

Ross Ulbricht's stance was admirably logical and unsparing, bereft of exceptions and implacable in its idealistic conclusions. Ross might be correct when it comes to government regulation of drugs versus letting the free market decide, given that prescription pill regulations have shown themselves to be a poor way of stopping the use and abuse of those drugs. (Six percent of Americans report having "abused" prescription drugs sometime in their lifetime—a massive number).[40] But Ross doesn't stop there; he wades into much more difficult territory with the clarity and assurance of an expert—or a true believer. The subject is child labor, which I had thought a battle waged and won long ago in the midst of English industrialization, when in the early nineteenth century laws were passed limiting or banning children's employment.[41] Apparently not. Ross Ulbricht had this to say about the subject:

> If the options available to a person are work or starve, why would you take away the work option? If people are voluntarily choosing to work in a factory under terrible conditions, it means the alternatives available to them are even worse. That work is an opportunity

for them to better themselves. Child labor regulations only hampered the development and expansion of the industries that were providing these opportunities.

Had they been allowed to develop freely, only under the constraints of supply, demand and property rights, they would have had to provide a safe work environment for their employees, if that's what the employees wanted. Let me give you a quick example. Nike and Reebok both have shoe factories in the same city. All of their resources and external conditions are effectively identical. The only thing they can vary is the quality of the work environment for their employees. Nike chooses to spend $1 per man-hour maintaining an improved work environment for its employees, while Reebok keeps that dollar as profit. Reebok will quickly find itself unable to attract the employee base it needs to produce its shoes as Nike takes its employees and market share. So, Reebok, instead of improving the work conditions, simply passes the extra $1 per hour on to their employees. Now we are seeing the market at work. Employees are now faced with the option of a safe work environment, or an extra dollar per hour. Some will choose safety while others will choose the extra pay.

And this is exactly what has happened eventually, where now employers do all they can to attract good employees away from their competitors.[42]

Ulbricht stresses that the free market solves problems better than any government possibly could. His argument seems consistent and relatively logical. It is true that when a poor-paying job is taken it's because the person taking the job doesn't have better options? Possibly. Is it really the best job they can hope for? Maybe. As Ross would say, why stop people from making *some* money instead of *none*?

It's important to look at the historical roots of this debate[43]— England originated many important early child labor laws—to see why they were proposed and adopted despite moneyed interests waging a campaign against such regulations. It's not difficult to find examples from the nineteenth century where a single factory or mine or manufacturing center dominates a given village or town. To state the obvious, one reason children don't have "other work options" is because, well, they are children. They can't walk or run to a neighboring district to increase competition for their labor. They don't qualify for many jobs due to lack of strength or height or a million other reasons, including a proscribed bedtime.

If, as was often the case, a dominant factory controlled much of a town's labor, the factory could force wages to the bare minimum since it was difficult, historically, for workers to move somewhere with better prospects (even if they had savings for such an adventure). If a factory could get the local children to do some of the dirty work, and pay them less than adults, labor costs would be reduced, a good thing in theory. That's the free market. What children should do in this situation, according to Ulbricht, is work, since it's the only job they have, despite their work depressing wages for other adults. Ulbricht advises unhappy adults to pack up and leave as soon as possible and go to another town where a big factory is paying a better wage. . . . Oh wait, everyone in *that* town is in the same boat, aren't they?

Journalist Elizabeth Bruenig[44] makes the case succinctly in her article "Libertarians Have a History of Horrifying Views on Parenting," where she states: "Libertarianism rests on the whimsical notion that all people are isolated, entirely free agents with no claims on others except those that they can negotiate through consensual contracts. The very existence of children flatly disproves this; any moral intuition indicates that children come into the world with claims on their parents at the very least, and their entire societies considered broadly. To avoid a hellish death spiral of infectious disease and neglect, we would all do well to reject [Paul/Libertarians] and his cohort on the subject of child rearing."[45]

Ross's highly theoretical free market discussions have a tendency to elide real-world issues, making many of his "proofs" difficult to whole-heartedly embrace. Labor, as in "workers able to be hired," is far from a frictionless resource, smoothly sliding around the economy to where it's needed and best compensated. Assuming labor knows where these "perfect jobs" are—and this is far from true—you simply can't overlook the fact that moving costs workers in time, money, and emotional effort. Many workers can't light-heartedly relocate; they might be taking care of a relative, or depend upon local ties for child care, housing support, or a million other things. It's always the case that a business can lower wages until it reaches the point of perfect "efficiency," attracting just enough skilled workers willing to do the job, but it's never the case that a worker is able to apply a simple function to determine their best economic position in the best location and cheaply put this mystical knowledge into practice.

The free market isn't moral, to state a truth no libertarian would dare argue; nor is it necessarily efficient, as anyone who has worked in modern corporate America can attest. The free market does respond alertly to incentives, however perverse, however obviously "wrong" to the man in the street. Consider a business that insures people's health and collects fees every year from those signed up for such a service. The legal system dictates that the insurer must do what it has promised to do, but the insurer is aware of these limits and doesn't do one iota more: even the *required* minimum effect is made with great reluctance. The endless hoops one must leap through in the American healthcare system, the proliferation of paperwork and required receipts and lost claims and endless phone calls—these are not incidental to the system but at the very center of the profit-making machine. This is nowhere made clearer than in the flexible spending account (FSA) regulations which allow participants to contribute a certain amount into an third party processor's account, tax free, to spend on healthcare-related items. What qualifies as a healthcare-related item is in constant flux, and the reason for this flux is the terrible incentive put in place at the end of every year: any money remaining in any individual's FSA account is handed over immediately to the employer. It's lost, gone. Use it or lose it.

This system produces exactly the results you would imagine. In many programs it's mind-numbingly difficult to spend your own FSA money. Receipts must be collected, scanned, and submitted. Accounts can be frozen while an irregularity or paperwork error is straightened out. There are few ways to easily and conveniently spend your FSA money; even claims related to treatment in a hospital, presumably a slam dunk as far as "healthcare-related items" is concerned, aren't automatically processed. You might have bought a bagel in the hospital cafe, for instance, or something equally egregious. The higher percentage of funds stuck in accounts at the end of the year, the more lucrative a third-party FSA processer's offer can be to an employer (a potential customer). It's become a rush to the bottom, with the "winning" FSA enabler being the one best able to inconvenience, slow down, hassle, and deny FSA customers the use of their own money.

The libertarian answer to this kind of complaint is always the same: the problem is government regulation, and when they're removed everything'll work out better in the long run. Perverse incentives are a product of legislation, not the free market. Ulbricht acknowledged this when he said, "Liberty is not a pill that makes men angels. What it does do is limit the extent to which evil can be expressed in the world." It's always the case that terrible companies will race to the bottom in various ways, hurting customers and employees in the process, but the answer to this is a new company springing up, rising from the entrepreneurial spirit of America, offering (slightly) better options with (slightly) better prices allowing for (slightly) better employee pay. Ross Ulbricht is surely right to say that liberty, by itself, doesn't necessarily fix anything. It isn't a magic pill. But he's surely wrong to resist applying that logic to *laissez faire* capitalism itself. Why is it true that a free market, and only a free market, is always the answer? Why will it always lead to better prospects for everyone down the road? How often in this messy, complicated, and chaotic world are broad theoretical certainties proven true, at least outside of the hard sciences?

Silk Road tested the libertarian idea of a free market for drugs. What was seen as a self-evidently insane method of dealing with narcotics (the "War on Drugs") would be contrasted with a pristine and uncorrupted free-market experiment. At long last, people would be able to purchase drugs without danger, anonymously, without social embarrassment, without state interference.[46] During a rare, secretive, highly encrypted remote "interview" published in the September 2, 2013, issue of *Forbes* magazine, recorded while he was still Dread Pirate Roberts, Ross states categorically, "We've won the State's War on Drugs because of Bitcoin."[47]

The government declared the war; the people broadly resisted; and the libertarians stepped in with the tools and expertise to get the job done. Now it's time to see how Ross Ulbricht's Silk Road fared.

CHAPTER 5

ROSS ULBRICHT: THE RISE AND FALL OF SILK ROAD

IN THE WORDS OF THE DREAD PIRATE ROBERTS

A t its height Silk Road listed over ten thousand illegal drugs for sale, along with a stunning variety of drug-related accessories and hard-to-purchase items—some legal, most not. Scales, syringes, bongs, and cocaine-sniffing devices (made of titanium) could be found, as well as alpaca socks, beef jerky, and good old-fashioned books. It wasn't always about Moroccan hash or pure molly; the market for "traditional" goods and services lagged the illegal one by a factor of 100 to 1, but it was slowly increasing. This was Ross Ulbricht's vision made real: a safe, automated, secure, and trusted online store. It was out of the reach of any government on Earth. There were no regulations except those imposed by Ross himself (no guns, no explosives, no child porn, no violent videos). Customers were happy. Honest vendors were happy. Sleazy vendors suffered from brutal customer feedback and were slowly winnowed out. A global community formed out of the Dark Web's void; an example of the free market spontaneously generating life.

If only it were that easy.

Nothing about Silk Road was accidental—nor inevitable. Silk Road required a sophisticated suite of cryptographic utilities unavailable a few years before, Bitcoin being the most notable. It also required a specific type of person to envision the site, build it, troubleshoot it, guide it toward profitability, and oversee its operation over the course of two busy years. A smash-and-grab money-obsessed scam artist could have created something like Silk Road but would have stolen everyone's bitcoins after six months. An entirely amoral web developer could have created something similar to Silk Road but without any limitations on what was being sold; blocks of malleable clay-like C-4 explosive could have been peddled, next to the most violent and filthy varieties of porn. Silk Road was far more "free" than the highly regulated American marketplace, but it too had boundaries and limitations, and it required a delicate balance to keep from spinning out of control. It also required a *highly* dedicated administrator, who even after becoming aware that the DEA and the FBI and the HSI (and probably a few more three-letter agencies) were hot on his trail nevertheless thought Silk Road important enough to risk significant jail time.

It wasn't about money—near the end, Ross Ulbricht could have pulled out of Silk Road with a hundred million dollars' worth of bitcoins. It wasn't even about the War on Drugs, making explicit the "right" way to handle people's innate desire for such chemicals. For Ross Ulbricht, Silk Road was an ideological test bed, a real-life implementation of libertarian principles and libertarian economic theory. What led Ross to such an extreme position—driving him to construct a site with manifest disregard of local, state, federal, and international law, soon to be the target of every drug-enforcement agency on the planet?

To understand how Ross arrived at this philosophical turning point it's necessary to look at what happened in 2008, after Ross abandoned academia and was left to his own devices. Despite his scientific background Ross began to see the world as sunny or dark, full of objects transparent or opaque. Certainties replaced conditionals. Ideology replaced testing. Ross slowly transformed into a fundamentalist, the hardening of his ideological viewpoint increasing with Silk Road's success.

This is the story of the founding of Silk Road and its growth and its eventual collapse, as well as a parallel story with a very different trajectory: Ross Ulbricht's transformation into a zealot.

How to View the World

Ross Ulbricht wrote a lot of posts on the Silk Road message board—a *lot*. Most of them were related to the messy business at hand but some branched into other subjects: what he happened to be reading at the time, the latest economic news, or random gossip gleaned from a random thread. Ross used the message board to host "The Dread Pirate Roberts Book Club," which discussed economics textbooks, libertarian tracts, and science fiction/Cyberpunk novels. The book club occasionally reviewed movies as well, notably the dystopian freedom-fantasy *V for Vendetta*, which everyone raved about.[1] Ulbricht's trial also furnished reams of material, including the so-called "Diary of the Dread Pirate Roberts," parts of which were divulged in open court. Altogether, these give us a detailed view of the Silk Road's timeline: its birth and growth and inevitable collapse. Whenever possible I'll be using Ross's own words to tell the story, occasionally distilled from longer passages but otherwise unedited.[2]

The first sentence of Ross's LinkedIn profile[3] is extremely telling: "I love learning and *using theoretical constructs to better understand the world around me*" [italics mine]. Most scientists would find this formulation backward; the scientific method urges a careful and open-minded survey of the world, which eventually generates a "theoretical construct," extending experimental results. Pick up a rock, drop it, and see how long it takes to fall. Pick up another rock, climb a ladder, drop it, and see how long it takes to fall. Repeat a few hundred times at varying heights. You'll end up with a sheet full of numbers that, if you happen to be mathematically astute, will suggest the following equation, precisely fitting the data: the time it takes something to drop is the square root of twice the height it was dropped at, divided by the Earth's constant gravitational force ($9.81 m/s^2$). Once this general equation is postulated,[4] it allows scientists to calculate the time it takes anything to fall from *any ladder ever made*. A discrete bundle of data furnishes an infinite supply of useful information.

The postulated equation can be periodically checked and re-checked and tweaked for precision as necessary—for example, including the effect of air resistance. Regardless, the equation is a valuable and significant result and seems to be getting at a deep truth about the world, not insignificantly that the mass of the object being dropped isn't a part of the equation. In other words, a heavy rock doesn't fall to Earth any faster than a smaller rock, because the mass of the rocks isn't part of the equation (only the height at which the object was dropped is used as input). This result isn't intuitively obvious, but the equation forces such a conclusion.

Ross Ulbricht looked at the world in reverse, attempting, in his words, to "use theoretical constructs to better understand the world around me." This is akin to parsing the equations relating to falling bodies in order to understand how things fall, spending a week or a month doing the math and plugging in hundreds of numbers and coming back with a list of results: it will take 1.414 seconds for a rock to drop 9.8 meters. I suppose it's a valuable exercise, but he could have gone outside and dropped the rock from a height of 9.8 meters and timed how long it took to fall, ensuring the correct result, since experience has shown the real world does, on occasion, perversely ignore theory.

Because the basic equations for falling bodies have been checked millions of times and form the basis for countless numbers of real-time applications that work perfectly and without failure, Ross's method makes sense, up to a point. Scientific "truths" as represented by fundamental equations allow rapid and deep understanding of how the world works. Read and study a physics textbook until it's fully understood and surely you will come away with a deeper appreciation of how water travels through pipes and the types of electrical resistors and how heat flows through bodies with varying heat transfer coefficients, all valuable ways of understanding how the physical objects around us function. If the equations aren't complete and perfect representations of how things work (and they never are), they get it mostly right, and with refinements can achieve 99.9999 percent or higher parallels between theory and experimental data.

Theories such as quantum mechanics, under constant scrutiny for the last hundred years, have undergone a rigorous sequence of ever-more-demanding tests by the most accomplished physicists in the world, and it's not unusual for theoretical results to match experimental results to an accuracy of eleven digits—surely the most impressive marriage of theory and data in the history of science.

It's tempting to conclude that the only way quantum theories could match reality so closely, often to the limit of the measuring machine's precision, is by representing a Platonic ideal. The universe *really does* distribute a particle in space according to probabilities laid down by its wave function, for it didn't how could millions of results match the equations so consistently and exquisitely? In this instance the universe functions like an intricate device with incomprehensible depths of machinery: to get detailed real-world results simply enter detailed input data.

Ross was trained in the so-called hard sciences, where the rigor of previous results is implicit yet testing is ongoing, and it's perfectly sensible to use a canonical equation and assume it will give useful and valid results. But Ross's LinkedIn page continues, far more worryingly: "Now, my goals have shifted. I want to use economic theory as a means to abolish the use of coercion and agression [*sic*] amongst mankind. . . . To that end, I am creating an economic simulation to give people a first-hand experience of what it would be like to live in a world without the systemic use of force."

This is a pseudoscientist at work, proposing and creating an economic simulation to give users the sensation of living, "in a world without the systemic use of force." Crucially, it's a simulation, not an experiment. Ross isn't wondering what the result will be, he's telling us what it will be. Ross has it backward when he states that in order to live in world without the systemic use of force, participate in this simulation. Shouldn't he instead run a simulation and see what happens? If you participate in this simulation, theory suggests it will reduce "the systemic use of force" (whatever that happens to mean). Did the economic simulation actually achieve this goal? Are economic theories, in general, rigorously tested and akin to fundamental physical equations such as the mass-energy equivalence $E=mc^2$, and able to inform through *theory* the particular and messy truths of the world?

It's not a new idea: in a previous chapter we read about how Utopian dreamers of the nineteenth century such as Josiah Warren and Charles Fourier crafted precise theories about the best way to structure a town or a local economy; the most efficient way to achieve happiness and sexual satisfaction; the demands upon the wealthy and the responsibilities of the poor; the importance of architecture and the crucial role of capitalism or communism or whatever –ism is being embraced, and they were put to the test in utopian simulations[5] again and again.

Silk Road is nothing less than Ross Ulbricht's vision of a libertarian utopia, an economic simulation with a built-in expectation of success, which qualifies as a tragedy not because everything fell apart in the end, or because of wantonly immoral behavior on the part of a few government investigators, or because bad people did bad things with money made using the site. The tragedy arises from the fact that an essentially good and modest man ended up doing terrible things.

To understand how it happened, it's necessary to go back to 2008, when Ross Ulbricht was finishing graduate school.

A Libertarian's Education

Ross could pass as a conventionally clever, academically gifted student, excelling in college and ultimately winning a full scholarship to Pennsylvania State graduate school (the 2008 Anne C. Wilson Graduate Research Award in material science). Ross took his work seriously enough to earn a master's degree with a thesis called "Growth of EuO Thin Films by Molecular Beam Epitaxy." In it Ross helpfully defined epitaxy this way: "Thin films can be grown on top of a preexisting single crystal that has a similar atomic spacing in order to enable the depositing species to extend the single crystal lattice into the deposited film." In other words a crystal with a desirable structure, such as a regular hexagonal pattern, displaying great strength or chemical/electrical properties, acts as a seed for the thin film layered on top, forcing the film into a novel hexagonal arrangement, creating a type of material that has never existed before. Note here the importance of the seed crystal's structure, which ultimately determines the growth of what's layered above.

At this point in his life Ross had fully embraced his political beliefs, going so far as to join the PSU College Libertarians and to engage in debates about universal healthcare. Ross naturally maintained that, "The United States has a 'massively regulated health care system' and that if deregulation occurred the system would work better."[6] Here Ross ignores, as do many deregulation champions, that certain markets, such as healthcare, have fundamental conflicts between what is most profitable (reducing expenses and refusing treatment) and what is moral (providing high quality medical care to all). This conflict isn't easily resolved, since health insurance is based on risk pools (the group of people insured) instead of direct competition. Insurers competing for low-overhead clients, poaching healthy customers from each other's risk pools, function to reduce premiums for the young and healthy types being poached. They are the perfect insurance consumers; they pay in and don't take much out. All this does for the rest of the population is increase premiums that are no longer subsidized by the healthy young—not the sort of "universal price decrease" many champion.

During this period of his life Ross attempted to become a convention delegate for Ron Paul's presidential run and spoke admiringly of the man: "[Ron Paul] is eloquent. He speaks very succinctly and straightforwardly and is very insightful and wise. . . . There's a lot to learn from him and his message of what it means to be a U.S. citizen and what it means to be a free individual. . . . He doesn't compromise his integrity as a politician and he fights quite diligently to restore the principles that our country was founded on."[7] Ron Paul failed to win the nomination of the Republican Party, garnering thirty-seven delegates when 1,144 were needed. This seemed to signal the end of mainstream political action as an effective tool for achieving libertarian goals. McCain easily won the 2008 Republican nomination and famously selected Sarah Palin as a running mate. Amidst the ensuing culture war Obama triumphed (a crushing 365 to 173 advantage in the electoral college), leading to the 2010 Affordable Care Act ("ObamaCare"), which greatly extended government "interference"[8] in the healthcare market. What was a deeply committed libertarian to do?

Silk Road, Ross's "economic simulation," was intended not simply as a money-making machine but as an idealistic experiment in free-market deregulation. The "force" Ross objected to as being omnipresent in our society is the incessant demands placed upon individuals, necessarily limiting their fundamental freedoms. Why was it wrong, much less illegal, to smoke a joint in the backyard, bothering nobody? Why was it wrong to purchase and swallow a

Valium to get through a long plane flight? Why was it wrong to resist being forced to purchase, or support through taxes, healthcare of a limited sort selected from a limited array of choices, none of which the individual desired nor chose? They all impinged upon a citizen's ability to choose freely. What was required was a regulation- and government-free marketplace, where anything (within reason) could be offered and sold with minimal oversight and maximum privacy.

The combination of anonymizing Tor and Bitcoin were the key technological features allowing such a development. They formed the basis for later growth; they were the seed crystal, structuring everything layered on top, guaranteeing (in theory) discretion and safety for all concerned.

By 2009 Ross realized an anonymous, safe, and secure online store was technologically feasible, and promptly got to work. But Ross's business plan had a few serious deficiencies: he wasn't a programmer, nor a cryptographer, nor particularly savvy when it came to Tor and its obscure requirements and features. Ross wasn't sure he was up to the task.

Ross needed help getting the site going, or at least expert advice on tricky programming issues, and this wasn't a skill set for which he could easily advertise. Dark Web programmers are a reclusive and capricious bunch. Ross wasn't going to risk exposing himself or his project to outside influences unless it was absolutely necessary, and as a result he was stuck. He wasn't capable of making progress on his own. Something had to be done, but nothing could be done without betraying himself. Luckily (or un-) for Ross, he bumped into an old friend, Richard Bates.

Ross first met Richard in 2002 when they were freshmen at the University of Texas–Dallas, and Ross stumbled across him again in late 2009 when they were both living in Austin. Bates was a far more experienced programmer than Ulbricht, having studied computer science and worked full time since graduation at PayPal, eBay, and other billion dollar, no-nonsense corporations. By 2010 Ross was chatting with Richard regularly, asking questions related to a "secret project" that was going to be hosted on Tor—that's as much as Richard knew. Richard was happy to help; he hung out with Ross socially, met at parties, and at first everything seemed low-key and friendly. But Ross needed constant assistance. Their chats became more frequent and Ross's questions more detailed and persistent. Richard began to wonder what Ross was up to; why it was taking so much of his time; why he was unable (or unwilling) to get help from other people.

The year 2010 was shaping up to be terrible for Ross. Nothing was working out. He wasn't in school anymore, he wasn't working as a scientist (surely what he had imagined for his future), and a short-lived attempt to make a living as a day trader had failed. He threw himself into Good Wagon Books,[9] a donation-based book "reuse" company Ross being run by one of his friends. The idea behind Good Wagon Books was straightforward. The online bookstore, based in Austin, Texas, would canvass various neighborhoods and ask for book donations. A percentage of all profits would be sent to local charities, and unsold books and magazines were either passed along to interested nonprofits or directly recycled. The company wasn't a nonprofit, but aspects of its business model rubbed people the wrong way. A Yelp thread sprang up, with suspicious Austinites airing their concerns. The most forceful of these critics argued that Good Wagon Books were doing little more than, "scamming free media (books, DVDs, etc.)"[10] for pure profit, not charity.

This led to a quick response by Ross's business associate:

> I am the owner of Good Wagon Books and I would like to kindly give our side of the story, while also accepting your feedback. Please understand that I am very upset about the way Good Wagon has been portrayed on this thread, especially since I've poured twelve months of hard work trying to create a company that I sincerely believe in. So while I have an unwavering belief that all feedback is good feedback, I apologize if I write with more emotion than is required. We do not claim to be a non-profit: To quote from our website at goodwagon.com/non-profit: "While Good Wagon Books is a for-profit company, we try to do as much Good with our collections as possible. To this end, we pledge a portion of every book sold to Explore Austin. We also donate the books we can't sell to the Inside Books Project and donate most non-book items to various other non-profits such as the Salvation Army and Any-Baby-Can."[11]

While this rebuttal makes sense, it's clear, at least from a distance, that there's a fundamental tension in the way the company is constructed. Good Wagon Books is for-profit, but their URL is http://goodwagon.com/non-profit. Good Wagon Books helps people get rid of books that are cluttering up their house, but it's not as "charitable" as directly donating those books to a nonprofit. A portion of all proceeds goes to charity, but the majority goes to a for-profit venture. Good Wagon Books positioned itself in the space between book donations and charities, taking the most valuable donations and passing on the least. While not illegal it nevertheless existed in an uneasy gray area. Some customers, particularly the elderly and infirm, were happy with the service: Good Wagon Books came to the door and helped clear attics and closets of unwanted books that might have clogged up their houses for years, if not decades. Others thought Good Wagon Books a scam.

Was the company doing the community much good? Let's do the math. If Good Wagon Books were given books that otherwise would have been directly donated to nonprofits, it reduced the overall rate of charitable giving. If Good Wagon Books were given books that otherwise would *not* have been donated, it generated a net increase in nonprofit donations (because a percentage of Good Wagon Books' profits were distributed to charity, and any percentage of the total is greater than zero). From a libertarian standpoint there's no issue here either way; people can choose to donate to Good Wagon Books or not. From a broader perspective it's not clear. Jaime M. summarized the basic objections in the same Yelp thread, speaking directly to the owners:

> Maybe *scam* is a harsh word, but "clever way of making money off of something that people usually participate in out of benevolence" is long-winded.

Good Wagon Books was already on the rocks financially, and after Ross took it over full time he realized it wasn't worth the effort. The generally negative community feedback was deeply depressing to an idealist such as Ross, who was genuinely attempting to "create a company that I sincerely believe in." I don't doubt him on this. I'm sure it's what he was trying to do; the question is what was the result? As a business model it sounds good in theory, but how does it work in the real world?

What's interesting about Good Wagon Books is the vague nature of its business model. On the one hand it was unobjectionably legal and, unlike other for-profit companies (such as check-cashing companies[12]) with far more dubious business models, it donated part of its profits to charity. On the other hand, because its profits were based on donations that might have been given to charity anyway, it wasn't clear it was contributing to the overall good. Free market libertarian dogma gives Good Wagon Books two enthusiastic thumbs up, but our common sense is troubled. Many people had exactly the same reaction to Silk Road[13]—which in late 2010 was more of a dream than a reality: "By the end of the year, I still didn't have a site up, let alone a server. I went through a lot over the year in my personal relationships as well. I had mostly shut myself off from people because I felt ashamed of where my life was. I had left my promising career as a scientist to be an investment adviser and entrepreneur and came up empty handed."[14]

Ross indulged in a little *The Secret*-style positive thinking in the depths of 2010's lows,[15] and wrote in late 2010 the following absurdly wish-based plan of action for the near future: "In 2011, I am creating a year of prosperity and power beyond what I have ever experienced before. Silk Road is going to become a phenomenon and at least one person will tell me about it, unknowing that I was its creator. Good Wagon Books will find its place and get to the point that it basically runs itself. . . . I will be happy. . . . I have many friends I can count on who are powerful and connected."[16]

What's surprising is that much of this did in fact happen, although wishcasting had nothing to do with it. It required dirty, difficult, sometimes dangerous work, leading Ross into strange places and involving him with projects unsuited for somebody with his background. Not only did he have to hack together a site, he had to become a drug dealer.

At the end of January 2011, Ross had managed to create a relatively functional though primitive site and was ready to release it to the world. He was also busy creating fake aliases and logins to popular drug and Dark Web message boards. His plan was to pose as a regular user and begin a thread or add to an existing thread, and announce his discovery of a new site, called Silk Road. This astro-turfing spiel is a typical sample from Ross: "I came across this website called Silk Road. It's a Tor hidden service that claims to allow you to buy and sell anything online anonymously I'm thinking of buying off it, but wanted to see if anyone here had heard of it and could recommend it. [Ross gives Tor address]. Let me know what you think."[17]

What's fascinating is one of the earliest responses to Ross's post, by the delightfully named ShadowOfHarbringer: "So here we go, the first Bitcoin drug store. We're going into deep water faster than I thought then. I wonder how long will it take for govs to start investigating Bitcoin?"[18] As it turns out, a scant five months later a Chicago Homeland Security Investigation into Silk Road was launched in response to a sudden increase of Mail Branch (postal) seizures of drugs and other contraband.[19] There wasn't any way the government was going to remain in the dark about *this* dark site, not when it was designed to be maximally visible to anyone with access to the Tor network.

The major stumbling block for any new online drug superstore was getting past initial resistance and suspicion. From the start, people viewed Silk Road as a scam, or a possible scam, or something that would inevitably lead to participants being scammed (or Goxxed, as they now say, following the $600 million Mt. Gox Bitcoin swindle[20]). Ross had a pretty good idea on how to get over this initial hump. From Ross's journal, as revealed in court:

> I began working on a project that had been in my mind for over a year. I was calling it Underground Brokers, but eventually settled on Silk Road. The idea was to create a website where people could buy anything anonymously, with no trail whatsoever that could lead back to them. I had been studying the technology for a while, but needed a business model and strategy. I finally decided that I would produce mushrooms so that I could list them on the site for cheap to get people interested. I worked my ass off setting up a lab in a cabin out near Bastrop off the grid. In hindsight, this was a terrible idea and I would never repeat it, but I did it and produced several kilos of high quality shrooms.[21]

Bastrop is a small town within easy driving distance of Austin which, crucially, borders Bastrop State Park, a protected pine forest well known on the Shroomery website (the oldest and most well-respected source for all things psilocybin) for, "Supporting *P. cubensis* during a wet spell. . . . You can [also] find *Panaeolus cyanescens* in the immediate area if the weather is right."[22] Ross's lab consisted of a series of sterilized jars or glazed ceramic containers, supporting a substrate (a mix of flour and vermiculite, for example) injected with mushroom spores. Once the spores produced enough fungus to completely cover the substrate, it could be removed and put into a damp, humid location, either outdoors in a secret location in the forest or in an everyday aquarium equipped with a basic heating apparatus and a plentiful supply of clean water. Ross began mushroom production in the cabin and, as soon as he could, set up colonies in the wild, which he could safely harvest without much possibility of being caught.

Growing shrooms was a decided shock for Ross. It's surely not how a former Eagle Scout imagined he would be putting his wilderness survival skills into practice. He had a bachelor's degree, a master's degree, and a successful academic track record. What was he doing coaxing mushrooms from spores? Ross accepted it as a necessary danger because he needed product for his fledgling site. Nobody was going to sign up for Silk Road until they saw, with their own eyes, another vendor take the first step and profit from it. Not only was Ross going to astroturf advertise his site, he was going to do the same to kick-start it. Silk Road's first vendor was in fact Ross Ulbricht selling under a fictional ID, peddling home-grown shrooms at a low price, promptly packaging and shipping the incoming orders. Customers were happy and wrote rave reviews. Potential vendors saw the customer feedback, became envious of the shrooms salesman's quick and safe profits, and took a small leap of faith: they signed up. And things worked out for them. It wasn't a scam, existing only to steal bitcoins. Other vendors saw and joined. Silk Road had achieved critical mass.

The early growth of Silk Road was relatively slow and controlled, and Ross was able to handle the increase in site traffic and process most of the transactions directly. In early 2011 he wrote:

Working on Good Wagon Books and Silk Road at the same time. Programming now. Patchwork php mysql. Don't know how to host my own site. Didn't know how to run bitcoind. Got the basics of my site written. Only a few days after launch, I got my first signups, and then my first message. I was so excited I didn't know what to do with myself. Little by little, people signed up, and vendors signed up, and then it happened. My first order. I'll never forget it. The next couple of months, I sold about 10 lbs of shrooms through my site. Some orders were as small as a gram, and others were in the qp range. Before long, I completely sold out. Looking back on it, I maybe should have raised my prices more and stretched it out, but at least now I was all digital, no physical risk anymore. Before long, traffic started to build. People were taking notice, smart, interested people. Hackers.[23]

The problem with a site attracting hackers is that hackers are interested not only in what the site has to offer but the site itself as a subject for exploitation or (at least) investigation. Ross had managed to cobble together a working site, but it wasn't professionally done and had a number of serious vulnerabilities:

Between answering messages, processing transactions, and updating the codebase to fix the constant security holes, I had very little time left in the day, and I had a girlfriend at this time! At some point, a hacker found some major flaws in my code. I sent it to him for review and he came back with basically "this is amateur shit." I knew it too. I tried to work with him but I think he lost interest and since I wasn't charging commission, I only had my shroom money to pay him with. Thankfully that quadrupled from bitcoin increasing in price, little did I know I could've cashed out at 8x higher for a total of 32x![24]

It was a perfect time for the site to undergo necessary growing pains. Ross was lucky the hacker hadn't done something underhanded, such as introduce a virus or bogus code into the site that could be later activated or accessed to compromise the entire operation. Instead, the hacker registered his disgust at the low quality of the code and faded away—he didn't think it worth his time to fix it. It's often the case that more effort is required to patch and correct an unstable codebase than to start over from scratch, which is what Ross eventually decided to do:

> I decided to rewrite the site as suggested by my benevolent hacker adviser. So, while still manually processing transactions and responding to a bigger and bigger message load, I began rewriting the site. At some point around this time, I also learned how to host my own site and was on my own servers. . . . I wanted control of my .onion domain . . . and that was yet another learning curve, configuring and running a LAMP[25] server, oh joy! But I was loving it. My ideas were actually working. Sure it was a little crude, but it worked![26]

Silk Road vs. "The Biggest Force Wielding Organization on the Planet"

Ross was no longer an amateur programmer. He had written a reasonably stable site using the correct tools, hosted on a Tor server under his control. All that was left was to switch the old site with the new; to point customers to the new server, leaving a link where the previous had lived. It wasn't easy:

> The weekend of the switch was the peak of stress for me. Updating a live site to a whole new version is no easy task. You don't realize how many little pieces lay on top of one another so it works just right (at least when you code poorly like my amateur ass was doing). So for about 48 hours it was stop and start on the switch, but I finally got there and it was working. It looked like I didn't have to process the transactions manually anymore, but then the rot started. Some where, the site accounting wasn't balancing, and I was losing hundreds of dollars every few hours. I started to panic. I tried everything I could think of, but couldn't stop the bleeding. It was getting to be thousands of dollars and I was losing sleep and getting slow. I didn't give up though. I rewrote the entire transaction processor from scratch and some how it worked. To this day I don't know what the problem was. AND in addition to these stressors, Silk Road got its first press, the infamous Gawker article.[27]

Before the site rewrite, Ross had been processing all the transactions himself; receiving bitcoins from customers for purchases and forwarding them to the vendor after the customers received their shipment. As the site grew larger, this payment flow became a serious liability and needed to be streamlined. That was the role of the transaction processor, which Ross created to automate the flow of money and free him from being intimately involved with every purchase made on the site. Just after the site was rewritten and made more sophisticated, the "Gawker article" was published on June 1, 2011, the first mainstream press coverage of Silk Road, and it (naturally) made hay with what they found there. The story was called "The Underground Website Where You Can Buy Any Drug Imaginable," and included screenshots of cannabis and hash as well as a soothing interview with a laid-back programmer who had purchased ten tabs of LSD from the site, paid using Bitcoin, and had them delivered by mail.

Suddenly the world knew about Silk Road. Interest spiked. Traffic increased tenfold. College students all over the country saw the listings and quietly went insane. Members of the establishment were shocked and appalled and knew what to do about it. Senators Charles Schumer of New York and Joe Manchin of West Virginia had this to say:

> "This audacious website should be shut down immediately," Manchin said.
>
> "Never before has a website so brazenly peddled illegal drugs online," Schumer said. "By cracking down on the website immediately, we can help stop these drugs from flooding our streets."[28]

It's amusing how Schumer's response is a knee-jerk reaction straight from 1955. Logic, as well as a brief overview of the vendors, show that nearly all the drugs listed on Silk Road for American consumption in fact originated in America (to better avoid customs/ import inspections). If these drugs are "flooding our streets" we're already underwater. Silk Road was a new distribution channel for existing drugs, and one obviously far safer than purchasing on street corners. What upset the two senators was the site's *audacious* and *brazen* nature; ignored entirely was a simple question about what *effect* shutting down the site would have. Would it make a significant change in how many drugs were consumed? Would it increase or decrease overdoses or street violence and robberies? Nobody knew or cared. It was selling illegal drugs ergo it must be shut down.

The sudden scrutiny wasn't easy on Ross:

> I started to get into a bad state of mind. I was mentally taxed, and now I felt extremely vulnerable and scared. The US govt, my main enemy was aware of me and some of it's [*sic*] members were calling for my destruction. This is the biggest force wielding organization on the planet.[29]

During this difficult period of updating the site, sudden publicity, and increasing FBI and DEA interest, Ross found himself leaning on his programming buddy Richard Bates more and more. But Richard grew frustrated with his friend's constant questions and demands for help. Finally Richard had had enough of the secrecy. In the following court transcript of one of their unencrypted Gchats, logged on Ross's computer and found by the authorities, Richard ("baronsyntax") told Ross ("me") that enough was enough:

> baronsyntax@gmail.com: *I'm officially forbidding you from men-*
> *tioning your secret project again unless you are going to reveal it*
> me: *can i ask you programming questions for "no particular reason"*
> baronsyntax@gmail.com: *yeah*

As an ultimatum, Richard's was pretty weak. Richard knew or suspected Ross was doing something illegal and wasn't interested in getting caught up in it. The fact that Richard was still willing to help "in general terms" confirms this reading—it looks like window dressing, supplying a reasonably solid defense should things turn sour. But Ross wasn't able to handle Silk Road's many demands all by himself and was soon forced to do something he promised himself he never would.

Ross invited Richard over one evening and did the unthinkable. He took a deep breath, loaded the site, and let Richard see it for the first time. He also revealed his role as the site's lone developer and administrator. As related in court, Richard's reaction to Silk Road was instructive: "I remember seeing that green camel for the first time, and pictures of drugs. I think my immediate reaction was, 'They're going to shut this thing down really, really soon.'"[30]

It's not clear how much of the following is true, and how much is a result of Richard spinning the truth after the FBI came knocking on his door, so take it with a grain of salt. Richard claimed in court that, while continuing to help Ross with Silk Road, he was at the same time pressuring Ross to shut it down and start a new business, a legal Bitcoin exchange. Ross wasn't, initially, interested in the suggestion, but on November 11, 2011, after somebody posted on Ross's Facebook wall the message, "I'm sure the authorities would be very interested in your drug-running site," Ross reconsidered.

Slowly, quietly, Ross began freaking out, and Richard says he urged Ross to do the only sensible thing: shut down Silk Road. It was the last thing on Ross's mind. For whatever reason, Ross decided to go all in and used the opportunity to cover his tracks. Ross told Richard he didn't have to worry anymore. He was out—he had sold Silk Road to somebody and was going on a trip around the world using the sale proceeds. From that point on Ross never asked Richard coding questions and always maintained the fiction that his interest in Silk Road was purely academic. He wasn't running it, profiting from it, and wasn't interested in discussing it. As time passed the two spoke less frequently. Richard would occasionally chat with Ross, but the chats usually petered out quickly. The following example is typical:

> baronsyntax [Richard]: *Did you see Slashdot last week?* [referring to an article about Bitcoin]
> me [Ross]: *negative*
> baronsyntax: *There was something posting on Friday that you might find interesting*
> me: *i'll take a look, thanks*
> me: *glad that's not my problem anymore :)*
> baronsyntax: *yes*
> me: *I have regrets, don't get me wrong*
> me: *but that shit was stressful*

me: *still our secret though, eh?*
baronsyntax: *yup*
baronsyntax: *I'm spilling the beans when I turn 65 though.*

Knowing he was a hunted man, Ross attempted to be professional and security conscious, using Tor and Bitcoin mixers and heavy encryption whenever possible. In other ways he was a pure amateur. He had a significant, if not large, presence on social networks. He created and uploaded YouTube videos. He saved chat logs and contact data and customer and vendor information far past the "one month destruction" time frame he required his vendors to use. When the authorities eventually grabbed Ross's laptop and unencrypted it, they came across a few of his chats with baronsyntax, leading to a subpoena requesting Google cough up all Ross's chat records, after which it was easy enough to track down the real Richard Bates.

It's hard to blame Richard for testifying against Ross in court; the FBI visited him a few days after arresting Ross and had more than enough evidence to charge him as a criminal associate for helping to code and maintain Silk Road, particularly after he knew what Ross's secret project was really about. The expected prison time for a (likely) conviction was shocking—multiple decades. Richard agreed to cooperate if the government dropped their charges against him, and that's how he ended up testifying for the prosecution.[31] Many people made money selling drugs on Silk Road, or indirectly by working for Ross as site administrators, but Richard was one of the few who hadn't. He helped Ross out of friendship. Although Richard had been deeply involved he hadn't a cent to show for it—and this fact saved his skin. The government could have prosecuted Richard, and probably won the case, but it would have been a hard sell: how much of a drug conspirator could he be if he never made a profit? The government's offer of immunity made sense on both sides. It's nice to see in the midst of this messy legal quagmire that being a generous friend kept Richard out of jail, even if he was forced to snitch.

Ross Ulbricht was right to worry about the federal government. By 2012, after his site had been up and running for a year, Silk Road had already caught the attention of Homeland Security Investigations (HSI), the FBI, and the DEA. HSI Chicago opened an investigation called "Operation Dime Store," gathering evidence from US Postal seizures and actively tracking Silk Road message boards and vendor pages. HSI Baltimore formed a special task force, targeting Silk Road and its administrators, and displayed a certain sauciness by naming it "Marco Polo," after the eponymous traveler who history (or myth) informs us was the first European to travel the Silk Road to Asia during the Middle Ages, a trip lasting twenty-four years. HSI Baltimore was hoping their journey would be substantially shorter, but the historical resonance isn't a throwaway connection: they were the first to take the Silk Road seriously, and the first to track Ross as he, in amateur fashion, attempted to avoid capture.

The biggest problem with an anonymous site such as Silk Road is that, by design, the administrator isn't able to verify vendor accounts. It was a relatively trivial matter for the FBI to find a Silk Road vendor (in custody on unrelated charges) who was willing, for a reduction of charges or other plea bargain goodies, to turn over his Silk Road password to the feds, allowing a government mole to assume the online role of a freedom-loving drug-dealing libertarian vendor with a wonderful history of past sales.[32]

Imagine somebody asking you to dance on the edge of a cliff. Imagine the security precautions you would take before agreeing, the harnesses and lifelines and mini-parachutes you would demand. Ross Ulbricht experienced this every day. Every communication he sent to Silk Road had to be encrypted. Every time he accessed Silk Road he had to be mindful about the connection he was using. He had to double check that he didn't accidentally give away anything in his forum posts or private messages; even something as simple as "It's night I'm tired" would cut the global possibilities for the Dread Pirate's location in half.

By 2012 the DEA, having infiltrated a few Silk Road vendors, was communicating with the Dread Pirate Roberts directly, working on an (entirely fictional) drug deal involving importation of millions of dollars' worth of contraband. It was the first Silk Road transaction of this size and scope, and Ross imagined it would take the site to a new level. It's one thing, I suppose, to sell drugs already in the country to users who want to buy them safely with known dosages; it's another to work on importing a massive new shipment, although for many libertarians it's all the same. Allow adults to make decisions about what they put into their bodies; the government can deal with any outliers who act irresponsibly after doing so.

Around this time Silk Road's sister site, the Armory, which sold weapons through the mail, closed its doors. Ross had created it a few months before, and he announced the closure in this way:

> As most of you have figured out, we are closing the armory. Your first question is probably "why?". Well, it just wasn't getting used enough. Spinning it off originally was done somewhat abruptly and while we supported it, it was a kind of "sink or swim" experiment. The volume hasn't even been enough to cover server costs and is actually waning at this point. I had high hopes for it, but if we are going to serve an anonymous weapons market, I think it will require more careful thought and planning.
>
> The next question is probably "can we now sell guns on Silk Road?". The answer there is most definitely NO. If we do support weapons sales once more, it will be on a separate site.
>
> As the banner on the site says, finish up your business there and withdraw your coins before the end of the countdown. If you recently bought a seller account and haven't made enough sales to at least break even on it, contact us on the armory and we'll get you a refund.[33]

Here we have the quintessential Ross Ulbricht: thoughtful toward vendors, not interested in stealing any bitcoins already invested, sad about the experiment failing, and principled in refusing to allow gun sales on Silk Road. In a country where guns are both legal and widely available for purchase from stores such as Walmart, hardly an exclusive merchant, what is the role of a black market arms store? Were the legal hurdles of gun ownership so burdensome they required a way to circumvent them? Why would you buy online if you could, legally, buy in public? Was it really wrong to keep firearms away from the mentally deficient, former felons, and a long line of extremists? Did libertarians want to fight for the right to keep fully automatic weapons in the hands of any and all private citizens, including light/heavy machine guns?

As it turns out, no. Ross was highly uninterested. He considered the War on Drugs far more damaging to civil liberties, as well as expensive and highly destructive to personal freedom (particularly for those in prison on narcotics charges). Silk Road members were broadly sympathetic; the Armory died an unlamented death.

Meanwhile, the feds were busy. They had cooked up a nice little cocaine importation scheme and wanted help from the Dread Pirate Roberts in finding a buyer who could handle at least ten kilograms. Ross contacted one of his trusted Silk Road administrators, Curtis Green, who said he was interested.[34] The sellers, federal agents, refused to use the US Postal Service to deliver such a large and valuable package and requested, from Ross, permission to send private couriers to hand the package to Curtis in person. Ross, amazingly, acceded, sent them Curtis's home address, and the sale went through. When he got the news, the Dread Pirate Roberts wrote to Curtis, "congrats on sale!" Everything was great. Except that the feds had arrested Curtis Green immediately after he accepted the cocaine shipment. The government finally had what they wanted: a cooperative arrestee with a trusted Silk Road administrator account ("flush").

Although he didn't know it, the world was closing in on Ross Ulbricht. He had gone from being the anonymous founder of an anonymous illegal drug site to somebody who asked friends for help programming the site; somebody who had extensive social media exposure, including remarks about his "illegal drug site"; somebody who had a trusted Silk Road administrator in the hands of the HSI. . . . Surely the house of cards was going to collapse. Yet at this crucial moment the government investigators began to go crazy.

A few weeks after Ross Ulbricht's trial and conviction, the US government filed charges against two former federal agents intimately involved in the Baltimore Silk Road investigation.[35] For the remainder of this book this "innocent until proven guilty" pair will be known simply as Slinker and Stinker.[36]

Slinker, a DEA agent, had been in on the setup, trapping, and busting of Curtis Green on cocaine charges. Both Slinker and Stinker interrogated Green after his arrest, and after he agreed to cooperate he turned over his Silk Road administrator account ("flush") to the Marco Polo task force. Slinker and Stinker used the "flush" account to squirm their way deep into Silk Road as a trusted user, vendor, and all-around fixit guy. It was an impressive infiltration: the government started with nothing, quickly arrested a low-level vendor, assumed his identity online, and used this access as a springboard to trap a Silk Road administrator in a bogus drug transaction, and thereafter assume his identity online. With administrator privileges on the site, surely the Dread Pirate Roberts's true identity would soon be revealed. Instead, something strange happened.

The Dread Pirate Roberts was contacted by a new user, Nob, who apparently had an "inside informant" in the Marco Polo task force investigation. Nob was willing to give the Dread Pirate a bit of information for free, but if he wanted more, it was gonna cost. Ross was curious and listened to what Nob had to say. Nob's story went like this: a corrupt federal agent was willing to talk and spill the investigation's secrets, but it would require bitcoins, a lot of them. Ross eventually paid $50,000 for further details and for once he wasn't ripped off: he got his information. The problem? Nob was actually Slinker, and Slinker was busy padding his e-wallet by peddling secrets, anonymously and under heavy encryption, to Ross from his own investigation of Ross.[37] It looked like a splendid plan.

Curtis Green was again interviewed by the Baltimore Silk Road task force on how to use his administrative password to gain administrative power over the site. Green was seated at a computer and made to show exactly how such a feat was accomplished. Slinker and Stinker, overseeing the debriefing, doubtlessly watched with desperate curiosity. Before noon, Stinker left the interview room while the rest of them continued to talk to Curtis about Silk Road, his contacts, and the other details. In an amazing coincidence, that very afternoon Silk Road suffered a major attack, and $900,000 worth of bitcoins were stolen.[38] Ross Ulbricht was shocked and angered by the theft and after an investigation zeroed in on Curtis Green's account, which he determined had been at the root of the incursion.

From Ross's perspective, Curtis Green was using his Silk Road account to reset vendor pin numbers, access their funds, and transfer money from one account to another (his own). Bitcoins were flowing out of the Silk Road coffers and the Dread Pirate Roberts had no idea where they were going—until he realized Curtis must have been stealing bitcoins to pay for whatever bad stuff was happening in his life at the moment (it seemed to be a long list). DPR (all activities alleged but not yet proven to be committed by Ross under the guise of the Dread Pirate Roberts will be noted by DPR)[39] wrote to his new pal, Nob,[40] whom he now trusted as a useful thug, and told him, "The Employee got busted! Also, he stole funds from Silk Road users. Beat him and get the money back, kthxbai."[41]

The cutesy *kthaxbai* (OK thanks bye) is particularly galling. What DPR was apparently hoping for was a visit by the drug dealer's "goons," who would smash Curtis's teeth in or carefully break five of his fingers in slow sequence or use another cinematic technique to convince him to return the bitcoins and stop being such a scumbag. That DPR wanted an undercover agent to spearhead this assault is hilariously inappropriate and led DPR deeper into an increasingly dismal swamp.

DPR was in a terrible position, deeply enmeshed in numerous cons and completely out of his league. His new friend Nob was Slinker, who was busy selling details of his own investigation of Ross for bitcoins; his other associate, Curtis Green, had been set up by Stinker, who stole bitcoins using Curtis's login and identity. DPR was hemorrhaging bitcoins at this point, but worse was yet to come.

DPR was annoyed he couldn't participate directly in Curtis's punishment: "I want to kick his [Curtis's] ass myself, but let's leave it to the pros. . . . I would have no problem wasting this guy." DPR realized he couldn't be directly involved and instead relied upon Nob to act as his intermediary. Nob supplied DPR with ever-more-fanciful reports about his quest to punish Curtis. But DPR was still worried. He was aware of how much Curtis knew about the operation, the site, its users, and its financial records, and he wasn't sure if Curtis had been arrested and was already working with the authorities. DPR sent Nob a customer service request: "Can you change the order to execute rather than torture? . . . [I] never killed a man before or had one killed before, but it is the right move in this case . . . considering his arrest, I have to assume he will sing." This was incredibly old fashioned of DPR; who speaks of criminals "singing" anymore, outside old movies and pulp fiction?

After a bit of haggling, DPR agreed to pay Nob $80,000 for the hit, $40K before and $40K after.[42]

It's hard to imagine the glee the federal agents must have felt. They quickly set up an account, had DPR wire $40,000 worth of bitcoins into it, and thereafter a fast-paced series of scripted events occurred. Curtis, still in custody, agreed to participate in the gruesome charade of being tortured, with photographic proof, before being faux executed—again with photographic proof. The federal agents kept in touch with DPR over an encrypted (but heavily logged) chat, where Nob revealed the status of his B-movie plan: he had a squad of assassins in place,[43] waiting for Curtis's wife and daughter to leave the house before moving in. Once Curtis was alone they would grab him, torture him, and not stop until he returned the bitcoins. Later, they'd remove him from the house, drive him somewhere, and "kill him."

DPR replied laconically, "Just let me know when it's done. It's still a go."

Three days later the putative assassins reported they were *still* torturing Curtis, who was being amazingly stubborn about returning the bitcoins. No worries though: they were sure Curtis would soon "break." DPR thanked them for the update and told them to carry on. Soon thereafter came graphic (staged) photos of Curtis's torture and death. DPR was a little rattled, and wrote back to the apparent killers: "[I'm] a little disturbed, but I'm OK . . . I'm new to this. . . . I don't think I've done the wrong thing. . . . I'm sure I will call on you again at some point, though I hope I won't have to . . . I just can't believe he was so stupid. . . . I just wish more people had some integrity."

Yes, that's what was needed: integrity. Unfortunately, things continued to spiral out of control. A former vendor contacted DPR with proof that he had been able to hack Silk Road, and had customer and site data ready to be released to the public unless he was paid $50,000 each week in bitcoins. DPR ground his teeth, resisted, complained, did some forensic searches on his own servers, and eventually agreed to pay his blackmailer. He also discovered the blackmailer's name and address—either through his own cleverness or because it was planted there for him to discover. DPR was so confident about the revelation that he got in touch with another new friend, a user known as Redandwhite, with whom he was arranging another large-scale drug deal, and asked for help. In the pulp fiction world DPR was living in, Redandwhite was a "well known" handle for the Hell's

Angels, which wasn't simply a merchandizing goldmine beloved by aging riders all over the land, featuring t-shirts modeled by tattooed models of the slightly naughty variety, cheesy leather garb, hats with bad words on them, and other "motorcycle" accessories. In DPR's mind the Hell's Angels functioned as an honest-to-goodness criminal enterprise capable of executions on demand. Which is what DPR demanded.

Redandwhite, surely pinching himself at the opportunity presented by this incredibly naive and inexperienced criminal mastermind, bargained and complained and bargained some more and eventually extracted $150,000 in bitcoins for a "hit" on DPR's latest blackmailer, who was becoming increasingly demanding. DPR asked Redandwhite, before killing the blackmailer, to acquire the location of another well-known Silk Road scammer, Tony76, who was apparently working in concert with the blackmailer to make DPR's life as difficult as possible.

Not surprisingly, Redandwhite managed to "kill" the main blackmailer, but not before getting Tony76's "real address and location." After scouting Tony76 for a few days, Redandwhite reported he was living and working with three other drug dealers, and it would be easiest to kill all four—since it was hard to know when Tony76 was going to be alone, etc.

This was DPR response to the killing of the blackmailer, from his personal log later seized and presented to the court in the trial of Ross Ulbricht:

04/01/2013
    created file upload script
    started to fix problem with bond refunds over 3 months old
    got word that blackmailer was excuted [sic]

It wasn't a big deal, just another aspect of business, reported along with stunning developments such as the creation of a file upload script. The Tony76 issue was more serious; was DPR willing to pay for his death along with three others, who were innocent as far as Silk Road was concerned? He was. Redandwhite drove a hard bargain but agreed that for $500,000 he'd off the whole bunch.

DPR transmitted the bitcoins. "The banality of evil"[44] comes to mind as DPR constructed scripts and troubleshot refunds and "with the energy of good bureaucrats"[45] finished off his final bullet point, scheduling and paying for a multi-person hit.

A few days later Redandwhite proudly stated, "That problem was dealt with. I'll try to catch you online to give you details. Just wanted to let you know right away so you have one less thing to worry about."[46] It wasn't until much later that DPR realized what should have been obvious from the start: no assassinations had taken place. Why would they? Redandwhite (still unidentified by the authorities) jumped at the chance to lure a gullible and insecure criminal who was already being blackmailed by an unknown enemy. DPR eventually discovered the truth and jotted it down in laid-back California style: "r&w flaked out and disappeared with my 1/2 mil." The authorities have no record of any deaths occurring, despite Redandwhite's claims; it's clear that DPR paid for assassinations that (thankfully) never took place.

Everything was unraveling. A hacker was hitting Silk Road with a concerted attempt to knock it offline, and generally succeeding. Ross was instructed to pay the hacker $100,000 worth of bitcoins the first week, and $50,000 every week thereafter, or risk further disruptions. Ross paid.[47] Feeling he needed an escape hatch, Ross attempted to purchase alternate identity documentation for $40,000: "I tried to get a fake passport from nob, but gave fake pic and fucked the whole thing up. nob got spooked and is barely communicating. said his informant isn't communicating with him either."[48]

Unfortunately for Ross, his shipment, stuffed full of fake passports, had been seized at the Canadian border by custom officials, who informed authorities in the United States, who came knocking on Ross Ulbricht's door in San Francisco where he was living under an alias. "The highest levels of government are hunting me," Ross wrote, and "I can't take any chances." Nob, the Silk Road user being run by the federal agent Slinker, had apparently produced via a third party a series of fake passports from photos and other details supplied by the Dread Pirate himself: what better way was there to track down the real person behind the alias? Ross Ulbricht was essentially handing over his personal information to the government, but Slinker and Stinker, busy feeding off the bitcoins spilling from Silk

Road via any number of channels, were uninterested in pursuing this obvious—very obvious—very juicy lead. The agents who knocked on Ross's door with a manila folder full of fake passports didn't know the Silk Road backstory, and they certainly weren't working with Slinker or his pals. The fake passports should have been enough to break the case, but it wasn't until a year later that Ross was arrested by another investigation entirely. In the meantime, Slinker and Stinker continued to shake down Ross as thoroughly as possible.

Ross wasn't able to corral the chaos. The FBI discovered an apparent misconfiguration in the Silk Road hidden service user login interface, revealing the IP address of the host server. This enabled them to send a legal request to Iceland, asking authorities to seize and copy the newly discovered Silk Road server. The Reykjavik Metropolitan Police shared the results of the Silk Road server image with the FBI who forensically investigated the data, leading to more servers in Pennsylvania. The US-based servers were quickly subpoenaed, seized, and searched, revealing full backups of the entire Silk Road site, including logs, chats, personal emails, and most importantly . . . Ross's real name.

The investigation at this point had been transferred to the HSI Chicago branch, who (unlike other sworn government officials) were not messing around. They flew into San Francisco and, since Ross Ulbricht had been previously interviewed over the fake passport debacle, they knew exactly where he lived and proceeded to stake him out. Slinker and Stinker, aware that the feds were moving in to arrest Ross, proceeded with a last flurry of shake-down maneuvers. Giving up his Nob alias, Slinker created a new one, French Maid, and sent Ross internal details of the Chicago investigation, promising that for $100,000 he would divulge more.

As recorded by Ross, "paid french maid $100k for the name given to DHLS by karpeles. He hasn't replied for 4days. Got covered in poison oak trying to get a piece of trash out of a tree in a park nearby and have been moping. went on a first date with amelia from okc."

I feel bad for Amelia from OKC, but she was lucky Ross had poison oak during the date, which surely prevented anything too exciting from happening. This was doubtless good for Amelia; Ross didn't have much time left. The fact that French Maid absconded with his bitcoins and never wrote back was, at this point, to be expected. (Slinker and/or Stinker also sent DPR extortion demands related to Curtis's fictional assassination, asking for hush money, but DPR, for once, brushed these threats aside.)

October 1, 2013—Ross Ulbricht's final day of freedom—wasn't distinguished by any unusual events. The Chicago HSI team had taken their time and had slowly built a profile of Ross's daily habits. They knew what he was likely to do and where he was likely to go. The weather forecast said it would be mostly clear, in the low 60s, slightly windy with low humidity—extraordinarily typical for San Francisco in early autumn. The sky was a cloudy, vaguely bright haze, everywhere the same, the dull light leaching color from the world for the poor mortals forced to live and work there.

Ross Ulbricht was renting a room in a small, shabby multimillion-dollar home in one of the most unfashionable neighborhoods in San Francisco, West Portal. It wasn't particularly close to downtown, and it certainly wasn't anywhere tourists visited. Rumbling Muni (the San Francisco Municipal Railway) trains popped out of underground tunnels at one end of West Portal, cut through the center of the neighborhood heading southwest, and lumbered clumsily through the flat streets. The neighborhood was full of businesses such as She-She Nail Salon, ThriveAbility, Eezy Freezy Health Foods, and others even more marginal. Most people, if they think of West Portal at all, register it as a bland waypoint while traveling to or returning from San Francisco State, a place to move through, not stop and visit. It combines the expense and hassle of a big city with a complete lack of cultural or architectural amenities that can, occasionally, in other contexts, make living in such a place endurable. Incredibly high rent and only-slightly-higher-than-average income result in constant economic pressure. Nobody lives easy in West Portal, not even putative Dark Road multimillionaires.

Ross was in the habit of leeching free and anonymous Wi-Fi from public cafes, and on the day in question took his laptop and headed in the direction of Bello Coffee, where he often sat for hours, drinking coffee and using the café's electricity and internet connection. Unfortunately for him, Homeland Security Investigations (HSI)—the professional branch, not the clown patrol headed by

Slinker and Stinker—was ready. They had been indirectly monitoring Ross's online activity via an encrypted chat room used by Silk Road staff. Yet another HSI agent had infiltrated Silk Road under the name Cirrus, and after proving his ability as a basic but honest vendor he slowly moved into a position of greater power, eventually attracting the attention and trust of the Dread Pirate Roberts. Cirrus worked for a time as a paid Silk Road forum moderator, and one of his first acts was to crack down on a Silk Road user who had resurrected an old thread, which began:[49]

> INFORMANTS,   SURVEILLANCE,   AND   UNDERCOVER
> OPERATIONS—"Good informant, good case. Bad informant, bad case. No informant, no case." (Police saying)

Cirrus wrote "Guys, please don't bump threads that haven't been posted in for months!" It's easy to see why a thread of this nature would make Cirrus nervous; he was, in fact, an undercover plant and wanted nothing more than to let such threads die a quick death. But he received pushback, and other users found Cirrus's comments heavy handed:

> What is the (unexisting) logic behind this?
>   If that guy hadn't bumped this I never would have read it or even have known I had missed out. This is such an active forum with constant new threads, this revival of good threads saves clutter and helps those who would have missed it.

It put Cirrus in a difficult position. He felt obliged to do what, looking back, was transparently obvious: tamp down concerns over possible infiltration. When Silk Road users got a bit nervous—a common event—they would often speculate wildly and start threads full of this sort of stuff:

> Aurelious Venport: whoever has been posting on the DPR account lately . . . is not the same person
>   joolz: whats that mean ? = its compromised be the police or L.E ? ???

L.E. being short for Law Enforcement. Cirrus jumped into the discussion and closed the thread immediately: "No, joolz, no one is saying or implying that. Please don't start that kind of rumor."

Even in his moderator introduction to the community, a thread begun by the Dread Pirate himself, there's fun to be had:

> forgettegrof on July 12, 2013, 06:59 am: OMG DIFFERENT OH.MY . . . GOD Three months ago DPR had a different grammatical structure then he does now, then. THEN, we get a new moderator. Conspiracy! DEA, KGB, Mole Men!

Cirrus deals with it in the only way possible:

> Cirrus on July 12, 2013, 07:01 am: don't forget ALIENS and BIGFOOT!! and especially ABOMINABLE SNOWMEN!!

Since Cirrus was in the encrypted chat room with the Dread Pirate, pretending to do work, he was able to see when Ross entered and (more crucially) left, which implied Ross (in the real world) had logged out and was moving to a new location. It also indirectly built the case that the Dread Pirate Roberts was Ross, since there was a correlation between Ross's movements and the absence or presence of DPR in the chat room.

As Ross started to move, agents tracking him saw him heading for the café and scattered around the block to avoid detection. Ross popped his head into café, saw there were no tables or outlets available, and turned around, heading for the Glen Park library next door. He passed a narrow alley that had been converted into a private parking lot, running half-a-block deep and terminating in the surprising green of three healthy trees. A collection of recycling and garbage containers were pressed against the left wall. Three dishwashers or cooks or waiters, spilling out of a back door of the café with cigarettes and repulsively dirty aprons, were clumped in a group, talking, passing the time. After a few seconds Ross reached the Glen Park Library.[50]

Glen Park library was a small, relatively empty library, as libraries go, not the best place to find an anonymous corner in which to run a drug empire, but equally difficult as a venue for espionage. It wasn't going to be easy to get close to Ross without making him wonder what another library patron was doing creeping up and sitting next to him when there were plenty of empty tables available. The agent working with Cirrus, on a street corner near the library but outside direct line-of-sight, had seen Ross disappear from the chat room during his walk to the café. His partners soon updated Cirrus via cell phone; Ross had entered the library.

Ross walked up the short flight of steps to the second floor and went to the so-called science fiction section, a grandiose title for what amounted to a four-foot-wide bookcase wedged between two tall windows. Romance, an equally puny bookcase, was situated on the other side of the window.[51] Ross sat at a small circular table in front of the central window, plugged his laptop into a convenient outlet, and got himself into a world of trouble.

When Ross reappeared in the chat room, Cirrus did something very clever. He requested a private chat with the Dread Pirate in order to ask him about a tricky "customer support" issue, Silk Road being big enough at this point to mimic the stultifying language of corporate America, which when adopted by illegal organizations of any sort always comes across as slightly ridiculous. Ross, who always took his job seriously, wanted to know more about the problem, and Cirrus quickly gave him a customer name, knowing any investigation would require Ross to log into his Silk Road administration panel, allowing Ross full access to everything occurring on the site—and proving beyond any reasonable doubt Ross's identity.

The operation was put on full alert when the Dread Pirate typed into the chat window: "ok which post?" Ross had successfully logged into the Silk Road administration panel and was waiting for more information. They finally had what they wanted: the Dread Pirate Roberts in a specific place at a specific time and logged into Silk Road in a way only its owner and operator could manage. All they had to do now was grab Ross (trivial) but more importantly seize his open laptop (tricky). HSI suspected, rightly, that Ross was using an encrypted laptop, and if he banged shut the laptop lid or logged out of the system all data on his hard drive would be unrecoverable. Assuming Ross wasn't using a short and obvious password such as

123456 or *mypassword*,[52] a locked laptop would render Ross's data fundamentally unrecoverable, useless as evidence, and likely torpedo any legal case.

The sting operation was more than ready. They had prepped and surveilled and planned the interagency arrest for months. After receiving the OK from Cirrus, three FBI agents entered the library and headed for the second floor, where they enacted a scripted scene. A male agent and a female agent, dressed in bland California casual and initially attracting no attention, raised their voices in what appeared to be a lover's tiff. Since they were in the library they had to whisper-shout, but they made sure it wasn't *much* quieter than normal shouting. They slowly headed for a corner near Ross's table. As their argument grew more heated, they moved closer to Ross, behind him, on either side of him. Ross looked up to see what all the fuss was about and that was all it took. The female agent reached down and pushed Ross's open laptop away from him, and it slid across the table to her partner, who picked it up and immediately handed it to the third agent, who sprinted off with an evidentiary goldmine. Five minutes later they had copied the entire hard drive onto a USB memory stick and were busy moving through Ross's browser history pages, revealing Silk Road page after Silk Road page, many accessible only by somebody with administrative privileges, and some only by the Dread Pirate Roberts himself.

At the moment Ross's laptop was confiscated, he was deep in a conversation with Cirrus. His final message as the Dread Pirate Roberts is perfectly in keeping with everything I had read or learned about him as a man:

> Dread Pirate Roberts: you did bitcoin exchange before you started working for me, right?
> Cirrus: yes . . . but just for a little bit
> Dread Pirate Roberts: not any more then?
> Cirrus: no, I stopped because of the reporting requirements
> Dread Pirate Roberts: damn regulators, eh?

Ross Ulbricht was convicted on February 4, 2015, of running the Silk Road website, and he was found guilty on various charges, including narcotics trafficking, computer hacking, money laundering, and running a "continual criminal enterprise." He was sentenced to life in prison, and faces further charges related to the Dread Pirate Robert's "murder for hire" schemes, for which he has not yet been tried (as of December 2015).

IDEALISM AND "THE GRAIN OF INSANITY"

Between complaints about bad vendors and scam artists and boring details concerning fee percentage adjustments (the increase or decrease thereof), the Dread Pirate Robert's voluminous Silk Road forum posts reveal Ross's open engagement with the Silk Road community and his deep affection and appreciation for them. A typical love letter runs:

> . . . to all the players in this crazy game we're playing: buyers, vendors, financiers, the leaders in the community, the mods and admins, the arguers and skeptics, the evangelists, the tech gurus, the post office, the open source developers and communities, all of the giants who's shoulders we stand on. . . . I love you all!

This isn't Ross being coy or ironic, playing the seemingly honest host of a hugely illegal drug superstore, hoping to boost his credentials and reputation. It's typical, rather than unusual. On other occasions Ross emotes: "I love you all! I know the feeling isn't mutual in all cases, but still my love for you persists"; "Doesn't matter though, I love you all. Of all the people in the world, you are the ones who are here, in the early stages of this revolution"; "Love you guys!"; ". . . love"; "Love . . ."; ". . . love . . ." Ross writes "love" again and again, hymns to the community, congratulations for the hard work of various volunteers, and heartfelt assertions about how Silk Road will change the world. If Ross is lying, his literary skill is enviable, given that he's prone, in every other post, to malapropisms, speedy misspellings, and awkward phrases (mangling whatever metaphors are within reach). It's hard to imagine somebody working so hard to pull the wool over a future reader's eyes given that none of this was supposed to have any historical or topical resonance. The easy answer is the right one: these posts are nothing less than heartfelt effusions.

Ross loved Silk Road, and a mutual admiration society formed between him and its vendors and users. Ross loved his customers and loved his vendors, and they loved him (possibly to an even greater degree) for running the site and enabling them to make huge profits in relative safety instead of facing the uncertainties of face-to-face sales on the street. It wasn't just a money-making machine for Ross, though it was that; it wasn't just a libertarian economic experiment, a full assault on the insanity that is the current War on Drugs, though it was that; it wasn't just a way for a frustrated academic to make an impact on the world, and achieve, if not personal glory, at least immortal internet fame. Silk Road was crucial on a personal level: it was the most important *community* in Ross's life. His deepest desires and greatest triumphs and highest ambitions could be found and realized there, which is why nothing about Ross as clichéd "drug kingpin" makes much sense.

Ross lived in a relatively dilapidated house in a relatively unglamorous neighborhood. He didn't own a car, bought clothes from whatever stores were proximate, and had a personal life that, while far from monastic, was anything but lively. His San Francisco roommates rarely saw him and when they did he was often hunched over his computer. Ross owned no real estate. He hadn't managed to offshore any of his profits, lagging behind corporate America in this type of legal thievery. He plowed everything back into Silk Road, both time and money.

Sometime in the middle of Silk Road's spectacular (though short-lived) success, Ross transformed from a libertarian activist into a militant revolutionary. He might not have started out that way, but that's certainly where he ended. The following collation of Dread Pirate forum posts makes this perfectly clear:

> Together, we can make the Silk Road market a place where you can buy with confidence and peace of mind. If we stay true to our principles of integrity, virtue, mutual respect and camaraderie that have guided us to this point, I believe our future is bright and this revolutionary experiment will be a success!

There are heroes among us here at Silk Road. Every day they risk their lives, fortunes, and precious liberty for us. They are on the front lines making tough decisions and working their asses off to make this market what it is.

Humanity is at a critical juncture. Either violence will dominate the future of mankind, or peace will. The way of the state is the way of violence, oppression and death. The way of the market is freedom, dignity and peace. If you understand this, it is your moral duty to protect the victims of the state in any way you can.

One final thing about economics you should understand that most university courses don't teach and most philosophy classes won't touch. It's simple, foundational, and changes your entire perspective on things once you have realized it. it is this: Every voluntary transaction is a good thing.

Ross attempted to run Silk Road as a strict "Rothbardian anarcho-capitalist model,"[53] a concept he first ran across in graduate school. Ross saw the damage the War on Drugs had inflicted on individual liberties. It was an ongoing assault. Somebody had to take a principled stand against this interference, and the anonymity of Bitcoin enabled such a stance without resulting in immediate loss of freedom. A mortar-and-brick superstore, peddling heroin and Quaaludes? From the libertarian point of view, acceptable and interesting. Moving such a store online was the only way to keep the government from shutting it down within seconds of opening.

Moving in parallel with Ross's increasing libertarian fervor was his emotional entanglement with Silk Road: it was impossible for Ross to become anything *but* a true believer, with all the benefits and drawbacks associated with such a position. Many of Ross's actions were dangerous and opened him to exposure: there wasn't a rational reason for taking massive personal risks for minor or invisible gains for Silk Road. Yet Ross took such risks constantly. He wasn't transferring bitcoins into a secret Bahamas account, converting them into dollars or euros and buying condos or art or stocks or annuities to expand his financial empire, helping to ensure its strength in the face of a prolonged assault by a foreign power. He didn't create special accounts for his sister or parents, or hide ten million under a childhood friend's name in an obscure Lithuanian tontine. Ross was, to all outward appearances, a perfectly nice and focused and busy man, nothing more. But it wasn't deep cover on Ross's part, playing a continuous real-life game of "just a normal Joe" while overseeing over a billion dollars' worth of drug transactions. Ross didn't have a façade, because he didn't need one. He acted like the person he had become: an ideologue.

The benefits are obvious. Imagine the early Mormon settlers, persecuted and driven out of Missouri, calmly walking (wide-eyed and hopeful) toward an unknown future in Utah. You couldn't pay people to do it, yet thousands made the trip, buoyed by their belief in the rightness of their cause and, crucially, after the sharpening of their beliefs through ongoing discrimination.[54] Libertarians of Ross's stripe felt the weight of similar, if not as dire, persecution. Daily life was a series of small or large imprecations in the form of national currency, or government regulations, or legal strictures whose existence contradicted Ross's fundamental beliefs. Want to a buy a cookie from somebody? That's fine as long as they have the appropriate food service certification from the state/local authorities. Want to hire somebody to install an electrical outlet? That's great, as long as he's been approved to do such work, and it does not violate code, and you get it checked afterward by the local inspector. Want to buy a plot of land from your uncle? Great, but it requires forms and lawyers and fees and more forms. Our economy is ruled by *mediated* voluntary transactions; there are few examples of pure transactions outside of cash-for-food at a carnival or fair (and even there you are paying more than you should because of regulatory barriers that must be overcome by the seller before they are allowed to run a food stand on the premises).

A necessary product of strident idealism is found in Ross's basic economic principle: "Every voluntary transaction is a good thing." The key word is *every*. There's no shade of gray. The proposition isn't a theory to be tested but an assertion to be vociferously articulated. At root, it's rationally justified extremism. Ross claims every voluntary transaction is a good thing, and this covers the voluntary sale of drugs, voluntary sale of one's own body (either donated organs or for sex/other purposes), voluntary work by children in mines, voluntary suicide shows (with proceeds going to relatives), voluntary—well, you name it. The possibilities are as horrific as they are limitless. The concept is so extreme and unlimited that it's quite easy to imagine a dystopia where Ross's assertion is the core principal of the society's founding documents—to dreadful effect. In such a world there would be almost no way to limit those in power from gaining ever-greater power and abusing those who are forced to agree with whatever "voluntary transactions" are available. It would be difficult to imagine how financial markets would function in such a place, as voluntary transactions between those with information and those with money would have an overwhelming advantage over anyone competing against them on the stock market or anywhere else. Unlimited voluntary transactions would make a mockery of the legal system, and it's pretty clear that the net result would be another pat little phrase: *might makes right.*

If you pay enough, people generally do what you want. Those with the most money will purchase a volunteer army; those without money will be left to their own devices. The problem here, which Ross wasn't interested in thinking about, is the power dynamic at work in any transaction, voluntary or not. Offer a starving man a loaf of bread in exchange for indentured servitude for fifty years: yes, he could shun the offer and die, or "voluntarily" accept the offer and live the rest of his life as a slave. What about this choice is *voluntary?* Isn't it a case of word abuse? On a less extreme level, why would anyone take a job paying well below the poverty line if they were not beset by conditions rendering them incapable of getting more money elsewhere? Since these conditions are often not of the individual's choosing (having a child with special needs; being injured in a freak accident; ongoing racial or sexual discrimination; etc.) the net result is the leveraging of undesirable nonvoluntary choices by those in power, who are able to make lower-than-market-value offers and have them accepted.

Note that this pressure never works the other way. Bad luck on the part of a business or corporation does not suddenly result in a salary windfall for its employees; if anything they are laid off. It's hard to envision the result of fifty years' worth of such downward pressure, except to look at the American middle class and double or triple its current rate of decay.

It's a commonplace that ideologues see the world not as it really is but through the lens of their particular viewpoint. Strident communists see "means of production" pushing everyone except factory owners into the mud; strident Christians see God's hand in every mote of dust; strident believers in scientism apply scientific methods to everything and deny the validity of any other sort of knowledge;[55] paranoiacs see the world as a series of sharpened spears slowly surrounding them, preparing for a sudden strike. Curing these afflictions requires ideological flexibility, achieved through careful debate, convincing argumentation, and sensible discussion. Yet experience has shown nothing is more difficult than converting an ideologue—even in the face of fatal factual contradictions. Once embraced, ideology has proven to be a sticky substance. Too much has been invested, both emotionally and materially, to make change a matter of choice. How could a reasonably sane paranoiac, after insulting and offending friends and family over the course of a difficult year; after squandering money and time in constant movement from city to city; after damaging his or her health from irregular food and broken sleep, be made to realize *it was all an illusion*: the world isn't plotting a devious attack, in fact the world doesn't care what happens. The previous year had been nothing more than self-inflicted pain and misery. Surely that's far more difficult to accept than the simple easy-to-summarize assertion "everyone's out to get me," no matter where it leads, be it decline or death.

The effects of ideology are far from innocent. Imagine trying to convince Average Joe, a nice normal fellow in his thirties, to kill somebody. The victim isn't somebody Joe knows, and isn't somebody he's got a personal grudge against. Joe is vaguely aware that other people consider the potential victim a bad guy, but that's about it. What sort of argument could you make to inspire Joe to do the dirty deed?

It's a tough sell. The punishment for murder varies from unreasonably light to appalling (often a crap shoot depending on legal representation and jury makeup). Since Joe has no real emotional investment in the action, there isn't any easy way to arouse him into a bloodthirsty frenzy. Greed is always a possibility: why not pay Joe a lot of money, assuring him that the victim had it coming; that his absence would make the world a better place; that he wouldn't leave behind a grieving wife and drove of hungry children? As arguments go it's not terrible, but it's far from convincing. Many people won't be swayed. How much money is enough? What's the point of taking such a risk? Is the victim really as bad as is claimed? Who can be trusted? Average Joe doesn't have anything to grab hold of, and there isn't much to use against him. Appeals to racial or religious hatred fail; there isn't a long history of simmering slights that demand to be rectified in the present; passion is certainly far from anyone's mind; jealousy and its associated rages impossible. What's to be done?

With an ideologue there's always a crack in the armor. Ross Ulbricht knew, absolutely, that the state had its dirty fingers in places where it was not wanted and was actively committing violence against those who opposed it. To work against the damaging status quo is an obvious good, both in the short and more importantly the long term. Ross wasn't content overseeing a libertarian paradise. His ambitions increased as Silk Road gained in power and prestige, and by the end Ross would settle for nothing less than *changing the world*, a goal made explicit in the most revealing passage he ever typed to his friends on the forums, incorporating abolitionist rhetoric into what amounts to a nearly religious exhortation:

> [From libertarian works of economics] I understood the mechanics of liberty, and the effects of tyranny. But such vision was a curse. Everywhere I looked I saw the State, and the horrible withering effects it had on the human spirit. It was horribly depressing. Like waking from a restless dream to find yourself in a cage with no way out. But I also saw free spirits trying to break free of their chains, doing everything they could to serve their fellow man and provide for themselves and their loved ones. I saw the magical and powerful wealth creating effect of the market, the way it fostered cooperation, civility and tolerance. How it made trading partners out of strangers or even enemies. How it coordinates the actions of every person on the planet in ways too complex for any one mind to fathom to produce an overflowing abundance of wealth, where nothing is wasted and where power and responsibility are directed to those most deserving and able. I saw a better way, but knew of no way to get there.

Just as the historical Silk Road linked Europe with Persia, India, and China, enabling goods and technology and information and manuscripts to flow back and forth to everyone's mutual benefit, so Ross fervently believed Silk Road would lead the way to a brighter and better and less violent future thanks to, "the magical and powerful wealth creating [*sic*] effect of the market." If you are working for the good of yourself, your fellow Americans, and global citizens in general—deserving individuals numbering not in the millions but billions—wouldn't achieving this goal be a massive step forward for civilization? Yes. Thus, by simple binary logic, anything getting in that way of this goal, which strives for the greater good, *must be evil.*

This well-known dichotomy leads to predictable if bloody results. As put succinctly by social psychologist Roy F. Baumeister in *Evil: Inside Human Violence and Cruelty*: "If you think that you are doing something that is strongly on the side of good, then whoever opposes you or blocks your work must be against the good—hence, evil. . . . [This conclusion] is central to the idealist's basic faith that he is doing the right thing."[56]

This leads, unfortunately, to a linked result; namely that "some people who commit evil deeds are motivated by high ideals and a zealous desire to make the world a better place, as they see it. It is mainly from the perspective of their victims . . . that these acts are bad."[57]

For the majority of people, idealism is a core requirement, almost a necessary precondition, for the consummation of a stranger's premeditated murder, allowing (at the very least) a redefinition of behavior otherwise understood to be starkly evil. Men slaughter men who have a darker or lighter shade of skin not because they are intrinsically evil and enjoy bloodletting (though some do) but because slaughter in this case isn't a sin to them: the victim isn't quite human, rather part of a subhuman species, allowing escape of ethical strictures by simple redefinition. The world's better off without *those* sorts around. You know the sorts: those who believe we are born with original sin or don't; who have an ancestor with Middle Eastern origins or don't; who have certain tattoos along the sides of their arms or don't; who believe communism is or isn't the perfect system. Completely assured judgments of this type require a robust black-and-white dichotomy of thought, revealing certainties of understanding and leaving no room for doubt—yet require constant ongoing assurance that they are indeed in the right. Insecurity is covered and drowned by bombast.

Silk Road gave Ross that assurance. There was hardly a moderate libertarian to be found on the site, much less a critic. The Silk Road's wild and sudden success was proof, if proof was required, that Silk Road was not just a marketplace for voluntary transactions but a philosophical rebuke to heavy-handed and ever-increasing statism.[58]

For Ross Ulbricht the world split and differentiated. He no longer looked for scientific truths, testing them against evidence. He wasn't running an economic experiment. Things had moved far beyond that. He now knew *the truth*, and *the truth* was confirmed every day in thousands of transactions, where people safely and peacefully resisted the state's power in flagrant disregard of oppressive laws. As Ross put it in his most emotional and strident confession:

> I am filled with inspiration and hope for the future. Here's a little story about what inspires me: For years I was frustrated and defeated by what seemed to be insurmountable barriers between the world today and the world I wanted. I searched long and hard for the truth about what is right and wrong and good for humanity. I argued with, learned from, and read the works of brilliant people in search of the truth. It's a damn hard thing to do too with all of the misinformation and distractions in the sea of opinion we live in. But eventually I found something I could agree with whole heartedly. Something that made sense, was simple, elegant and consistent in all cases. I'm talking about the Austrian Economic theory, voluntaryism, anarcho-capitalism, agorism etc. espoused by the likes of Mises and Rothbard before their deaths, and Salerno and Rockwell today. From their works, I understood the mechanics of liberty, and the effects of tyranny. But such vision was a curse.
>
> [A year or two after the Silk Road was started] . . . the pieces started coming together . . . and what a ride it has been. No longer do I feel ANY frustration. In fact I am at peace in the knowledge that every day I have more I can do to breath [*sic*] life into a truly revolutionary and free market than I have hours in the day. I walk tall, proud and free, knowing that the actions I take eat away at the infrastructure that keeps oppression alive. We are like a little seed

in a big jungle that has just broken the surface of the forest floor. . . . Will we and others like us someday grow to be tall hardwoods? Will we reshape the landscape of society as we know it?

What if one day we had enough power to maintain a physical presence on the globe, where we shunned the parasites and upheld the rule of law, where the right to privacy and property was unquestioned and enshrined in the very structure of society. Where police are our servants and protectors beholden to their customers, the people. Where our leaders earn their power and responsibility in the harsh and unforgiving furnace of the free market and not from behind a gun, where the opportunities to create and enjoy wealth are as boundless as one's imagination. Some day, we could be a shining beacon of hope for the oppressed people of the world just as so many oppressed and violated souls have found refuge here already. Will it happen overnight? No. Will it happen in a lifetime? I don't know. Is it worth fighting for until my last breath. Of course. Once you've seen what's possible, how can you do otherwise? How can you plug yourself into the tax eating, life sucking, violent, sadistic, war mongering, oppressive machine ever again? How can you kneel when you've felt the power of your own legs? Felt them stretch and flex as you learn to walk and think as a free person? I would rather live my life in rags now than in golden chains. And now we can have both! Now it is profitable to throw off one's chains, with amazing crypto technology reducing the risk of doing so dramatically. The opportunity to prosper and take part in a revolution of epic proportions is at our fingertips! I have no one to share my thoughts with in physical space. Security does not permit it, so thanks for listening. I hope my words can be an inspiration just as I am given so much by everyone here.

This is Ross the prophet, Ross the futurist, Ross the true believer. He's spearheading a rebellion, showing the world the path to change, allowing a peaceful revolution to overthrow what had previously taken war and blood to accomplish. The state must and will be resisted. Although in general I don't much care for European philosophers of Theodore Adorno's ilk, I've always remembered a remark he made when asked about a student rebellion taking place in France: "[It] contains a grain of insanity in which a future totalitarianism is implicit."

A "grain of insanity" can always be found in the clear-eyed purity of the ideologue, enabling behavior which might otherwise be impossible. This leads us directly to the crucial question: how could the Dread Pirate Roberts justify, contract out, and pay for Curtis Green's killing? Isn't this the most fundamental example of a *nonvoluntary* transaction? Assassin: *Do you want me to kill you?* Victim: *Uh, no thanks, I'll pass on that transaction.* Assassin: *Well, too bad, you are dying anyway.* Stab.

Whatever happened to: "The way of the market is freedom, dignity and peace?" What about this one: "Silk Road is an example of a moral culture where peace, cooperation and ethical competition are the norm, and violence and fraud are found only on the margin." There is only one answer: the Dread Pirate Roberts was convinced Curtis Green was a threat not only to his personal safety but more importantly to the continued existence of Silk Road. As we have learned from Ross the Preacher Man, Silk Road was a massive force for good in the world, in fact one of the few ways humanity could progress in the face of governments run amok, and anything endangering Silk Road had to be stopped. Because not good equals evil, and that which is evil may be killed.

It was that simple.

Ross put all his emotional energy into Silk Road. He had "friends" in the forums, with whom he regularly chatted. They were thinkers and hackers and programmers, whom he loved and respected; they told Ross he was doing a noble thing, which was all Ross wanted to hear. Curtis Green was going to tear this apart? It was emotionally impossible; logically it seemed wrong; a "hit" on Curtis Green was the natural solution. Anyway, he had it coming didn't he?

I don't believe that if you put Ross and Curtis in the same room Ross would have picked up a loaded gun and shot Curtis in the chest. The internet's anonymizing empowerment, turning otherwise normal people into verbally abusive trolls the world over, acts in the same way for illegal or immoral activities. Things you would never say to a friend you shout in a forum. That which you would never indulge in person you indulge virtually, paying for and enabling behavior you would squirm to admit in public.

Ross Ulbricht is a smart man, hardworking and multitalented, as well as phenomenally naive and unsophisticated. It's my personal belief, ridden as a hobby horse on more than one occasion (to the detriment, over Christmas eggnog, of all within earshot), that the humanities should not be thought of as an amusing sidelight for well-off or deeply irrational students. Ross's scientific education, reasonably sophisticated and certainly to be admired, was nevertheless narrowly targeted and left gaping holes in his ethical and cultural knowledge. It's a bit of a cliché to imagine scientists as experts in their narrow chosen field but hopeless in all others. There are plenty of counterexamples, broad-minded and sophisticated scientists managing all aspects of their life with enviable flair and success.[59] But it's also true that this isn't the case for the majority. It's not unusual for a graduate student in chemistry to have gone a decade without reading any history; to have assiduously avoided a survey course on philosophy or economics even as an undergraduate; to respect what is broadly thought of as "the classics" but not engaged with them on more than a superficial level. For many this isn't a problem. If a scientist stays in his chosen realm, most of the world's knowledge is indeed superfluous.

Yet if he or she steps out, it can lead to trouble. The list of scientists famous in their chosen field who have given absurd, spectacularly wrong, or unsophisticated opinions of neighboring academic disciplines is impressive. High on the list is Lord Kelvin's 1885 quote, "Heavier-than-air flying machines are impossible," which the Wright brothers disproved a scant eight years later. This is perhaps a simple matter of a master theoretician stumbling over what turned out to be a hands-on process of trial and error; far more common are Nobel winners opining about religion, politics, or medicine in cringingly silly ways.[60]

Ross Ulbricht found himself in the same situation. He was well-educated as far as it went but had had little exposure to subjects outside science. When he started to read about economic theory and libertarianism in 2008 he was filling what he perceived as a void in his understanding of the world, but without prior exposure to traditional economics or philosophy he lacked an apparatus for critically engaging with what he was reading. Ross was in danger of accepting only those opinions that happened to match his personal, political, and emotional inclinations, unmediated and without an analytic eye.

The core concept of libertarianism is appealing in its simplicity and complete faith in the individual. That Ross read what he did, attempting to broaden his horizons, was certainly not wrong and clearly to be admired. Most idealists don't do themselves or anyone else much damage, apart from conversational boredom inspired by too-frequent proselytizing, but it was different for Ross. Wholehearted acceptance of the material, mixed with an ability to put these theories into action, proved a disastrous combination.

There isn't any way to read Ross discussing child labor, and his method of solving the problem (hey, let the kids work!), without wondering if it's a parody, a Swiftian moment of light levity. If not it's perilously close, and reveals the author to have an extremely shaky understanding of both history and the functioning of society. It's not that everyone else has an answer and Ross's answer is wrong. It's that everyone else knows that such questions are vastly complicated, the only certainty being that any easy answer is *certainly* wrong. It's hard enough for one human to understand another; bunch them together in massive groups and call it an economy and suddenly one simple assertion is the answer to every problem?

Nothing can be taken to extremes with the confident expectation that it will work in predictable ways. Even quantum mechanics fails if pushed hard enough. The shutdown of Silk Road, and Ross various crimes, don't *necessarily* indicate something wrong with the core tenets of libertarianism, however broadly stated. Almost everything is fine in moderation, including claims about moderation, which opens the door to the following statement of categorical truth: it's a rare theory, a surpassing rare philosophy, and an as-yet-undiscovered economic theory that when pushed to the extreme edge (and possibly right over the cliff) fails to produce warped and perverse effects. The shining light of truth, reflected in an apostle's eyes, gazing with placid love at a congregation or those attending a business conference or at a fellow passenger stuck adjacent during a transatlantic flight, attempts to inspire hope by revealing a way out of our squalid, horrifically complicated, and endlessly bustling material world. It indicates the existence another way of living, one of greater peace, simplicity, and prosperity. They are often young, these true believers; often beautiful in their own way; often alluring even in the absence of any obvious religion or ideology. Old ladies blink their eyes and smile; stewardesses are unusually nice about tracking down pillows, sometimes slipping into first class to grab a luxurious specimen; hardened businessmen relax even before their first drink. I see their happy calm demeanor, envy their certainties, and wish (always) that I could face the world with a similar amount of cheerful joy, which seems limitless and takes nothing from their apparently endless supply of energy, but deep down I can't deny it: they scare the hell out of me.

Ross Ulbricht was a good man, and a bright and ambitious man, but like many bright and ambitious men before him he was blinded by ideology. That the Dread Pirate Roberts attempted to kill Curtis Green is beyond question; that he attempted to kill four others is highly probable. You can make claims about what Ross was or wasn't, what he wished to accomplish or what he truly believed. You can (and many do) find it hard to believe that a handsome, young, white gentleman, with an upper-middle-class family and a perfectly bland and safe and easy-to-understand suburban childhood, was capable of doing what he has been accused of doing. It feels wrong somehow. Surely it can't be true: *look* at him. Objections of this sort are entirely backward. Legally, morally, and ethically, an evil man who plots and schemes in the safety of his own head, who carries out frightful mental crimes with the greatest of pleasure, slaughtering thousands and raping and pillaging and concocting horrors only imagined by the most gifted artist—a monster entirely without respect for another's life or limb or endless screaming pain—such a person is at root entirely unobjectionable from a legal standpoint. What's thought but not put into practice doesn't matter.

A man whose fear of prison inhibits him from acting on evil desires is just as worthy of our respect as a man without evil intent who, not surprisingly, fails to act in evil ways. Yet a good man, with a blameless past and an apparently bright future, who commits an evil act for whatever reason—be it ideology or a thousand others ways we weak humans fail to live up to our own low standards—can no longer be considered good. Action matters. What was *done*, not *thought*. Curtis Green didn't have to be the focus of a contract killing. Ross's life was in no danger; killing Curtis wouldn't have stopped a nuclear bomb from going off, to cite a hoary and beloved example from every torturer's handbook; children were not at risk; no dam or ship or passenger plane was slated for destruction. Silk Road, a website, was in danger of being exposed and taken down. That's all.

The great villains of history are comforting in their uniform and all-encompassing evil. They are bad, they know they are bad, and they don't care. It's them against the world, and if blood be spilled so be it. If it's enjoyable spilling the blood, even better. Such types are easy to oppose, at least in theory: they aren't hiding their behavior from anyone. When they fall, as they always do, and are put on trial or shot in a cellar, it's clear to everyone that the world has become a better place. More disturbing, and vastly harder to discover and root out, are self-styled "good" people who nevertheless and with disturbing frequency commit acts of frightful evil. Ross considers himself, at root, to be a decent person. Possibly misguided; possibly someone who's made mistakes, but fundamentally a good egg. Ross's supporters point to governmental misconduct on the part of Slinker and Stinker, and create legal funds for his defense, and launch websites lamenting his imprisonment and conviction.

I find this understandable if a little sickening, for Ross Ulbricht is that most scary of modern monsters: an evil man who's completely unaware of his evil. Psychologists call people "entirely without empathy or remorse" psychopaths, but even psychopaths have a redeeming feature: they recognize they are responsible for doing ill. It's just that they don't care. Ross represents the flip side: without remorse or empathy not due to mental defect or internal deficiency but because of an amazingly strong ability to redefine his own behavior—killing for a good cause isn't something to apologize for, it's a necessary and praiseworthy act.

This is the "grain of insanity" at the root of every extreme ideology: a mediating lens so powerful and distorting it turns sin into virtue. The story of Silk Road seems, from a distance, pretty fun and crazy—drug sales and FBI sting operations and bad behavior on the part of investigators, followed by even worse behavior by the Dread Pirate Roberts. It's possible to view Ross as nothing more than a petty criminal, in over his head, getting what he deserves, the plot of Emmy-winning TV shows. But I couldn't help finding it upsetting.

The Ross who started Silk Road was not the Ross who ended it, and watching the steady progress of his moral decay raises the obvious question: could things have gone differently? It might not have taken much, a talk with a real-world friend or an inspiring lecture or a trip to a medieval cathedral town or something small and random, unnoticed by anyone else, shifting his perspective, opening a window otherwise tightly sealed.

It *might* have made all the difference in the world, but Ross had no Father Brown, and there was no twitch upon the thread pulling him back from the brink. Silk Road is a tale of birth and wild growth and sustained popularity and sudden destruction, leveraging the Dark Web and bitcoins and supported by a global community of enthusiasts. It's original and fascinating and gives us room to cheer or bemoan its eventual fate, infused as it was with the lively energy of many thousands of committed users. Ross Ulbricht doesn't inspire similar feelings. His is a simple tale of degeneration: not unusual, not original, rather trivial in its outlines, and experienced by millions before and surely millions to come.

CHAPTER 6

THE WINKLEVOSS TWINS: BORN ON THIRD BASE, HIT A DOUBLE

PRIVATE FACT VS. PUBLIC FICTION

Indisputable facts: the Winklevoss twins, Tyler and Cameron, were born on August 21, 1981, in Southampton, New York, to Howard Edward Winklevoss Jr. and Carol (Leonard) Winklevoss, who never revealed to them which was eldest. After the family moved to Greenwich, Connecticut, the twins attended the Greenwich Country Day School (grammar/middle school) and the Brunswick School (high school), both small, private, and expensive institutions. Following the lead of their next-door neighbor Ethan Ayer, who had rowed at Harvard and Cambridge, the twins took up the sport at the age of fourteen. After being accepted by Harvard in 2000 they promptly joined the Harvard varsity rowing team, propelling it to the 2003 and 2004 NCAA championships. This success led to international competition, a place on the USA Olympic team, and the 2008 Summer Olympics in Beijing, China, where they placed a respectable sixth.

While at Harvard they had a run-in with a social-networking site developer, leading to massive complications, both financial and legal. This part of the story, far more than high-level athletic competition, propelled the Winklevoss twins into the public eye, which probably wouldn't have noticed a pair of Olympic nonmedalists with perfect hair and engaging smiles.

207

Public fiction: Armie Hammer[1] played both twins in the 2010 film *The Social Network* (with the help of some special effects magic). In the movie they squabbled with Jesse Eisenberg (playing Mark Zuckerberg) over the founding of Facebook and the fabulous wealth it generated, and the visual contrast between them couldn't have been more stark. Mark Zuckerberg was depicted as a slender, clumsy, slightly unpleasant nerd with poor social skills and a habit of treating his friends badly; the Winklevoss twins were hulking Übermenschen, fantastically successful athletes, socially adept, and part of the most exclusive Harvard "secret society" (the Porcelain Club, founded in 1791). The Winklevoss twins majored in economics, were proud members of the elite, and were blessed with both money and contacts. They looked capable of picking up Zuckerberg and breaking his body over either knee.

The conflict in *The Social Network* was of the David and Goliath variety, one we have grown accustomed to in the late twentieth and early twenty-first century, perfectly formulated by another movie title: *The Revenge of the Nerds*. Apple computer and Bill Gates and Google and all the other canonical technology success stories featured similar protagonists: brilliant nerds fighting the good fight and ultimately triumphing over the entrenched forces of boring callous business. The little guy who was picked on and bullied in high school buys a Ferrari when he's twenty-eight. The programmer nerding out in his garage tinkers his way into a multimillion dollar fortune. It's what we expect: the nerd wins in the end. And if the nerd triumphs, his opponent must represent the other side—those doing the bullying, who don't have the brains or competence to keep up with where the world is heading. The best *they* can hope for is to cash in on another's brilliance.

Movies don't necessarily (or even often) reflect the truth, but they do an amazing job at defining and solidifying public opinion. In *The Social Network* the Winklevoss twins came across as the *ne plus ultra* of aggressively annoying white privilege—inheritors of status unrelated to accomplishment. In real life, they've stayed in the limelight due to the successful lawsuit they filed against Facebook for "stealing the Facebook idea" and the sixty-five million dollar settlement that resulted. The media tracked their subsequent appeal of this decision, as the twins claimed Facebook knowingly overvalued its stock price in the settlement, allowing the company to use fewer shares to make up the overall total.[2] As the twins continued their legal maneuvering, angling for more Facebook millions at a time (2009) when the American and world economy was crashing, public opinion nosedived—and it wasn't particularly favorable to start with.

In the court of public opinion the twins are broadly regarded as spoiled, undeservingly lucky, and obnoxious. To cite a typical example, Max Read, writing for *Gawker*, laid his emotions bare in an article titled "Idiot Dick Facebook Twins Now Own One Percent of All Bitcoin": "Best of luck to these two idiot dicks and all their computer money and their hard drives around the world."[3]

What about the business community? J. Webster sums up the zeitgeist pretty well, writing in 2012 under the heading, "The Winklevoss Twins Are Now 'Venture Capitalists'":

> So everyone is sort of laughing at the Winklevoss Twins, Cam and Tyler, and how they're now venture capitalists in the "cloud" space. What knowledge do they possess to invest and support new companies? They have money. And this is mainly because of the money they're going to make on the Facebook IPO. Money they earned by suing Mark Zuckerberg because he stole their idea for a social network.[4]

The Winklevoss twins are apparently in over their heads—though to be fair they've got the number-one qualification for any venture: capital.

Moving away from narrow web-based news sites, for whom Winklevoss bashing and Winklevoss hating is a small but stable industry, let's inspect the mainstream media. Mike Vilensky at *New York Magazine* writes:

> When you grow up, say, tall, rich, and handsome, you might not have to work to attract the other (or same) sex, and then you might never develop certain evolutionary pluses, like the ability to overcome adversity, accept defeat, and learn humility. Because, frankly, why would you? Anyway, we're not bitter about this at all. We're just saying.[5]

I'm not sure irony protects against bitterness as much as Vilensky thinks it does. The last line of the article is particularly telling, and arrives *apropos* of nothing: "Ah, pretty people: Sometimes life is hard for them, too."

A more subtle takedown can be found in *Vanity Fair*'s 2011 feature article, "The Code of the Winklevii,"[6] a relatively early example of the expected assessment. The title gives us an indication of where the rest of the article is heading, using "Winklevii" (college-level wit, pluralizing a singular Winklevoss), which was first coined by Zuckerberg as an insult back when everyone was still kicking around Harvard. Much of the article is dismissive: "The Winklevosses seem almost a parody of the Jazz Age sportsman. . . ." "[The Winklevoss twins are the] Carriers of the Torch of Justice. . . ." "We decided that a chaos-flouting journey into Mexico would be a good idea. Los Winklevoss." Particularly damming: the Winklevoss twins "really, really, really don't like to lose."

The Winklevoss twins are depicted as obsessed (perhaps traumatized) by their Facebook experience, forever striving to "win" a hopeless battle against Zuckerberg in court, attempting to ham-handedly slant public opinion (in interviews, through PR outlets) in their favor. Despite world-class results at the 2008 Beijing Olympics, the fact that the Winklevoss twins' training regimen includes yoga is picked out as a "funny" detail, given their assumed role as unthinking scions of Western privilege. It's described this way: "The brothers sat in sloppy lotus positions," and were urged to visualize the pain of losing.

What happened next? "Tyler's face tightened against the memory of failure. 'Now let's go do some weights,' said [the trainer], 'and never feel that way again.' Late American Nobility."[7]

It's possible, though difficult, to find Winklevoss supporters and Winklevoss fans on the internet, but they're outnumbered a thousand-to-one.

Why this desperate desire to criticize? What is everyone so angry about?[8]

The Winklevoss twins "discovered" Bitcoin in 2010 and became enthusiastic supporters and investors, but even their Bitcoin proselytizing is (often) negatively impacted by their association with Facebook and a general cultural unease about their success and status. What's the root cause of their bad reputation, reviled state, and generally hated nature? There are plenty of tall, dark, and handsome millionaires in the world, and most of *them* are widely celebrated and envied and actively praised: what makes the Winklevoss twins so different?

To get to the root of the public's unease it's necessary to investigate issues popping up again and again in movies and articles and feature-length *Vanity Fair* investigations: the Winklevoss family's wealth, the Winklevoss family's origins, and how the Winklevoss twins benefitted (and ways they didn't).

THE "CURSE" OF WEALTH

The Winklevoss twins were born into a wealthy family and made a fortune at a shockingly young age due to their legal dispute with Facebook. The twins were doubly blessed, and with such riches isn't it understandable, even expected, that whatever else they do with their lives, fortune will smile upon them? That they continue to be in the news, and are running one or two successful businesses, isn't worthy of note. Wouldn't everyone succeed if they had a great pile of Facebook money to use as a springboard? The answer is *no*, and we know it's no from the very public experiences of other "lucky" millionaires. Lottery winners are a perfect example.

The most interesting thing about lottery winners isn't the amount of money won nor the initial moment of shocked joy when the numbers, inexplicably, line up and match those displayed on the television screen, but the statistical likelihood that, five years later, the winners will be broke and far more unhappy than if they had never won in the first place. The same sort of dynamic occurs with many professional athletes, who despite players unions and so-called financial advisers are often profoundly incapable of competently handling money and wind up destitute a few short years, if not months, after they retire.[9] There isn't any reason to be surprised by this, or opprobriously abuse those unable to deal with sudden wealth—few of us would manage better, acting soberly and rationally and taking the advice of dry accountants who advise against a gimmicky BMW and who instead suggest an equally useful and far more reliable Toyota.

Wealth is difficult to handle even for sober and experienced businessmen. The story of Jack Whittaker is immensely instructive. President of a successful contracting firm, with a personal fortune in excess of fifteen million, Jack was fifty-five years old when he took home $93 million after winning the 2002 Powerball lottery. You would think a millionaire would know what to do with money and have sufficient education to avoid common temptations. This simply wasn't the case.

Jack quit his job, started going to strip clubs, and carried $500,000 cash in his car's trunk—soon stolen. He spread the money around his family, giving allowances to his daughter and granddaughter. Soon everyone felt under siege. His wife was continually bombarded by requests for money, help, support. Jack was subject to unrelenting "business suggestions," chances to invest in one-time-only opportunities, and as the mark for every grifter in West Virginia he was the center of an endless series of cons and scams. Jack started to drink heavily. He was twice arrested for DUI. Nine months after winning the lottery his granddaughter died of an overdose from drugs purchased from the lottery windfall. A month later his daughter died of another drug overdose. Some say money can't make you happy, which might be true, but it can certainly make you miserable. After taking an inventory of the year and asking if she would have done anything different, Jack's wife sobbed, "I would've torn that [winning] ticket up."[10]

Modern America is a particularly difficult place to gain sudden wealth. Money is envied and worshipped as an end to itself, the reason to work brutal and unforgiving seventy-hour work weeks, the ultimate reward for those with talent or ability or the guts to achieve riches. Money defines the American Dream, and it's not how millions are made that matters. . . . What matters is the end result: money. Turning down a higher-paying job or career for reasons of "personal happiness" is thought odd if not actively perverse. Yet in the long run money's just a tool—a powerful tool, enabling the building of dams or the accumulation of a world-class collection of art, but tools work best when guided with a firm purpose. Money in the hands of a completely happy and fulfilled individual doesn't change much; money in the hands of a driven individual serves as a force multiplier; and money in the hands of somebody valuing money for money's sake is necessarily, and sometimes shockingly, disappointing. It's like the unhappy traveler. Wherever he goes he's still the same person. A philosophically naive individual who happens to inherit millions remains the same person beneath the gaudy gilt, yet imagines things are very different.[11]

It doesn't have to be this way. In a religious society a sudden influx of wealth might not, quite so often, lead to personal or familial trauma, since the winner's religious certainties remain fixed and the winner remains enveloped in a supportive social and cultural milieu. These are distinctly *not* features of modern America, where we are constantly told paradise can be yours (if you just had enough money), and happiness is within reach (for those with enough money), ergo if you have enough money—what's the problem? Who wants to hear about the trials and tribulations of the top 1 percent? Yet the latest research has shown that the wealthy, up to and including billionaires, are significant more unhappy than the average American.

The American Dream isn't simply materialistic and shallow; it's also fundamentally a lie. The trick isn't to get rich, it's to do something that makes you happy and that you can continue doing for the rest of your life. If you get rich in the process, great—otherwise, don't worry about it.

Howard Winklevoss Jr., father of the Winklevoss twins, is a pension-expert multimillionaire. Howard was peculiarly well-adapted for his rapid and somewhat amazing business success, having worked with large sums of money all his life and taught students at the Wharton Business School the best methods for building and retaining capital assets despite ongoing payments. When Howard went into the pension business for himself, and money started pouring into his personal coffers in what soon became a flood, he was nearly immune to its peculiar temptations. First, Howard honestly loved working with pensions and consulting about pensions and thinking about pensions and writing books about pensions and wasn't about to stop no matter how much money it made him. Second, he was constitutionally unable and unwilling to fritter away money. If anyone knew the value of long-term yield US government bonds and a hundred other immensely safe and productive securities it was Howard Winklevoss

Jr. As for friends and family pestering him for handouts—not going to happen. Are you really going to run up to, say, your pension-loving serious-minded, quiet and confident and unapproachable uncle and beg him for $50,000 for a new car or SUV? It's hard to imagine it happening, harder to actually plan and carry out such an appeal, and impossible to envision a result other than a calm, measured *No*.

There would be no Winklevoss twins' investment in Bitcoin, no Bitcoin entrepreneurial fever, no Harvard or Facebook lawsuit or any of the rest had not Howard Winklevoss Jr. been so spectacularly successful. Without understanding the father's history it's impossible to understand his famous sons, and to do Howard Winklevoss Jr. justice we have to delve into the extraordinary story of pensions. Where do they come from, how do they work, and what business opportunities did Howard Winklevoss Jr. see and exploit, resulting in immense personal gain?

The Strangely Fascinating History of Pensions

Mentioning a pension invites people to look the other way, and discussing pensions forces immediate yawns, and if you dare to lecture on pensions the likely result is shameless catatonic slumber. The very word *pension* bring to mind a dreary English attic, dim even at the height of noon, with rows of scribbling scribes scrawling figures on endless reams of curled parchment, pens moving in small bursts producing a sequence of scratching sounds like the struggles of a trapped and dying rat, a dry and infinitely attentive Scrooge of a supervisor circulating and making sure nobody stops calculating for an instant and nobody lacks for ink in the inkwells and nobody's having any fun at all. This isn't a personal failing of mine, a knee-jerk reaction against the absurd anal-retentive labor involved; pensions are often described as "The Most Boring Important Topic in Economics"[12]. Even accountants working in the field can't seem to muster up a lot of enthusiasm: "Pension plans are about as boring as it gets."[13] If you still doubt, bring up pensions at your next poker game, book group, biochemistry faculty bagel scramble, or manicure. Glazed eyes from wall to wall.

Yet I'm here to tell you that despite what you might have heard, notwithstanding deep cultural reluctance to tackle the topic with anything close to an open mind, pensions are mathematically interesting, historically important, and for experts such as Howard Winklevoss Jr. the direct source of a $100,000,000 fortune, which, as anyone worth $100,000,000 will likely tell you, is about as far from boring as something can be. Our reluctance to engage with pensions is more than a little strange, particularly when we remember gold and silver fortunes in the not-so-distant past, often the result of removing dirt and rock from a prospective strike with little more than pick and shovel. Is there anything more fundamentally repetitive and dreary than shifting soil from one place to another? Isn't this the sort of thing sadistic prison wardens force prisoners to do, often forcing a mental breakdown? Yet nobody in 1849 San Francisco viewed the owner of a successful gold mine and winced at the thought of the tedious work involved in its creation. They just saw piles of accumulated gold and yearned and desired and envied. Why should pensions be any different?

Anti-pension prejudice goes all the way back to the invention of pensions. (It sounds weird to say they were invented, but they were.) When pensions were first implemented they were looked down upon by the majority of the populace despite being a tool for the masses, ensuring greater financial stability in the long run. To understand what happened it's necessary to go back to Greece, the "cradle of civilization," circa 500 BCE.

Solon of Athens, whose governmental reforms helped create Athenian democracy, was an open-minded legislator who famously established state-regulated brothels (*dicteria*) with fixed pricing for basic services, catering to the pent-up demands of the common man unable to afford the expensive dancing girls (*auletrides*) who took part in more sophisticated shenanigans. The *auletrides* were a class above the common *dicteria* prostitutes and better able to indulge aristocratic whims during public and private banquets when their services were hotly engaged, in acts limited only by the guest's imagination.

The aristocrats of ancient Athens wished to distance themselves from the filthy lucre produced by filthy trade and filthy farming, even if their own family was less than a generation removed from such filthy concerns. Solon wasn't concerned with such mores and was intensely interested in the pedestrian, crass, and "boring" business of trade and economic activity as well as, naturally, pensions. Solon argued and eventually wrote into legislative statute the principle that, "Persons maimed in a war should be maintained at the public charge."[14] That was it, the very moment of birth, the start of publically funded pensions. It was an idea that when put into practice proved surpassingly difficult to modify or change: a drop of blood coloring a glass of otherwise clear water, easy to mix but impossible to extract.

Military pensions became increasingly widespread in the ancient world, and by the time of the Roman Empire had become not only an expected benefit but something codified in poetry and important enough to weigh heavily upon the head of every Emperor. In 509 BCE the Roman army officer Publius Horatius Cocles, despite overwhelming numerical disadvantage, managed to defend and destroy a bridge over the Tiber River against an invading Etruscan army, inspiring the 1st Baron Macaulay's *Lays of Ancient Rome* (1841), which included the poem "Horatius," detailing the hero's well-earned rewards:

> They gave him of the corn land
> That was of public right,
> As much as two strong oxen
> Could plough from morn till night;
> And they made a molten image,
> And set it up on high,—
> And there it stands unto this day
> To witness if I lie.

This verse defines the early Roman pension plan, particularly for soldiers such as Horatius who returned wounded from battle (he took a spear to the rump). If you did something spectacular you might get a statue, but everyone got a land grant. As a pension scheme it had certain clear advantages: nobody snubbed their nose at real estate, since land ownership (gazing upward at the nobility) was valued even if the soil was rocky or thin and the plot size small. It was, literally, something you could depend on; it was firm and solid and seemed to answer the question posed by old age and eventual infirmity. The problem for the Roman empire was twofold: 1) grievously wounded soldiers didn't make the best farmers even if they knew what they were doing, and almost none did, and 2) land was scarce even in 500 BCE, and governmental sequestration of quasi-public lands for use by veterans, removing income traditionally granted to their informal aristocratic overseers, caused a whole lot of blowback. What you ended up with were a lot of solders limping around tiny "estates" doing not a lot of growing of anything in particular, which, when seen as a collective enterprise, reduced the agricultural output of an empire already dependent upon grain imports to meet its ever-expanding needs. More crucially, returning soldiers were given lifelong exemption from Roman taxes, including those associated with their land grant.

While difficult to spot in the moment, from a historical perspective the long-term effects of the pension scheme were obvious and deleterious. The empire was essentially giving away, in many cases permanently, both land and all future revenue associated with the land, reducing not only its agricultural value but destroying forever an ever-increasing fraction of its tax base. Soon it became clear that Roman soldiers, who had come to expect pensions and demand them in ways more-than-occasionally bloody, must be appeased, yet the status quo was no longer sustainable. What to do? The clever Romans transformed a liability into a strength. Soldiers were no longer given small plots of land in Italy but larger, grander holdings on the borders of the empire. It was reasoned, correctly, that soldiers cared more about size than location, and when invested via ownership of land in an outlying province they would readily serve in a local militia to defend their new homes. It looked like a perfect compromise, and staunched the fiscal bleeding for a while, but it was still the case that land grants, no matter how distant and seemingly insignificant, corroded the tax base. What had been fifty years ago an obscure outpost was now a bustling town, yet the rapidly appreciating land owned by soldiers was immune to taxation. The empire not only reduced the present but actively mortgaged the future.

Around 25 BCE the first Roman emperor, Augustus, decided to fix things once and for all. He established the *aerarium militare*, the official military treasury, responsible for dealing with the troublesome pension problem of retiring solders via direct monetary payment. Gone were the days of land grants and allegiance to whatever local powers were proximate to the soldier's holdings; now it was the Imperial Rome Military distributing cash benefits, therefore ensuring (they hoped) veteran support and loyalty to the emperor. The *aerarium militare* was funded by new and unpopular taxes as well as loot from military expeditions, and its existence immediately generated a series of interesting if somewhat gruesome questions: given an army of size X, what percentage of X will retire after fifteen, twenty, twenty-five, or thirty years of service (the pension payout increased with time served)? How might these estimates be made, and how accurate would they be, and what does it imply for the tax rate needed to sustain the *aerarium militare* over a ten or fifty or one-hundred-year period?

These sorts of questions form the base of Howard Winklevoss Jr.'s intellectual life work. For thirteen years he taught as an adjunct professor of actuarial science and insurance at the Wharton School of Business and published widely respected foundational texts such as *Pension Mathematics with Numerical Illustrations* (second edition, 1993), precisely outlining the minimum incoming contribution levels required to achieve "expected" output given a vast and often bewildering set of options and pension structures. The book also features necessary and important but nevertheless disturbing sentences such as: "Active plan participants are exposed to the contingencies of death, termination, disability, and retirement, whereas nonactive members are exposed to death." Utterly dry and rational yet fundamentally correct.

The advent of personal computers allowed actuaries to hone their calculations, projections, methodologies, and assumptions. Combining software with pension planning was an obvious step but required expertise to produce a product polished enough to impress the most demanding corporate clients. That's exactly what Howard Winklevoss did in 1987, creating Winklevoss Technologies to handle the software side and Winklevoss Consultants for hands-on benefit funding assistance. As far as pensions are concerned the big questions boil down to three major issues: what's the expected input, what's the expected output, and how can the accumulated money be safely invested and distributed?

The latter issue is far from trivial. Whenever a pension fund gets big, such as the heap of sestertii piled in the imperial treasury on top of Rome's Capitoline Hill, there's a temptation even for the officially appointed *praefecti aerarii militaris* in charge of the pension fund to wonder to themselves: would anyone really notice if ten coins went missing? What about a hundred? Given the constant inflow and outflow of monies, wouldn't it be difficult to pin down exactly how much the treasury should have at any given moment, making claims of theft nearly impossible to prove? What if the official books were lost, or burned, or baked in a financial oven, cooking at precisely the right temperature to give the results desired? Would anyone really notice the loss of one one-hundredth of a percent? What about one fiftieth of a percent?

We've already seen this problem illustrated quite clearly with Bitcoin. That which makes bitcoins so attractive to a certain segment of the population (digital, relatively anonymous currency) also leave it open to theft, even if those being tempted are federal agents.

Some have argued the fall of the Roman Empire was due to poor pension planning and the relentless accuracy of actuarial mathematics. Emperor Augustus capitalized the initial *aerarium militare* with his own money, and thereafter used tax revenue to keep the fund at a reasonable level. This was as stable and sustainable as the pension fund ever got. Once the pension money started to be doled out, and soldiers saw retirees walking away with what was for them vast lumps of cash (equivalent to ten or fifteen years of service), there wasn't any question of reducing or cutting pension payouts. The pension was seen as a birthright, and woe to anyone tampering with the system. Emperor Caligula was notorious for his insane whims, his love of bloody spectacle, and behavior perfectly in line with his reputation as one of the worst humans ever to blight the face of the earth—but it wasn't until he abolished war pensions that he signed his death warrant (the pensions were immediately reestablished following his assassination).

Corruption in pension fund distribution, widespread fraud, double- and triple-dipping, bribery and outright robbery drained the fund far faster than it was replenished. Rome was forced to debase its currency at a steady rate from roughly 13 percent silver to half a percent two hundred years later, stamping ever more coins to pay their unfunded obligations, hoping to outrun inflation and compensate the soldiers before they took matters into their own hands. When coins proved insufficient, land grants were reinstituted, creating an ever-faster spiral of financial irresponsibility. At some point the system just broke down. Rome had utterly exhausted herself. When the barbarians swept away the last of the empire its death throes were little more than a polite, slightly dusty cough. One can't help but wonder what might have been accomplished had they more fully aligned themselves with responsible actuarial principles!

THE DESPERATE AND
UNHAPPY WINKLEVOSS ANCESTORS

The Winklevoss twins are famous during interview for highlighting and repeatedly stressing the humble origins of their grandparents, great-grandparents, and anyone else in the family tree deriving from "common" stock—which according to them is nearly everyone. As Dana Vachon put it, in his long *Vanity Fair* interview with the Winklevoss twins: "It was deeply important to the twins that I understand the humbleness of their roots."[15]

This isn't something the public really cares about. If the Winklevoss twins didn't insist on talking about their family tree and its many (distant) branches, it's unlikely to have ever reached the public record. Yet they do insist, and it makes for puzzling reading. Why do the Winklevoss twins continue to talk about their extended family, and what would they have us believe about them? Both the question and its answer are artifacts of their poor public image—it's a way for the Winklevoss twins to fight back, even if it's a cowardly weapon to wield.

The rough sketch that's usually supplied by the Winklevoss twins goes something like this: Howard Edward Winklevoss Sr., their paternal grandfather, was born on May 21, 1911, in Jackson Center, Pennsylvania, and never managed to attain more than an eighth-grade education. His father, the Winklevoss twins' great-grandfather, worked in the local coal mines for so long that in hunched old age he suffered from debilitating back pain. At least he escaped the fate of *his* father who died of "black lung," a Victorian coinage for coal workers' pneumoconiosis, a fatal condition resulting from breathing in too much coal dust for too many years. According to the twins, and as reported by the *New York Times* and with slight variations in many other sources, Howard Winklevoss Sr. was a simple "garage owner," leading a quiet life until his death in 1993.

As "humble origin" stories go it's acceptable but scarcely noteworthy. Hardly anyone's grandparents, born in the 1910s, had a particularly fun time of it. First came World War I (1914–1918), then the Great Depression (1929–1935), striking this unlucky generation just as they entered the work force. With skyrocketing unemployment, low wages nationwide, and hunger spreading throughout the middle class, it wasn't a good time for anyone except the very wealthy. Working in a Pennsylvania coal mine seems like a pretty bad job by today's soft standards, but compared to not having a job at all (and possibly starving) it's got a certain appeal. I don't mean to downplay the hardships involved in mining, nor the toll it takes on a miner's health. It was difficult and dangerous work and miners were certainly underpaid for much of it, laboring in an environment current standards would certainly term wildly unsafe. Yet in 1935 many jobs were difficult and dangerous and likely had a long line of desperate unemployed workers praying for a chance to work them (the national unemployment rate stood at a shocking 20.1 percent).[16]

Howard came from a huge family, of the type once common and now impossible to imagine, with no less than eleven siblings—brothers Carl, Donald, Stanley, Frederick ("Ted"), Paul, and Alfred, and sisters Helen, Esther, Pearl, Hazel, and Mabel. I'm sure there were difficult times at home, with many mouths to feed and only one overburdened coal miner bringing home the metaphorical bacon, but, as the eldest, Howard likely had it better than those who followed. As was typical for the period, the miner's eldest son didn't find the prospect of life in the mines very appealing, and despite the national depression and his lack of formal education he wasn't about to trudge underground and pick up a mattock. Simply put, he left home looking for a better life. He married Marian Virginia (Minnis) Winklevoss on August 20, 1935, and his son, Howard Jr., was born eight years later. Apparently the Winklevoss brothers were car crazy, or at least serious enthusiasts, and were busy from an early age fixing, buying, selling, and swapping them. This might be the origin of the Winklevoss twin's laconic description of their grandfather as a humble car lover and garage owner, which is true as far as it goes—not far at all.

It's not entirely clear what Howard Sr. was doing in his early days in Mercer, Pennsylvania, where he moved after fleeing coal country, but he was certainly busy. By the time he was forty-one he was on the First National Bank of Mercer's board of directors[17] when it aggressively purchased the assets of Farmer's Bank in what was considered, at the time (1952), a very complicated transaction. In 1956 Howard Winklevoss Sr. created, on the site of what used to be a Ford garage, the Universal Wholesale company, which replaced or at least greatly expanded a previous auto-parts supply store. It boasted a broad inventory, including electrical gadgets, toys, paint, hardware, and major home appliances, and it was successful enough to employ nine people full time. In 1958 he chartered the Pittsburgh Life Insurance Company, offering a broad array of insurance options for fellow Pennsylvanians. Given his experience in the field, in 1966 Howard was named vice president of the strangely titled 20th Century Corporation, which was busy becoming the state's largest life insurance company (it also acquired a mutual fund company on the side).

This was a very busy period for Howard, as he jumpstarted a series of successful ventures, such as the Greateastern Insurance Corporation, founded in 1967, which had the following modest goal: "to seek long term capital appreciation by investing, acquiring, and controlling life insurance companies." Howard wasn't a man interested in the trivial act of owning and running a single insurance company, which might be enough for a modest millionaire; he wanted to set up a container company, guiding a suite of insurance companies, whose interactions and synergies could be exploited for profit. While officially a high school dropout, it's clear that Howard, since leaving home, had educated himself far beyond a typical undergraduate of the period.

In 1971 Howard and brothers Stanley, Don, and Carl set up a grand concern called "Interstate Auto Auctions." It was housed in a fifteen-thousand-square-foot building located on twenty-six acres of land, and served 4,800 car dealers throughout Pennsylvania and neighboring states. Employing fifty workers, the auction house moved over five hundred cars a week, bringing in and turning over a million dollars of automotive stock every Sunday. Howard Sr. was the president of the board of directors, and of course had plans for further expansion. His idea was to gather up and recondition leased cars, selling them after a week of refurbishment for higher prices and increased commissions. The operation has the feeling of something an older, financially savvy brother might do for his less successful siblings, as at root it's nothing more than a souped-up car dealership where sales are made via auction and inventory is an extremely fast-moving stream of dealer-supplied "traded in" cars. Howard Sr. handled the finances, talked to his bank buddies about what loans would be required to get the concern off the ground, and after it was fully operational returned to his high-finance ventures in insurance or whatever else struck his fancy.

To be fair, the Winklevoss twins aren't lying when they claim their grandfather was a "garage owner." But it's more than a little absurd as a summary of his career, which gives every indication of an intelligent and ambitious man succeeding far more than he failed, and achieving immensely more than your average Pennsylvania coal miner's son.

Let's turn to the distaff side. As reported in "The Code of the Winklevii": "In [the Winklevoss twins'] mother's family, unwashed vaudevillians roamed the Wilsonian countryside in canvas-covered flatbeds, living off pratfalls and song."[18]

The Winklevoss twins claim their mother's parents, or perhaps that side of the family in general, roamed the country performing for a living, a stark contrast to taciturn Pennsylvania coal miners but not, at root, more prestigious even if it sounds a lot more fun. According to records, this story is even more problematic than painting Howard Sr. as an undereducated grease monkey lording over a single-bay garage. The Winklevoss twins' maternal grandmother, Mildred Leonard (née Lotz), grew up in Belle Harbor, an affluent neighborhood of Rockaway Beach, Queens, New York. If you don't know about Rockaway Beach, either from the Ramones song or personal experience, it's essentially a four-mile long strip of public beach located on a long and narrow peninsula jutting into the Atlantic. It became popular and populous in the 1800s but remained a playground for the rich until 1900 when railway stations linked it to the mainland and all the boroughs of New York City. An amusement park, Rockaway's Playland, opened in 1901 and featured a terrifying wooden roller coaster later called "The Atom Smasher" due to the violence of its motions. Playland's success solidified the transformation of Rockaway into an open-to-all vacation destination, and Rockaway was soon given the name "New York's Playground." The wealthy still had enclaves, but now everyone could afford spend a day or two at the beach in the summer.

Mildred's parents, Gustave and Gesine Lotz, were at the forefront of this transformation and worked at the Palace Hotel in Rockaway. They didn't have to worry about job security even in the midst of a national depression because not only did they work at the hotel—they owned it. Mildred had, by all accounts including her own, a blissful childhood, growing up in the Belle Harbor neighborhood, living a block-and-a-half from the ocean. In 1910, Mildred's year of birth, Rockaway was already a prestigious location and Belle Harbor one of the most exclusive neighborhoods, and her parents owned a hotel. Hers was a comfortable childhood.

In her early twenties Mildred moved to New Hyde Park, Long Island, another prime location, and taught at the New Hyde Park Road School, an elementary. She married Francis J. Leonard in September of 1935, and they lived in what is now a modest half-million dollar house on their combined income as a teacher/thirty-five-year detective on the Manhattan South homicide squad. Far from luxurious, it was nevertheless an exciting and desirable location, with quick commute times into Manhattan and everything the city had to offer. Francis Leonard won citations for his police work and as part of the homicide division dealt with the most serious crimes, such as the incident breathlessly reported by the *New York Age* in July 1934, "Jealous Cripple Held Without Bail for Murder of Former Paramour and Man in Park."[19]

So much for the Winklevoss twins' history of "unwashed vaude-villians." At this point I'll stop rifling through the archives. If the

Winklevoss twins want to make myths of the past, fine. If they wish to imagine their family, as a whole, little better than drunkards lolling in the dirtiest gutters of 1930 New York City, sustaining themselves through petty crime and the most sordid cons perpetuated against the weakest and most vulnerable citizens—have at it. I guess it helps them sleep at night.

But it's ridiculously unnecessary and comes across as little more than a hypersensitive knee-jerk reaction. What is it the Winklevoss twins fear? Why are they so unwilling to state the bland, somewhat boring, and certainly not incriminating fact that their grandparents, on both sides of the family, lived happy and prosperous lives? That their paternal grandfather was an entrepreneurial stud? That their mother's mother was a noted Belle Harbor belle? That the coal mines and vaudeville (if it existed) were at least three generations removed, a purely nineteenth-century phenomenon? What's the point of downplaying the past?

The answer can be found in the American Dream

THE AMERICAN DREAM

The Winklevoss twins, to judge by their public interviews, are certainly guilty of the crime of timidity. They obfuscate their family's past, obscure details, and slant the facts. They shy away from the truth because they worry, not without reason, that the truth will make people uncomfortable. It's not the case that most people have the financial resources at age thirty-two to invest in Bitcoin and purchase 1 percent of the extant currency. It would be nice, and "easy" I suppose, if the Winklevoss twins had done it "all themselves"—been born poor, struggled through childhood, excelled in high school, managed to get a scholarship to a prestigious school . . . business success and millions of dollars to follow . . . it's something we can all feel good about. We could point to them and say, "Look, it's possible, anyone can make it if they just have guts and determination." But that's an alternate universe; let's return to our own humdrum reality.

The root cause of most people's Winklevoss discomfort is the American Dream and the terrible burden it's forced to support. You hear it all the time on talk radio and from presidential candidates such as Mitt Romney[20] ("bitter politics of envy") and in casual conversations outside football stadiums and in cocktail bars early on Friday night: "They want to punish people for getting rich." Who *they* are and what the punishment entails varies, but it's often *liberals / excessive taxation*. At root it's thought to be a simple matter of envy. Those who *can't* envy those who *can* (and *do*). If you work hard enough and are smart enough and do everything you can you'll be rewarded by the American Dream, which grants everyone the opportunity to achieve prosperity. If you don't get rich you don't have anyone to blame but yourself. Given this doctrine, taxing the rich is exactly the same as taxing our most successful citizens because the American Dream rewards success. And that's unfair, isn't it?

Always lurking in the back of people's minds is hope born of desperate optimism: one day, however unlikely, the American Dream might shower me with gold, and when this happens I certainly don't want to be paying 35 percent or 45 percent or even higher taxes on my hard-earned income. What's fair for *them* will be fair for *me* when I reach that point in ten, twenty, or a million years.

This dream, this dogma, is so deeply baked into the American consciousness that it's essentially impossible to extricate. It's often hard to see, much less acknowledge.

Because the United States, unlike almost all other first-world nations, funds public schools using local property taxes, poorer neighborhoods, with lower real-estate values, generate smaller school taxes resulting in lower school funding. Lower funding results in lower-quality education, directly impacting real estate values because few prospective home buyers want to move into an underfunded and poorly performing school district, resulting in what's been called a "death spiral."[21] The rich get richer and the poor get poorer. Wealthy neighborhoods have great schools because they can afford them, leading to upward real estate pressure for people looking to buy homes near good schools, increasing real-estate prices leading to more funding for the already highly performing schools. . . . While the opposite occurs in the poor neighborhoods. Real estate prices stagnate or decrease due to underfunded schools, resulting in more of the same.

State and local government step in to help moderate the more extreme school funding inequalities, but these types of subsidies are often dependent upon political whim and the strength of the current budget. Even if per-student spending between districts is roughly equal, there's no guarantee that the educational outcome will be the same. In fact, studies consistently show that money alone can't fix poorly performing schools, yet when students are moved from poorly performing schools to better schools their educational outlook almost always improves. There also exists huge differences in per-student spending between states: in 2013 Utah spent an average of $7000 per pupil, while New York State spent $20,000.[22]

What is it we see when we look at the Winklevoss twins? They stand resplendent in high-tech athletic gear, thighs thick as poplars, six-foot-five and broad shouldered, looking very much the Olympians as they pose, disturbingly doubled, the image of young and aggressive and WASPY confidence. *Success.* They made it. They are winners, global jetsetters, dedicated world-class athletes, instant multimillionaires, perfect representatives of the top 1 percent of the top 1 percent. As such our culture should celebrate them, hold them up as examples for our children to emulate; laud them as products of intense athletic competition, their Olympic berth a reward of stubborn effort. But they don't function in that way. As symbols of the American Dream they fall significantly short. It's hard to point to one of the twins and imagine the same for your own son because he won't be attending the Greenwich Country Day School, featuring alumni such as George H. W. Bush, with a tuition of thirty-five-thousand dollars a year (this is roughly equivalent to the cost of Exeter's day students). It's unlikely your son will attend high school at the Brunswick School ($40,000 a year), or make it into Harvard, *or* be able to afford it if he did ($60,000 a year) without crushing debt (even if he manages to qualify for reduced tuition). Each Winklevoss twin had, in today's dollars, a $500,000 education before they even started applying to colleges, giving them access to the best teachers and facilities money could buy.

In one sense they are the perfect realization of the American Dream; Howard Winklevoss Jr. made it very, very big and wanted the best for his sons. We would like to think we would all do the same.

His decision to educate his family using the best schools money can buy is noble and to be admired. But it also makes us uncomfortable. The Winklevoss twins succeeded, sure, and did a lot more than their similarly blessed classmates, but there really isn't much to root for here. Compared to the average student in a poor school district in Memphis, Tennessee, the Winklevoss Twins have an almost overwhelming suite of educational, social, cultural, and structural advantages. These advantages are so visible and so clearly a part of what allowed them admittance into Harvard, which was the source of fantastic opportunities and all their later wealth, that it's very difficult to really get behind them and hold them up as exemplars of the American Dream.

> Approximately 45.6 percent of Harvard undergraduates come from families with incomes above $200,000, placing them in the top 3.8 percent of American households. Even more shockingly, only about 4 percent of Harvard undergraduates come from the bottom quintile of U.S. incomes and a mere 17.8 percent come from the bottom three quintiles of U.S. incomes.[23]

This isn't a level playing field. It's barely a game. On the one hand, yes, the Winklevoss twins succeeded beyond their wildest dreams; on the other hand, they had a lot of help. They climbed the ladder of success so quickly because the rungs were very, very close together. For many others, including the unfortunates in the "lowest quintile," the ladder has been stretched upward as in a Looney Tunes cartoon, making the rungs so far apart they're impossible to reach and ascend.

The Winklevoss twins must get this all the time, either explicitly or implicitly. Yeah you are rich, but you had help didn't you? Isn't your dad well off? Do you really think you deserve what you have? Would you have done as well if you had lived my (less privileged) life? It's defensive on both sides. It's hard to ignore the success of the Winklevoss twins and easy to rail against them in a spasm of envy, but it's also possible to ask the question in a more sober and measured way: had the twins been born in a tract home to an alcoholic mother in Oklahoma would they have made it to Harvard? If no, or very, very unlikely, what's the real cause of their success?

This is why the Winklevoss twins play up their (fictional) humble origins. It's not the American Dream on an individual level but the American Dream writ large, a generational tale of rags to riches, a slow but constant ascension from the coal mine to the middle class to the upper class and beyond. . . . Global celebrity, paid appearances, multimillion dollar LA mansions . . . *look at them now.* It's the only way the myth can be made to work. Nobody will ever view their father as anything other than insanely rich; or their upbringing other than the best money can buy. But if placed within the context of generational striving it becomes more palatable. Your son might not have all the privileges the Winklevoss twins had, but his son might, or his son after that.

The American Dream isn't descriptive. It doesn't explain how somebody got rich. Nor is it predictive. You can't believe in it wholeheartedly and work as hard as you can and be guaranteed, after forty years, of retiring comfortably from your accumulated financial gains. Nor, as it turns out, does the American Dream describe the on-the-ground reality of much of America. I'd suggest jettisoning the myth entirely, but if that's not possible at least understand what it means and doesn't mean. The Winklevoss twins didn't have a choice about whether to accept the great gifts they were given—and even if they had a choice, surely we all would have done the same, shouting *Yes, please.* That their opportunities exceeded our own isn't surprising; isn't it how the world works? You might as well strike the sun for burning your back one hot summer day.

I do wish the Winklevoss twins were more upfront about their family history and less willing to pander to those who feel "uncomfortable" with the truth. How wonderful it would be if they simply stood up, tall and imposing, confident and unapologetic, and explained how much they owe to their family; how lucky and privileged their lives have been; how a family impulse toward entrepreneurship had been instilled in them from an early age, running three generations deep; how business contacts and family connections help them in innumerable ways; and thanks to this great upward push they bent their powerful knees, waited for the right moment, and leaped toward beckoning opportunity.

If anyone finds this version of the Winklevoss career arc offensive it really doesn't have much to do with the Winklevoss twins them-selves—any objection implicates the United States of America. It's certainly possible to pass laws adjusting or reducing the types of benefits enjoyed by the wealthy, via higher taxes, restricting inheri-tances, equalizing teacher pay across both public and private schools, requiring blind college admissions, and a million other ideas that, no matter how mildly voiced, inevitably generate loud cries of "socialism" or "class warfare" and go precisely nowhere. We have the America we voted for and, apparently, deserve. The Winklevoss twins reflect the reality of America, not the myth of the American Dream. That the two are fundamentally in conflict isn't their fault, and they really shouldn't be blamed for our collective lack of courage to face the facts without flinching.

CHAPTER 7

THE WINKLEVOSS TWINS: THE FOG OF SUCCESS

CREDIT WHERE CREDIT IS DUE

The Winklevoss twins leveraged their privileged upbringing to gain admittance to Harvard, become professional athletes, and spot (or create) an opportunity that later became Facebook. After graduating from Harvard they remained busy, kept their eyes and ears open, attended Oxford business school, didn't sit on their Olympic laurels, and when they heard about Bitcoin (a friend of a friend cornered them during a party and gushed the news) they looked into it. They read Satoshi's white paper. They talked to the principals involved. They discussed Bitcoin's possible future with each other, peers, whomever would listen. They became if not converts at least excited supporters, and thereafter threw their business and financial weight behind the currency.

Bitcoin was the Winklevoss twins' next gamble, and their relatively early investment in the currency has already paid off in millions—with millions more surely to come. They live smack dab in the middle of the hothouse atmosphere of New York City Bitcoin startups, which are (collectively) growing so rapidly they almost put Silicon Valley to shame.[1] The Winklevoss twins have regulators on their side; Wall Street banks are listening to them; Big Money is about to move into Bitcoin.

Satoshi created Bitcoin, Ross Ulbricht popularized Bitcoin, and the Winklevoss twins are mainstreaming Bitcoin. The currency's maturing, if not yet fully mature.

What's really going on with the Winklevoss twins' second taste of success? How much "credit" do they really deserve for their Facebook idea, and is Bitcoin fundamentally more interesting and important than Facebook? How nimble have the twins been with their Bitcoin investments, and where do they see the currency heading? Were they right to embrace Bitcoin regulation and use it as a cornerstone of their business model, or is it nothing less than a rejection of Satoshi's ideals?

From private schools to Harvard to Facebook to the Olympics to Bitcoin and Bitcoin regulation and whatever's beyond: it all started in Greenwich, Connecticut, with the twins' magnificently privileged childhood. How much credit to they deserve for their accomplishments, given their great childhood advantages? As it turns out, more than most think.

PRIVILEGED BRATS OF WEALTHY PARENTS

There isn't any doubt that the children of the poor suffer as a result of their desperate living conditions. "Economically disadvantaged" children have behavior issues in school, get tangled up in the legal system, graduate high school at lower rates, and are admitted to prestigious colleges infrequently—this is one of those rare cases where statistics and common sense perfectly align. Poor nutrition, high stress, and lack of a "stable home environment" can combine to suppress achievement, putting the poor at a significant disadvantage compared to their well-fed, safe, and "bored" suburban peers for whom the bland comfort of cookie-cutter neighborhoods isn't something to be celebrated but decried—neighborhoods that would be the envy of the working poor living in mostly urban, mostly desperate, mostly unsafe conditions.

Children in the lowest 10 percent income bracket suffer high rates of drug abuse of every sort: cigarettes, marijuana, alcohol, prescription pills, cocaine in various forms, and all the rest of the "more serious" stuff. What's become increasing clear is that the children of privilege, those in the top 5 to 10 percent, have rates of substance abuse approaching those of the poorest among us, both far greater than the middle class. "The high rate of maladjustment among

THE WINKLEVOSS TWINS: THE FOG OF SUCCESS   233

affluent adolescents is strikingly counterintuitive," writes Suniya S. Luthar, PhD, in the leaden terminology of her profession. "The evidence suggests that the privileged young are much more vulnerable today than in previous generations."[2]

Pressure to succeed drives bad behavior. Wealthy kids know how much money is being spent on them. Most are painfully aware of their privileged position and the high expectations that go along with it. A recent study done on a group of upper-middle-class youth being groomed for the most prestigious universities summarized their outlook this way: "I can, therefore I must, achieve: Strive for the top, to attain what my parents achieved. This is the central, imperative life goal; nothing else is as important. Without such success, I will be left behind as a failure as others soar to great heights."[3] One natural byproduct of "pressure to succeed" is overwhelming stress, and "reducing stress was the most common reason offered for drinking, drug use, and smoking."[4]

After being given the best music lessons using the best instruments with the best teachers in New York City, success won't (can't) lag far behind. That's the default expectation: the best tutoring and the best education should (will) result in the best outcomes. If somebody fails, and doesn't achieve what's expected, it's doubly damning. Failure is magnified. Handed a high-end Porsche and sent to the track only to lose a race to a patched-up jalopy . . . a jalopy? How did *this* happen? For many the stress is too much to bear.

While it would be silly to argue it's better, in the grand scheme of things, to be born poor versus wealthy or middle-class versus wealthy, wealthy parents don't guarantee either happiness or lifelong success. Failure is easy regardless of situation. That the Winklevoss twins, as youth, navigated these minefields is creditable; that they became Olympic athletes laudable (how many of their peers managed this feat?); that they were admitted to Harvard and graduated four years later, attended Oxford and graduated with MBAs, and continue to work with Bitcoin and invest in Bitcoin and do everything except sit back and live off the interest of their Facebook lawsuit. . . . It might not be noble, but at least acknowledge it's noteworthy.

HOW TO BECOME A BILLIONAIRE

The Winklevoss twins first heard about Bitcoin sometime in 2010, and unlike many others they took it seriously and read about it and talked about it and decided it might be *The Next Big Thing.* Cue lightning. Let's remember the not-so-distant past. The Winklevoss twins had the idea for Facebook before Facebook was a thing, and built a proto-Facebook (called ConnectU) before Facebook was up and running, and claimed, in court, to be the "inventors" of Facebook and were so convincing that Facebook awarded them multiple millions of dollars to go away and be quiet. They went away but weren't quiet. They continued to fight against Facebook, appealing their legal settlement after claiming it was undervalued, causing anyone within earshot to roll their eyes: *You got your millions, now shut up.* The legal squabble finally ended when a judge, reading their latest appeal, applied a hammer to their coffin's final nail: "At some point, litigation must come to an end, and that point has now been reached."[5]

Facebook has been extravagantly successful as a financial and cultural force, but this wasn't obvious when it was first created. What made it take off as it did? And what does it say about Facebook? American capitalism is full of oddities that made their investors wildly rich: the "Have a Nice Day" yellow smiley face is estimated to have brought in half-a-billion dollars for the two brothers who trademarked it. The *I Can Has Cheezburger* web site, which introduced us lolcats and lolspeak and kicked off the internet meme craze, made millions for its creator. Selling "pet rocks" in 1975 generated a profit in excess of $15 million for advertising executive Gary Dahl—in one year. Dr. Eamonn Butler, director of the Adam Smith Institute, explains that "The free market works in mysterious ways"[6]—the success of a given product indicates the product was purchased *en masse.* That's all it says. It's possible for lower-quality products to win out over higher-quality, lower-priced products. Worthless products and worthless ideas occasionally make their lucky salesmen rich; wonderful products based on incredible ideas occasionally make their investors rich, or not—depending. That Facebook is now worth billions of dollars is a financial fact; that the Winklevoss twins played an important role in its creation is beyond dispute; what's not clear is how Facebook reflects upon the twins. Is it an invention worthy of global acclaim?

Facebook is a good, perhaps canonical example of "mature" American-style capitalism and how billionaires are currently minted. This process used to follow a well-trodden path: in order to earn a billion dollars (adjusted for inflation), a man (it was almost always a man) either had to rule a relatively prosperous nation and continue his royal family's ongoing accrual of wealth via taxation, annexation, and occasionally outright war/asset seizure, or be a particularly successful businessman in the right sector at the right time. Nathan Rothschild was a famously wealthy banker/mover-and-shaker in early 1800s Europe, with financial resources large enough to prop up Prussia and save England from the so-called "Panic of 1825," a fascinating financial disaster paralleling France's much earlier "Mississippi Bubble." The panic started when a world-class swindler, Gregor MacGregor (his real name even though it sounds phony) took "the long con" to an entirely new level, and furnishes a good example of how, under capitalism, riches occasionally accrue not only to peddlers of useless objects (pet rocks, etc.) but peddlers of fictitious objects as well.

Short cons are small swindles ("grifts"), gaining part or all of the mark's cash. Low-level thievery of this sort is often accomplished using card scams (three-card Monte and the like), weighted or magnetized dice, or simple sleight-of-hand. The payoff is small and so is the risk.

The long con requires preparation, time, and one or more coconspirators. There is no assurance of short- or long-term gain. Risks can be great—long cons require elaborate ruses with thin substantiation; once the conman's fiction is pierced there's often no way to escape a subsequent police investigation. However, if the sucker ("gull") is caught up in the scam, and believes it wholeheartedly, a large payoff is guaranteed. Fictional shares in a fictional company are purchased for thousands of dollars; a deed for hundreds of California acres is signed and notarized; a "sure fire" track horse ends up losing, and an all-or-nothing bet fails to come through. After a successful long con the victim is often so ashamed of their greed/gullibility that the loss goes unreported.[7] The con artist makes a bundle, and the bundle's not reported as theft. What could be better? The swindle cooked up by Gregor MacGregor.

Born in 1786, Gregor MacGregor left Scotland at the age of sixteen and joined the British Army as an ensign, a rank purchased by his family. A few years later, following a squabble with a superior officer, MacGregor requested and was granted discharge, after which he visited Venezuela, where he impressed the locals with tales of his military experience and managed to get appointed brigadier-general. His deeds, however, failed to match his words, and after his side lost the Venezuelan civil war MacGregor was forced to flee the country. Missing the excitement of battle as well as the military's fabulous uniforms,[8] MacGregor became involved in campaigns in Columbia, Jamaica, and anywhere else that looked interesting. In 1817 he decided to "liberate" Florida from Spanish rule and attacked a fort on Amelia Island, taking it despite commanding only a handful of men. He established the "Republic of the Floridas," and things might have gone well if President James Monroe hadn't already been negotiating with Spain over purchasing Florida and had little patience for a new republic rising out of the swamps. The United States army squelched the nascent revolution, and Gregor MacGregor fled to England, where he uncorked one of the most outlandish schemes in the long and sordid history of confidence tricks. Calling himself the *cacique* (prince) of the *Principality of Poyais*, he began proselytizing about the beauty and fecundity of Poyais, a country encompassing 76,000 miles of tropical paradise near the Bay of Honduras.

This excited many of his well-off friends, and in 1822 Gregor MacGregor started to sell land in Poyais for three shillings, three pence per acre, which might have netted sufficient profits for your everyday conman. Not Gregor MacGregor. Since the newly founded countries of Chile, Columbia, and Peru had recently received loans from England, why couldn't Poyais do the same? In October of 1822, a 200,000 pound "Poyais Bond" was offered to investors, and it fared no worse than more substantial country's bonds, at least until two ships, stuffed with Poyaisian colonists, straggled back to England with a fatality rate of over 50 percent and the sad news that, shockingly, Poyais did not exist. The Poyais Bond immediately became worthless, precipitating a stock market crash and widespread panic—*if Poyais was fiction, what else might be?*[9] Better grab what you can before it all goes up in smoke. This was the bank run Nathan Rothschild and only Nathan Rothschild quelled, via a vast infusion of French bullion rapidly shuffled across the channel.[10]

The great American billionaires followed the general path of industrialization. Leland Stanford built railroads, oversaw huge rail systems, and amassed hundreds of millions.[11] Andrew Carnegie fed American's appetite for steel and became a multibillionaire in the process.[12] J. P. Morgan was busy with everything; the electrification of New York, merging Carnegie's steel empire into US Steel, buying banks and consolidating them. John D. Rockefeller became America's first billionaire thanks to Standard Oil, yet Henry Ford left him in the dust, dying in 1947 with a net worth a bit shy of two hundred billion.[13] Between these five we have the founding of industrial America—cars, oil, steel, electricity, railroads, and high finance. They were men who created things, leaving the world changed in visible and material ways. We were given cheap cars, cheap oil, bright lights at night, and cheap transportation of goods (thanks to trains), allowing cheap or at least vastly more affordable consumer products. The previous generation of European billionaires was busy saving countries from bad economic decisions and allowing new ones to get started via loans and expert oversight.

What happened when Silicon Valley took over the world? Steve Jobs and Bill Gates enabled the personal computer revolution, leading to the internet and all the madness that followed. They built the foundation for what was to come. And what came? Implementations built upon this foundation. Brick-and-mortar stores thrust onto the internet (Amazon). Garage sales hosted on the internet (eBay). Airline ticket and hotel listings on the internet (Expedia). Internet-specific companies soon arrived, allowing us to search (Google) and watch streaming video (Netflix) and do "social media" stuff.

The development of social media sites has a strange and inverse correlation to complexity. Back in the day, 1992, when the internet was relatively new, if you wanted to publicize yourself you could register an IP address, create a personal website, code it on your locally hosted web server using HTML, and populate it with text, pictures, and whatever other meager options were then available. This was a lot of trouble, but not hugely difficult; an existing website could be used as a template and customized, but it did require expertise to get all the pieces working together. The next step simplified the process: companies sprang up allowing you to build a web page (or write a blog) hosted on their site, meaning you no longer had to register your own domain name or run your own server. You just had to create content. This was much easier, but still a bit daunting.

In 2003 LinkedIn and MySpace appeared within months of each other and removed the ability to create a "specific" site within their broad portal. Instead, you could customize a basic "profile" template, but options were limited and one user's "profile" ended up looking much like another user's. This was intentional; by the time Facebook arrived in 2004, what I'm calling the "mass simplification" trend continued. Facebook was significantly less customizable than MySpace, and fewer options led to less "garish" and over-the-top profiles, giving the entire site a rather austere (at the time) look and feel. It seemed like a place for grownups, not music-obsessed teens.

But even this was a little too much freedom. The next step, predictable but still shocking, was Twitter, with a self-imposed 140-character limitation ensuring that nobody, anywhere, at any time, would ever be accused of poor writing or insufficient content. Given the space constraints, messages were soon stuffed with abbreviations and short-form jargon—rendering it an instant hit. Twitter was incredibly safe to use—even the most insecure and computer-averse Americans were able to sign up, type a few words, and send a "tweet" into the soulless void without any fear of criticism.

Next came Instagram and Pinterest, which essentially made text (even a 140-character limit) redundant with their nearly exclusive focus on visuals. What mattered were photos and images and short video clips—there wasn't room for anything else. The end point of this reverse textual evolution is Periscope, enabling personal video streaming. No text, no design decisions, no profile, no nothing. Simply a narcissistic stream from a user, depicting whatever their phone happens to be facing. I'm not sure it's possible to go any further in this direction; we seem to have reached a cultural cul-de-sac. Greater "innovation" in this space, the latest and greatest and newest thing, will necessarily include more options for the end user.

What's less demanding than a picture? A stream (you have to frame and compose and take the picture—with a stream you just let it run). What's less demanding than a stream? Wait and see.

When viewed in the context of the history of social network sites, Facebook wasn't the first, nor (initially) the most popular, and it wasn't festooned with any "killer app" features. What it had was a simple and clean interface, excellent advertising and press, and a more "mature" vibe compared to its competition. That this should spawn billionaires is strange; it's hard to find any other historical "innovation" succeeding due to such marginal improvements. Facebook has since grown to support a vast variety of economic activity, but its initial development was wildly unlike the business of any nineteenth- or twentieth-century billionaire. Facebook wasn't creating things, or building physical infrastructures, or electrifying the world. Facebook didn't kick off a transportation revolution, or help settle the West, or build steam ships capable of powering across the Pacific. If there was no Facebook there would still be something very much like Facebook—it didn't beat its competitors to the idea, it simply outmaneuvered them. Never in the history of the world has so much money been made so quickly by means of such trivial "improvements" to readily available alternatives.

That the Winklevoss twins were part of the Facebook story is notable but not, I think, up there with the invention of the telephone, the development of the Model T, perfecting the light bulb, or saving the economy of England from imploding. The world economy is so huge that anyone able to skim a tiny percentage for themselves, no matter how absurd or trivial the cause, can reap billions. What they did next was far more impressive.

The Winklevoss twins turned to Bitcoin—the most remarkable event in their evolving story. Sure, they had already profited from one the biggest internet startups in the short history of Silicon Valley, but this was different. They became involved with what might be the most important revolution in financial history, equivalent to the creation of a monetary internet.[14] It's extremely unlikely they would have randomly discovered and pursued two opportunities of this sort by chance. The Winklevoss twins have the extremely rare ability to spot (and react to) opportunities as they arise. Sure, it was crucial that the twins were at Harvard at exactly the right time and place to start ConnectU, but a lot of people attended Harvard and none of *them* created ConnectU. In 2010 Bitcoin was freely available to anyone who wanted to read about it, research it, download it, and invest. The twins looked, thought, looked again, got excited, and ran with it. By 2013 they claimed to own (or at least control) at least 1 percent of the entire Bitcoin currency. This isn't something that can be directly proven, but even if the number is far lower they were clearly invested in the market and buying bitcoins when they were around thirteen dollars, and the price has multiplied fifteenfold since then.[15] Bitcoin certainly earned them a few million, and possibly much more.

Purchasing bitcoins was only the start of their Bitcoin investments. In 2012 the twins founded Winklevoss Capital Management,[16] which funded internet (and particularly Bitcoin) startups. In late 2012, they created Math-Based Asset Services LLC,[17] underwriting the Winklevoss Bitcoin Trust, which released one million shares of Bitcoin-focused assets. Investors could purchase shares and if the price of Bitcoin increased so did the value of their holdings. By 2013 everything seemed to be happening at once; Bitcoin was getting a lot of press as its price surged over two hundred dollars. It stopped being a silly little virtual currency and become something ambitious and smart people wanted to learn more about. Everything looked like it was going great; the Winklevoss twins had a golden touch. Along came BitInstant.

BitInstant was a Bitcoin exchange founded in 2011 by Charlie Shrem,[18] allowing customers to purchase and sell bitcoins for dollars. BitInstant was located in New York City, putting it directly in the government's regulatory eye, which was both curious and unsure about how to treat the upstart Bitcoin currency. In 2013, the Winklevoss twins invested $1.5 million in the exchange, which was already processing a large number of transactions and didn't seem to be one of those "never turned a profit" businesses that typified so many startups in the heady dot.com bubble years. This was a real business, with real cash flow, serving an obvious need.

What it didn't have was a stable management structure, or much regulatory expertise in what was turning out to be a growing and complex field. BitInstant was a typical Bitcoin startup of the time; it was relatively easy to find a niche and fill it, but difficult to handle the volume of resultant sales or meet the increasing demands of regulations that were, at the time, somewhat murky. By 2013 it had grown to sixteen employees, including Alex Waters, its COO and CIO, who had previously worked on the core Bitcoin development team with fellow Bitcoin pioneer Gavin Andresen. Back in 2012 Alex and Gavin had been sponsored by a private company to help strengthen, test, and stabilize Bitcoin's core features, and they were the first developers paid to do Bitcoin development—and surely the first to have their salaries dispensed in Bitcoin.[19] From a technical standpoint, BitInstant had enough skill and sophistication to handle the demands of business and growth; however, from a structural view, things were not going well. Everyone was young and new to this, or any other, business. Accounting standards were low, and cash flow was complicated enough that it wasn't always known even to the CEO how much money was in the bank (assuming BitInstant had access to a bank—banks were wary of the unregulated exchange, and eventually all of them abandoned the company).[20] It also wasn't clear who was using BitInstant and for what reasons, and this was going to be a serious problem very soon.

Back in 2013, when Silk Road was still active and profitable, a large percentage of overall Bitcoin transactions were involved with purchasing illegal material or enabling its purchase by buying and selling bitcoins. BitInstant had nonexistent or (at the very least) lax "know your customers" policies, meaning that it was possible to set up an account and, with some low-level subterfuge, anonymously buy and sell bitcoins ultimately destined to be used on Silk Road or sites like it. Back in the "good old days," when Bitcoin entrepreneurs and advocates took a hardline "all or nothing" approach to Bitcoin privacy and anonymity, this type of exchange was thought to be ideal: it's nobody's business who's buying or selling bitcoins, so it's not necessary for an exchange to have rigorous records of transactions, detailing what customers are buying and selling and in what quantities. This obviously flung open the door for what soon transpired: money laundering and an influx of tainted "drug-derived" funds.

It wasn't that criminals or potential criminals used BitInstant to funnel profits or enable Bitcoin purchases; the BitInstant CEO

Charlie Shrem was working directly with Robert M. Faiella, a plumber-turned-Bitcoin advocate who operated a small bitcoin exchange on Silk Road itself.[21] Clearly any money transfers between BitInstant and Robert Faiella were tainted by his association with Silk Road. Shrem knew the source of Faiella's bitcoins and cash but didn't much care. In his own words: "I knew that much of the business on Silk Road involved the buying and selling of narcotics, and I knew that what I was doing was wrong."[22] This admission came in court on September 3, 2014, following a federal indictment of Shrem on money-laundering charges, during which he pleaded guilty to one count of "Aiding and abetting an unlicensed money transmitting business." Shrem was sentenced to two years in prison—a relatively light sentence, as the charge carries a maximum of thirty years.[23]

Shrem had been a rising star in the Bitcoin community. He was an eager advocate and energetic communicator, a founding board member of the Bitcoin Foundation (once the premier Bitcoin trade group, now fallen into relative disarray),[24] and had a strong media presence, lecturing and giving interviews as fast as requests arrived. His rapid rise and inglorious fall were the triggers for a regulatory sea change.

In the wake of Silk Road's seizure and BitInstant's collapse in July 2013, it was looking increasingly unlikely that Bitcoin was going to be left to fend for itself in a regulatory vacuum. The collapse of the Mt. Gox exchange in early 2014 made it clear, even to those in the Bitcoin community, that self-regulation and self-governing weren't working. At this point a significant minority of Bitcoin enthusiasts thought regulation not only inevitable but necessary for the currency's long-term stability. The Winklevoss twins, whose $1.5 million investment in BitInstant had gone up in smoke, certainly learned their lesson; they immediately pivoted toward participating in regulatory discussions with an eye to guiding the eventual results.

On January 28, 2014, the Winklevoss twins testified before the New York State Department of Financial Services "Virtual Currency Hearing," and supported the concept of a BitLicense which would be, "Built off of existing regulation and licensure of money service businesses and/or check cashing services."[25] The idea was to require Bitcoin exchanges to be licensed and follow the same rules as other currency exchanges.

While Charlie Shrem knowingly accepted funds originating from Silk Road, it wasn't clear to investors or entrepreneurs that a new, as-yet-unlicensed Bitcoin exchange wouldn't be held liable for transferring funds arising from "suspicious" sources, regardless of precise knowledge of their origins. The sight of Charlie Shrem in jail made it highly unlikely other Bitcoin exchanges would be set up in the United States; there was too much risk and too few guidelines. What if a drug dealer purchased $1,500 worth of bitcoins from an exchange, got caught by the police the next day, and had his bitcoins confiscated while his laptop clearly indicated their origin? What sort of blowback might there be for the exchange selling him the bitcoins? Nobody was in a position to know. In early 2014 the government hadn't taken a firm stand; public prosecutors weren't making iron-clad guarantees that an exchange would or wouldn't be held responsible. Bitcoin was in regulatory limbo, and nobody in their right mind was going to invest good money in a business that might, the following day, be ruled illegal. Lack of clarity inspired entrepreneurial paralysis.

THE MT. GOX BITCOIN EXCHANGE DISASTER

Mt. Gox is short for **M**agic **T**he **G**athering **O**nline e**X**change, an online exchange set up in 2006 to allow players of *Magic: The Gathering Online* (an online collectible card game) to buy and sell the online cards used in the game. Its author, Jed McCaleb, did all the coding himself, and it went "live" for a few months before McCaleb decided that supporting the site, which was only seeing limited use, wasn't worth his time and effort. That was pretty much the end of Mt. Gox as a card exchange, but a few years later, in 2010, when McCaleb read about Bitcoin, he immediately realized that another type of exchange was needed: from Bitcoin to fiat currency and back again. An extraordinarily gifted programmer,[26] responsible for widely respected peer-to-peer applications such as eDonkey2000, McCaleb wrote the Bitcoin exchange in one week and had it running live by July 18, 2010, when he announced it on the Bitcointalk.org forums:

mtgox (Full Member): Hi Everyone, I just put up a new bitcoin exchange. Please let me know what you think. https://mtgox.com[27]

By March 06, 2011, McCaleb had had enough of the exchange. He announced he was selling it to MagicalTux (aka Mark Karpelès), again on the Bitcointalk.org forums:

Hello Everyone
    I created mtgox on a lark after reading about bitcoins last summer. It has been interesting and fun to do. I'm still very confident that bitcoins have a bright future. But to really make mtgox what it has the potential to be would require more time than I have right now. So I've decided to pass the torch to someone better able to take the site to the next level.
    MagicalTux has already contributed a lot to the bitcoin community and in many ways he will be better at running the site than I was.[28]

Mt. Gox began to take off, and by April 2013 was responsible for 70 percent of all the world's Bitcoin traffic. People were buying and selling bitcoins at a dizzying rate, and since the exchange took a small slice of every Bitcoin transaction it was slowly banking huge profits. By November 2013, when Bitcoin briefly traded over $1000 due to extreme public demand (driving up the price), Mt. Gox's accumulated hoard of customer and company bitcoins suddenly spiked in value, creating what must have been an almost impossible temptation. That's when things started to go haywire. Customer withdrawals to North America were briefly suspended, and quickly reinstated, but remained incredibly slow; it sometimes took weeks to extract money from Mt. Gox accounts—if you were lucky. The unlucky ones, which turned out to be 99 percent of those with money at the site, lost everything. On April 2014, the company abruptly announced that hackers had stolen a vast number of bitcoins from the site, totaling "as much as 6 percent of the Bitcoins in circulation—worth more than $300 million at current exchange rates."[29] The total was actually closer to $600 million, from 850,000 "lost" Mt. Gox bitcoins, making it (by far) the biggest heist in world history.[30]

(At the time of writing, Mark Karpelès had been arrested in Japan for allegedly "illicitly add[ing] $1 million [in customer funds] to an account under his control,"[31] surely not the last charge he will face.)

What was the effect of this disaster on the Bitcoin community? Serious and far-reaching. The sudden disappearance of so many bitcoins, and the obvious lack of security at the premier Bitcoin exchange, shook the community to its core. Bitcoin's most ardent supporters had been hardest hit by the theft, and while other exchanges were still up and running it wasn't initially clear that Mt. Gox's collapse wasn't a harbinger, pointing toward the end of Bitcoin as a viable currency.

I got in touch with one of these unfortunates, Joshua Scigala, who had lost "a few hundred thousand" dollars at Mt. Gox. Who is Joshua Scigala? From his website, vaultoro.com: "Joshua Scigala is an entrepreneur whose focus is to make the world a better place by giving people back control of their money and to help develop financial solutions for people in developing countries."[32]

Mr. Scigala explained the effect of the Mt. Gox disaster during a discussion one evening (I'm in the United States, he's in Berlin): "Yes I lost a heap of bitcoin to Mt. Gox, or 'empty gox' as we all now call it. That event was really terrible not just for me personally but the whole amazing Bitcoin movement. It inspired me to show the world how a transparent exchange can function and drove me to develop Vaultoro.com [their motto: 'In math we trust'] with my brother Philip Scigala. We worked very hard to give the tools to our users to regulate us, not the state. This is done by developing our *glass books* protocol."[33]

"Glass books" is a transparency protocol that attempts to make it clear to the public how much money is held by the exchange: exactly how many bitcoins and where they are located. Regular audits are conducted, and the exchange's public holdings are visible on the public block chain. It is the exact opposite of how Mt. Gox was run, which was externally opaque, customer-unfriendly, physically remote, cryptic in its utterances, and impossible to audit. Sending your money to Mt. Gox involved an act of faith, which is a perverse way to treat Bitcoin, the most (theoretically) open and transparent currency ever invented.

Because Bitcoin uses a public ledger, which is visible to everyone who cares to look at it, it's possible, in theory, to set up an exchange using an e-wallet address that is "known" and publicly broadcast. Anyone, at any time, could go to a site such as https://blockchain.info and enter the public address for such an exchange and see exactly how many bitcoins it holds; the speed of input and output; track daily Bitcoin churn due to buying and selling; and in general have a good idea of how many bitcoins are being held at the exchange at any given time. This is an incredibly reductive example, as actual Bitcoin exchanges typically use private systems to track internal trades, and the public ledger is only used for either incoming or outgoing monies—but it's still far better than the alternative, which is nothing.

Scigala remains optimistic about the future, and he doesn't think the Mt. Gox disaster caused a fundamental slowdown of Bitcoin acceptance:

> Mt. Gox's collapse was a normal market process of educating consumers (the hard way) on what to look out for and what to demand from exchanges before becoming a member. Bitcoin's vision was to be money without interference, without middle men. We as users should demand proof of liability [from exchanges], and proof of reserve otherwise we shouldn't do business with them. The block chain is an extraordinary tool for both transparency and privacy and gives us all the power to regulate markets without the dangers that come with entrusting and empowering the force of a state.
>
> It was really really shocking when it happened but my passion about the technology, the disruption to global finance and the separation of money and state, was as strong as ever. What pissed me off most about the situation was that it put a negative image on Bitcoin and really took the wind out of a movement that was gaining massive velocity. With ridiculous uneducated headlines going something like 'The CEO of Bitcoin goes broke.' Really silly stuff.[34]

Joshua Scigala's a libertarian in deed if not in name, yet his ultimate goal is more humanitarian than strictly antigovernment (or wildly pro-individual-freedom):

In life money come and money goes. If you do something that you love with a passion, if you do something for a bigger cause than money, you will ultimately make money because you do that thing so well that people will want to pay you for it. So yes, I lost my money but I have my health and I have used the anger and sorrow arising from my loss and transformed it into energy and passion to create an exchange that will be an example in transparency. Hopefully it will inspire and teach the market to aspire for a higher benchmark before doing business with centralized exchanges. I think the [Bitcoin price] bubble was going to pop anyway, but the negative press really did Bitcoin a disfavor and put the brakes on. Then again maybe Bitcoin was growing too quickly.[35]

Joshua Scigala might be hopeful, but the rest of the world reeled from the collapse of Mt. Gox. Some agreed with Mr. Scigala that it was business as usual: "This was an amateurish and incompetently managed company . . . it will be replaced by competent operators who run better exchanges,"[36] but Jacob Donnelly, writing for insidebitcoins.com, wasn't so sure: "The entire bitcoin ecosystem was in complete chaos when [the Mt. Gox collapse] occurred. . . . Yet, despite the catastrophe, Bitcoin survived. But Mt. Gox serves as a constant reference point, particularly in mainstream media—and an event held up as evidence by regulators for the need to impose stricter controls on the cryptocurrency."[37]

This was the big question: was Mt. Gox a normal (and expected) effect of the free market weeding out poor performers, or was it a call for regulators to get involved in what had been, for too long, a "Wild West" where anything and everything was allowed?

THE NERVOUS, LUKEWARM EMBRACE OF BITCOIN REGULATION

The Mt. Gox debacle, along with the collapse of BitInstant and the arrest and eventual jailing of its founder and CEO, shook the still-small and somewhat delicate Bitcoin community. Alex Waters, former COO and CIO of BitInstant, fled the soon-to-be-bankrupt exchange along with a number of developers, hardware designers, and Bitcoin-savvy entrepreneurs. They founded Coin Apex, an umbrella company / Bitcoin incubator[38] that included, notably, CoinValidation, which in the words of the company, "helped businesses gain awareness of the regulatory and compliance issues with operating a digital currency company."[39] Nobody wanted to experience another BitInstant disaster, and CoinValidation focused on regulation as the crucial issue.

Let's remember that in 2013, as far as Bitcoin media coverage was concerned, the most exciting story was the FBI raid on Silk Road and Ross Ulbricht's arrest. For a while Bitcoin was only mentioned in conjunction with illegal drugs, the Dark Web, and the relative insanity surrounding Silk Road and its users and merchants. On the heels of this story came BitInstant and Charlie Shrem's arrest in January 2014 (and his subsequent conviction). Bitcoin was experiencing some serious growing pains. In February 2014 the Mt. Gox Bitcoin exchange blew up, "losing" around $600 million of its user's bitcoins. It was a brutal trifecta of bad press and highlighted the poor business practices endemic in the still-young Bitcoin startup community. It was a real question at the time as to whether Bitcoin was going to survive the year, much less in the "pure, unregulated" state still extolled by the hard liners. Debates raged—and still rage. Had "unregulated" Bitcoin been attempted, and (repeatedly) failed? Was "regulated" Bitcoin the only answer?

I got in touch with Alex Waters, who had survived the BitInstant meltdown and as a long-time Bitcoin insider could probably articulate the pros and cons of the regulation debate. Alex didn't think there was much to discuss—regulation was a given:

> After I left BitInstant, CoinValidation was definitely a reaction . . . a sort of *Oh crap we need to figure out this regulation thing.* So I spent a lot of time lobbying in DC and getting a sense of where policy makers were at, and where they saw Bitcoin and what we could do to educate them as well as encourage businesses to take on best practices. A lot of our advice went unheard because we martyred ourselves to the community for saying we wanted to work with the regulators. But at the end of the day, you know, I think we accomplished our goals . . . which [were] to help the industry to get more recognition in DC and not be laughed at.[40]

Alex Waters, like the Winklevoss twins, had felt the pain and understood the danger, not of regulation but its lack. Had BitInstant existed in a well-regulated environment, with clear expectations and processes in place ensuring compliance, things surely would have gone much better both for the business and its jailed CEO. There is a natural and necessary tension between the desire to regulate and the desire to control, and it wasn't initially clear to Alex that the government's early interest in the BitInstant exchange was really about anything other than giving themselves time to understand Bitcoin.

Alex laid out the timeline:

> I think initially in 2013 [regulation] was a way to put the brakes on Bitcoin. And not just in the United States, we saw it in China, in the UK, and in Russia at various different points in time. I think what happened is that Bitcoin came on the radar of governmental entities and they were moved to take action quickly to put the brakes on before Bitcoin spun out of control in order to get a sense of what it was. Before they really took a stance. That's what played out here in New York. . . . We are *past* taking a stance now. I think the US has actually been fairly lenient compared to their initial perspective. A lot of lobbying efforts have made the requirements less onerous, and it's been a lengthy process to get to where we are today, but we finally have regulatory clarity, which allows larger institutions to step into the space.[41]

The fundamental question for the Bitcoin community was, again, taken by ideological purists to be strictly black-and-white. Either Bitcoin was going to exist in the way they imagined Satoshi wanted it to exist, anonymous and private, with no expectation or desire for governmental oversight of any sort, or it wouldn't. The other side wasn't arguing for global control, for example requiring documented proof of a person's existence before allowing them to create an e-wallet, permitting bitcoins to be accurately tracked through the system and traced back to specific users. This is a nightmare scenario where Bitcoin is transformed into something infinitely worse than cash, as every purchase and every transaction is precisely mapped to a specific customer, a data miner's dream and a privacy proponent's nightmare. No, the other side was arguing for moderate regulation, of the sort that already exists for other currencies. It was hard for the Bitcoin traditionalists to hear this message, much less accept it. As Alex explained it:

> It might have been an overreaction, because we very publicly and maybe mistakenly said *Hey, we want to operate a regulated Bitcoin business*, which at the time was *heresy* for a lot of people. BitInstant was feeling the pain of regulation at a time when nobody else was, yet we were treated as *heretics* for even talking about it. . . . If the same things were said today I don't think people would care as much, because most of the Bitcoin entities now take regulation very seriously. People have become used to that.[42]

Alex Waters was in a peculiarly good position to argue for moderate and controlled regulation. He had been involved in Bitcoin from the very start and couldn't be accused of being a governmental shill or a woefully naive puppet of some larger power intimidated by Bitcoin and attempting to destroy it from within. Alex loved the way Bitcoin solved the problem of third-party trust, was intensely excited about its many future applications, and if he was wrong, or doing something to undermine it, it was out of misguided love rather than enmity.

Alex's introduction to Bitcoin had been typical. Growing up, Alex had a natural talent for computer programming, and in his teenage years became interested in cryptology and its applications, subscribing to a large number of rich site summary (RSS)[43] feeds reporting the latest proposals and developments. At some point in 2009, while living in his parent's basement and doing freelance programming gigs on the side, he was exposed to Satoshi's ideas, but they didn't really stick. In 2010, after the term *Bitcoin* popped up again and again in various online discussions, Alex read Satoshi's white paper and was so impressed he immediately downloaded the client and began mining, first using his computer's CPU and later with specialized mining chips. He started to get more involved in the community, avidly reading Bitcoin message boards and eventually participating in development discussions with whoever was interested. In 2011 Alex attended the first Bitcoin conference in New York City, where he met Gavin Andresen and many other notables who had previously existed only as names in a chat room or as message board avatars. After this introduction he was offered a chance to work on Bitcoin as a paid developer, sponsored by a company who believed in Bitcoin and wanted it to have a strong and reliable foundation. (They also wanted their product, built on top of Bitcoin's infrastructure, to work smoothly and reliably.)

Alex is remarkably down-to-earth about both Bitcoin and his early involvement. When asked for his overall take on the digital currency, he has this to say:

> I'm super grateful for Bitcoin. I was lucky enough to stumble across it. . . . I wasn't so clever that I sought it out, it kinda fell in my lap and I ended up being like, this is fun and experimental. Many of us thought it wasn't going to be anything significant, at the most something that may be coopted into something else that will be useful down the line. I didn't anticipate the price of Bitcoin going anywhere around $40. I was astounded it was at $36.
>
> I was mining Bitcoin when it was in the cents. There wasn't really a market for it, it was a PayPal kind of situation, and I actually sold a lot and gave away my coins at pretty low price levels—a substantial amount of coins that would be worth a lot today. Going into 2012/2013 my Bitcoin holdings were not significant and were never very high after that. . . . I didn't have the financial mindset for it. I didn't understand the economics of it; it was more a utility, an experiment. . . . I wasn't focused on turning a profit.[44]

When asked about the Winklevoss twins, who as major BitInstant investors necessarily interacted with everyone at BitInstant, Alex defended them against what he viewed as a general cultural prejudice:

> That's the tough part of being public figures you know . . . they draw a lot of criticism for several reasons. I spent a lot of time with Tyler and Cameron Winklevoss, and interacted with them professionally and socially, you know, I sort of considered them friends. I also had these expectations, getting involved with them. . . . There was all this material online and in the news and stuff but I found

they are actually really nice guys, far from what other people or social media claims. They're super intelligent and I think they have a good understanding of Bitcoin as a technology and recognized its value far earlier than most investors and political figures. In some ways they are champions of Bitcoin, bringing it to the notice of a lot of the influential people. In working with them the thing that strikes me is that, well, here are guys who don't need to work, they could retire to an island but that's not what they are doing. They work really hard when they don't have to. I've noticed this with other Bitcoin millionaires I've met; it's a sort of inverse thing that happens when people make a lot of money. They work even harder. In my interactions with them they are good people, well intentioned, and very professional.[45]

The Winklevoss twins continued to focus on regulation, viewing it as the key to creating a viable long-term Bitcoin exchange, leveraging their extensive business contacts and post-*Social Network* notoriety to raise Bitcoin's profile and interest those who normally would not care much about "niche" technological developments. (The entire Bitcoin ecosystem could comfortably fit inside the profits *earned in one quarter* by Wall Street's biggest banks.)

There is currently a race between two startups, Coinbase and Gemini, to create the first fully regulated Bitcoin exchange in the United States.[46] Coinbase already launched a Bitcoin exchange, however it's not currently licensed in all fifty states, leading critics to claim there's a substantial legal risk in using it. The Winklevoss twins aren't going to launch Gemini until all the regulatory issues are completely resolved and there is uniform regulatory clarity from everyone involved. It's hard to overstate how intensely the Winklevoss twins are engaged in Bitcoin regulation—it's not only central to their view of Bitcoin's ongoing evolution but is the cornerstone of the Gemini exchange itself. From a recent interview about "The Future of Cryptocurrency," the Winklevoss twins had this to say:

> We see [Gemini] as the Nasdaq of bitcoin, it's a US-regulated, New York-based platform to buy and sell bitcoins. . . . [I]t's a US home for people . . . where they can buy and sell bitcoin from a company that's regulated and has consumer protections. We see this as really

critical infrastructure to building bitcoin and realizing its potential.
. . . We've had open dialogue with regulators for almost a year now
and we feel that we're close and we want to make sure that we truly
area [*sic*] licensed, that's one of our principles. We don't want to
half bake it, or hack our way through and be on the fringe of it, we
really want to do this the right way and get the blessing of the regulators. And we do feel that that's around the corner.[47]

It's easy to understand the business rationale behind this. The
Gemini exchange has secured an account with an American bank,
allowing it to transfer money back and forth between US-based
financial institutions, as well as access to FDIC insurance for money
deposited into Gemini accounts.[48] The twins assure us that only a
small fraction of all funds at Gemini will be held by the online service
connected to the internet, as most of the Bitcoins will be held off-site in
secure storage to protect against human error, internal malfeasance,
and other factors that have led to problems in the past. In other
words, they have pledged 1) to embrace and guide regulation, and
2) to learn from the Mt. Gox disaster and take obvious security
precautions with money deposited at their exchange.

The Winklevoss twins are acting like adults in the still-young
market, and are busy getting other adults involved. Gemini has the
backing of Wall Street banks, hedge funds, and major institutional
investors. When it opens it will likely be the first fully regulated Bitcoin
exchange, doing business with the blessing of New York State and
every other state (most of which copied New York's regulatory framework). Deposits will be insured; accounts will be validated; internal
and external audits will be regularly performed; security standards
will be top-notch. This might sound like shilling, but rest assured
I don't have a stake in the success or failure of Gemini, nor am I
associated in any way with the Winklevoss twins and their complex
financial maneuvers. I have, however, spoken to a number of people
deeply involved in Mt. Gox and its failure and seen the damage it
caused, not only in people's lives but to the Bitcoin community in
general. I feel it's inevitable that if Bitcoin is going to survive and
prosper the only way is through reliable, insured, safe exchanges.

The Bitcoin community has had plenty of chances to create

stable exchanges without regulation, and the inevitable boom/bust cycle of their many attempts nearly destroyed the currency before it had a chance to stabilize. I'd be far more open to criticizing regulated exchanges if reasonable alternatives were proposed and "wild west" style exchanges had proved stable and safe. It's not always the case that history teaches lessons. Sometimes it's just a jumble of coincidence and happenstance. But when amateur businessmen running amateur code with amateur or nonexistent security measures continue to steal bitcoins, or allow them to be stolen thanks to simplistic safekeeping procedures, you can't blame people for choosing a regulated, insured alternative.

If the Winklevoss twins get their fully regulated and well-funded exchange off the ground, it's possible that in ten years it will look like one of the best business decisions of 2015. It has the chance (not infinitesimal), if not to make more money than Facebook at least have a far more transformative effect upon the US and global economy.

PRIVACY AND BANKING PUSHBACK

An Interview with Gavin Smith

Gavin Smith is an international businessman living in Switzerland, who, along with his cofounders, started First Global Credit in October 2014.[49] It is one of the first, if not the absolute first, of what I am terming a third wave of businesses crashing upon the unstable shores of Bitcoin. It's a company entirely uninterested in mining, storing, and exchanging bitcoins (first-wave concerns), or creating better e-wallets, extending the Bitcoin network, and enabling merchants (second-wave infrastructure building). Nor is First Global Credit one of those overheated Silicon Valley startups colonizing a narrow, occasionally nonexistent, sliver of the Bitcoin ecosystem, desperately hoping to exploit it. The third wave isn't about expanding Bitcoin or making it easier for Middle America to use, and it isn't even (much) about Bitcoin for Bitcoin's sake, the idea and the network and the block chain and all the rest. Third-wave businesses accept the fact that Bitcoin is a viable currency that will be around for decades. As such, Bitcoin deserves the same rights as every other national or international currency. First Global Credit is focused on Bitcoin's underutilized status as a pure investment vehicle.

I spoke to Gavin on May 14, 2015, and the discussion began with business boilerplate but soon moved into something more real and, ultimately, falsifiable. I'll present selected quotes from Gavin word for word and include, afterward, a brief translation from cosmopolitan business-ese into standard American English:

> We saw a possibility of Bitcoin's evolution into a genuine investment currency with its own capital markets. . . . The next move is creating a digital currency capital market with its own investment opportunities, and its own possibilities to earn a return. . . . Offering people the opportunity to use bitcoins as collateral or as bitcoin investments in their own right.[50]

Translation: back in ancient times, say 2013, if you had bitcoins and you wanted to make money off them you had exactly one option—stuff them into the digital equivalent of a mattress and hope Bitcoin's price rose. If it did, pull out the valuable wadding and sell it before anything bad happened. This is the "gold ingot" model of asset growth: keep it hidden, hope others are doing the same, and let scarcity drive up the price. It might work but it's a) inefficient and b) highly risky, as there is no room for hedging, either real or metaphorical.

> [Your bitcoins] are sitting there, and they might go up in value, but they are not working for you. To make a transformation into an investment currency there needs to be a mechanism available in native bitcoin form allowing people to use that currency to make investments. To earn an interest rate. A reason to hold it, over and above its long-term potential.[51]

Translation: Bitcoin requires the same level of support as traditional fiat currencies. Nobody puts money into a savings account without an interest rate (however low), and even if banks didn't pay interest they would still provide a significant hedge against loss by theft, via insurance and thick steel doors. Since bitcoins have traditionally been safest in "hard" wallets controlled by a single owner, online Bitcoin banks can't offer this level of security. Handing over your bitcoins to an online exchange has given you, historically, a 7 percent chance every month of losing everything, equal to an interest rate of minus 84 percent per year—a shocking, depressing, and entirely unacceptable state of affairs.[52]

This is a widespread and well-known issue with Bitcoin storage of any sort. The fact that bitcoins are anonymous, or mostly anonymous, or able to be made anonymous with a little effort, makes them tempting for insiders to steal and transfer into a private wallet (exactly the sort of greedy impulse that overcame Slinker and Stinker). There are many solutions to this ongoing problem but from the standpoint of an average customer it boils down to one thing: insurance. If you have a reliable third-party insurer covering Bitcoin deposits, doing for digital currency what the US government does for banks (for free) via deposit insurance, a large measure of worry would drain out of the Bitcoin ecosystem. Insurance would pay in the case of catastrophic bitcoin loss, and since insurance companies require well-organized layers of security protocol before agreeing to insure anything, the fact that insurance is available is noteworthy. That a company is able to procure such insurance is as important as the insurance itself. With both, the issue of theft is largely mitigated. The Wild West period of Bitcoin's history would then be relegated, firmly, to the history books.

First Global Credit offers such insurance and such guarantees. What it does not offer is anonymous investment and anonymous money exchanging, which was possible in the early days of Bitcoin. When asked about anonymous Bitcoin use, Gavin had this to say about privacy in general:

> [Privacy expectations] depend on what you are doing with bitcoins.
> . . . It's no different from the real world. If I go to a broker and
> trade stocks, they are going to need to know who I am and what
> my resources are, if I got my money legally or not—this is an inter-

nationally accepted convention. On the other hand if I buy something from the local video store I pay in cash and take it away and nobody asks or cares why I am buying it.[53]

If you accept Bitcoin as a legitimate currency, you must in fairness apply the same rules to Bitcoin as you apply to the rest. Why should an investor imagine it's possible to buy ten thousand shares of IBM anonymously via Bitcoin when it's not something you are able to do anonymously using dollars, euros, or a briefcase full of gold? Large transactions must be tracked and are the subject of numerous legal regulations. The same thing is happening with Bitcoin. In order to open an account involving massive piles of money, it's necessary to supply a legitimate form of identification capable of being checked and confirmed. Leveraging a large number of bitcoins must be linked to a specific person and these transactions tracked and saved for possible use in later legal investigations (should such an unfortunate event occur, and a subpoena appear). If Bitcoin is going to be embraced and folded into everyday reality it has to follow the path of more traditional currencies. Privacy, however, can be maintained.

> Safeguarding customer privacy is a critical feature. When we speak to people about privacy we frame it like this: not anonymity, as it's unreasonable to expect complete anonymity, but there is a reason to expect privacy. A lot of people in the Bitcoin community lump them together, but we draw a distinction. . . . People do have a right to privacy of information, if not to anonymity. If they are engaging in legitimate business, that should be allowed in a private manner.[54]

Just as banks can't be forced to divulge customer accounts barring a specific court order, savvy Bitcoin companies can incorporate themselves in jurisdictions like Switzerland or Iceland, which have strong privacy laws and corporate guarantees. Some countries are not as suitable as others: both England and the United States have few specific privacy laws applicable to Bitcoin. The United States in fact features what many call *anti-privacy* laws, and has indulged in questionable legal maneuvers in the past, such as seizing internet domain names via judicial order without allowing the owners of the domains due process (or even warning them in advance).[55] Fortunately, it's hard for a customer to tell if a server is sitting in Florida or Norway, allowing companies who care about privacy to pick and choose among the world's many options and select a jurisdiction with both strong privacy laws and a historical record of respecting them.

The general rallying cry of Bitcoin has always been financial efficiency, featuring frictionless transactions, free or nearly so, reducing what had been a sequence of laborious steps into a smooth and easy glide toward the ultimate goal: greater customer control of money and how it is invested, with few (if any) middlemen involved in what should be a simple and private transaction. Banks haven't innovated because it hurts their bottom line; allowing people to freely transfer money would reduce fees and profits by a significant margin, which is why it's never been implemented. Why doesn't Bitcoin concern them? Gavin has a few tentative answers:

> To be honest, people are at a certain stage of development and see Bitcoin as an opportunity, which I think it is. People are looking to use this technology within their business model. . . . Change will effect this profession or that one. . . . It's like the early years of the internet. People knew it would lead to disintermediation[56] but nobody was quite clear where that was going to be; it's still very fluid . . . People are looking and seeing Bitcoin is much more efficient, so how can I fit in, change my business model to take care of it. Adopt it and not be one of the ones left behind. Up till now, a lot of banks wanted Bitcoin to go away, didn't want to give it credibility by getting involved in it. I think we have moved beyond this. They are not going to risk a lot; at the moment Bitcoin is just worth 3.5 billion[57] in total. In Goldman Sachs terms, it's not worth the risk getting involved in a market that size.[58]

Two or three months ago, in a different era of Bitcoin's existence, banks didn't want to associate with Bitcoin, and if they did notice it they invested in research using millions of dollars rather than hundreds of millions—the latter would have been sufficient to become important players in the market. This was either an absurd disregard for what might be the most important financial innovation of the last hundred years, or a calculated attempt to downplay Bitcoin's importance by ignoring the (comparatively) small Bitcoin market, barring it from achieving respectability by association. It turns out that banks, such as Citibank, which brings in billions of dollars in quarterly profits, had other plans. Why get involved in Bitcoin when it's easier and far more profitable to create a new digital currency from scratch, replacing it?

In a response released months after the actual event, Citibank was asked by the English government for input regarding digital currencies, with Bitcoin as the general focus of the survey. The following question/answer session was part of the final published result.

> Q: Should the government intervene to address [money laundering, terrorist financing, and fraud with digital currencies] or maintain the status quo?
> Citibank: Yes the government should consider intervention.
> Q: What are the outcomes of taking no action?
> Citibank: A first step should be to provide immediate guidance to [*sic*] regarding existing digital currencies. There are clearly benefits for businesses and consumers in using these currencies. The existing cannot be controlled unless a better, safer alternative emerges unless governments and banks are at the centre of this technological shift beyond paper and credit cards, it will continue to support financial crime. To be a key participant may mean that banks and governments need to work together to develop digital currencies that supersede the existing physical and electronic solutions.[59]

To repeat: "Banks and governments need to work together to develop digital currencies that supersede the existing physical and electronic solutions." When I read it I thought it brazen, and, when asked, Gavin Smith called it both brazen and shocking. It's an incredibly bold and cynical stance, though perfectly sensible as a purely capitalistic ploy. Since it's obvious Bitcoin is a useful though flawed tool, why not get rid of the flaws? If banks and the government were to issue a new type of digital currency in order to deal with money laundering and the rest of their stated objections, likely removing any real hope of privacy, is there any chance at all that the digital currency would 1) be free of bank-controlled transaction fees, and 2) feature immutable structural barriers stopping the government and/or banks from issuing more digital currency in times of "crisis"?

It's incredibly strange to hear international banks explaining the money-laundering dangers inherent in "anonymous" Bitcoin transactions when they are the same entities accused of participating in money laundering on a global scale, often for years on end. Simon Johnson put it bluntly in his article "Money-Laundering Banks Still Get a Pass from U.S.":

> Money laundering by large international banks has reached epidemic proportions and U.S. authorities are supposedly looking into Citigroup Inc. and JPMorgan Chase & Co. . . . There may be fines, but the largest financial companies are unlikely to face criminal actions or meaningful sanctions [for money laundering]. The Department of Justice has decided that these banks are too big to prosecute to the full extent of the law, though why this also gets employees and executives off the hook remains a mystery. And the Federal Reserve refuses to rescind bank licenses, undermining the credibility, legitimacy and stability of the financial system.[60]

The case of Raul Salinas (brother of Mexico's ex-president) and his $200 million bank account is instructive. When Raul Salinas was arrested and his large-scale theft of government funds exposed, Amy Elliott, his private bank manager at Citibank, testified before a Senate panel regarding the bank's alleged laundering of Raul's money: "This goes in the very, very top of the corporation, this was known . . . on the very top. We are little pawns in this whole thing."[61]

The General Accounting Office of Congress eventually concluded that Citibank had ignored its own safeguards against money laundering and failed to verify the source of Raul Salinas's money. On a more recent note, from 2013:

> Last year U.S. authorities reached settlements with HSBC, Citigroup and UK-headquartered Standard Chartered Bank over alleged money-laundering compliance failures. HSBC agreed in December

to pay more than $1.9 billion to settle an investigation into evidence it shifted cash for rogue nations, terrorists and Mexican drug lords.[62]

Examples abound. While it's certainly possible Citibank is honestly concerned about money laundering and various forms of Bitcoin-related fraud, the activities of the largest multinational banks over the last fifty years have proven that money laundering isn't an issue linked to currency, nor to regulation. The key is prosecution, or lack thereof. If large banks don't suffer from poor press or (more importantly) from sufficiently scary legal or financial penalties after being caught laundering money, there isn't any reason for them to stop. Experts estimate that only 1 percent of all money laundering ever comes to light, and less than 1 percent of 1 percent of money launderers are ever prosecuted and thrown into jail. Lax or nonexistent penalties ensure that such behavior continues unabated, even for banks already charged and convicted with money laundering:

> To see this perverse incentive program in action, consider the recent case of a big money-laundering bank that violated a deferred prosecution agreement with the Justice Department, openly broke U.S. securities law and stuck its finger in the eye of the Fed. This is what John Peace, the chairman of Standard Chartered Plc, and his colleagues managed to get away with March 5. The meaningful consequences for him or his company are precisely zero.[63]

Money laundering, black-market sales of illegal items, and fraud are serious issues that deserve serious attention. What they don't require is a digital currency. By far the biggest "black market" currency in the world is American dollars; by far the largest money launderers are international banks. There aren't any studies showing Bitcoin money laundering is larger, by percent, than that taking placing using old-fashioned greenbacks. To argue for sensible regulation of Bitcoin is one thing; to argue for the abolition of Bitcoin because of illegal activity on the part of a small minority is tantamount to calling for revocation of nearly all bank licenses due to prior accusations, convictions, and ongoing investigations. And that's not going to happen, is it?

I'll let Gavin Smith explain the transformative and possibly world-changing power of Bitcoin:

> As a digital currency enthusiast, I love the idea of digital currency, it's got huge benefits on a societal level that we're only starting to touch on, to do with keeping government in check and making them act more responsibly. People are only starting to talk about the real benefits of digital currency, not just economic benefits of lower fees.
>
> People talk like they're anti-government, but I don't think anti-government is the right way to phrase it. [Bitcoin] enforces responsibility on government, which is different. I think a lot of the community would not want the government to disappear, and obviously people are in favor of government—if the government chooses to be responsible, great, if not there is something that can force a level of discipline or responsibility. . . . I used the word before and I think that sums it up. People want their government to act responsibly, and not mortgage the future for votes now. I think a larger proportion is in favor of this than just the libertarian element.[64]

Argentina, after a long series of economic shocks, found itself in 2013 saddled with moderate but rising inflation. The government responded with what observers call a "loose" financial policy, printing money faster and faster in order to pay for public spending, with the predictable effect that by 2014 the inflation rate was over 41 percent (meaning that any currency you keep in your safe will purchase 41 percent fewer products/services a year later). As a result, everyone converted Argentinean pesos into far more stable American dollars on the black market as quickly as they could. This was a poor solution for all the obvious reasons: it enriched illegal money changers who charged a percentage from every transaction, removed expected tax revenue from the government, and forced people to carry around sacks of cash—which often isn't the safest option. If Bitcoin was more broadly available, open to anyone with a smartphone, the money-changing black market might soon dry up.

Bitcoin allows citizens to escape local economic problems and enter into a global network of exchange. It also points toward a way for citizens to escape from or punish profligate (or irresponsible) actions on the part of their national leaders. Before, citizens were held captive by a despotic government's whims. Foreign transfers of money could be cut off and the local currency manipulated in ways helpful for the ruling elite but damaging to everyone else struggling to survive. After Bitcoin, people have an alternative. There isn't any way to ban Bitcoin unless you shut down the internet, in which case everyone suffers from top to bottom. Should the government start messing around with interest rates or printing scads of currency, or else arbitrarily peg the currency value to a commodity or foreign note or do something widely understood to push the economy into dangerous territory—many might shift their money into Bitcoin. If this happens the government and its rulers are directly impacted through loss of tax revenue, lack of ability to control lending, and a hundred other factors. Banning Bitcoin, as was attempted in Argentina, proved to be all but impossible. Governments are forced to work with Bitcoin, not against it.

For the first time in history, governments can be punished by its citizens for acting irresponsibly. It's a large and powerful stick, unlike any previously available. Instead of a bloody revolution, featuring bombs and guns and jingoistic speeches, Bitcoin opens the door for another possibility: a clean financial revolution. Throw away your money and pull out of the banks and punish everyone who created the ridiculous situation in the first place. Adopt Bitcoin. This time, unlike all the other times, we won't be the only ones to suffer—or even suffer the most.

HEY, LET'S SAVE THE WORLD

Sarah Tyre, COO of Coin.co, a Bitcoin processing solution developed under Alex Waters' Coin Apex "tech incubator" umbrella, is enviably young for her position, remarkably savvy about the nascent Bitcoin ecosystem, and endearingly open about what motivated her interest in Bitcoin.

The story goes something like this: Once upon a time there was a bright young woman who received an undergraduate business degree, followed by a master's degree in business communication, followed by travels to Spain where she kept her eyes wide open about what was going on around her. The Spanish economy had tanked, or was in the process of tanking, and unemployment was high. Her friends cautioned her to be careful, imagining mobs of unruly jobless Spaniards descending upon tourists in a greedy wave. What she found was different—people struggling (no doubt) due to the faltering national economy but engaged (on all levels) with a relatively safe and widely accepted "black market" for goods and services, greatly lessening the pain of the struggling "traditional" economy. The euro functioned as a black-market currency of choice, as anything earned in Spain could be spent in Portugal or France without requiring a currency exchange. Sarah took note.

When she returned to the United States she landed a plum job at a small, successful company that made a lot of money and paid a good salary and expected, in return, its employees to work hard, stay late, and buy in. According to the laws of capitalism, and the glowing promise of the American Dream, she had "made it." She could settle down, pay off school loans, and really start living. The only hitch? She hated it.

> And it just, it was a really good job, it just wasn't for me, like the fit was not good, and so I quit and moved to New York City and decided I'm not taking a job until it's something I can really get behind. These aspects of what was going on with me, it got me to this place where when I heard about Bitcoin . . . of course I was a little confused like everyone is. I wanted to know where to go next, like how can I find out more, so I read Satoshi's white paper. . . . I'm not going to lie and say every word in that made sense, but I had a decent understanding and realized the magnitude of which it could influence the world. I said *Wow this is a big deal.* . . . I'm already thinking about a ton of ways it can be used. . . . There are a lot of different countries that could benefit from it. . . . Not just the currency but the public ledger. If some countries had their spending on the public ledger, think about how much corruption could be avoided.[65]

This is the sort of thing that we imagine died out years ago. What happened to the hard-nosed kill-or-be-killed capitalism of the Gordon Gekko variety?

> I wanted to be part of making a difference, if it's at the operational level or just being part of a company I believe in, I want to work in a sector I can get behind. I also wanted to work with people that were from a similar frame of mind and . . . ethical. This type of new technology attracts people who wanna make money and the technology is so new you can always find ways to get in and [disparaging tone] *make money*, but ultimately it's bigger than that, it's something that can change society across the world. I met some of the people I work with now; they had been around awhile, clearly weren't just in it for the money. They wanted to make a positive change. There was no doubt in my mind this is something I wanted to be a part of. So I started consulting for Coin Apex and CoinCo and ended up running their operations as COO, and I've not looked back since.[66]

I guess it worked out for her OK.

It's often difficult to explain Bitcoin's potential to Americans. This isn't because of fundamental financial ignorance; the reason has everything to do with their privileged position in the world. It's like the clean drinking water problem from the perspective of somebody living in New York State: it's something I vaguely associate with earnest TED lectures and visions of dusty African plains and pestilential disease in eastern Yemen (not to mention absurd California water laws), but since the East Coast typically has fresh water in abundant supply (in fact 21 percent of the world's fresh water is on the American side of the Great Lakes) it's not something I worry about on a daily basis. Fresh water might become the *new oil*, but if that happens the United States is confident in its ability to handle the "problem."

If an American, let's call him George, installs a Bitcoin e-wallet he will suddenly have the ability to use Bitcoin for transactions—but not much else has changed about his life. Like most Americans, George already had access to a credit card, a checking account, banking services, and a strong and well-respected legal system. If George takes out a loan with a bank, the bank quickly issues the agreed-upon amount and expects George to repay it in full. If George uses a credit card, he assumes it will work, barring an error of his own making. Bitcoin is thought of as a first-world luxury, a type of super cash, the (inevitable) integration of money and the internet, an evolution of the Netflix type where we went from unhappy bulky video tapes to slim DVDs to rentals over the internet to finally, for many of us, streaming video anytime and all the time. The internet is a convenience, enabling what we could already do but making it happen faster.

From this perspective it's easy to understand how many Americans, or Europeans, or anyone living with a stable banking system, might view Bitcoin as "the latest gadget," gadgets being (by definition) gee whiz and glitzy and neat but not essential. You play with a gadget but you don't fight wars with it—or use it to change the world.

Let's leave the comfortable surroundings of Ross Ulbricht's cold and clammy San Francisco, or Satoshi's presumed Japan, or the over-heated hothouse atmosphere of New York City's Bitcoin community and wander instead over the Atlantic Ocean to a country of forty-seven million people, wedged between Kenya and Mozambique: Tanzania. Its name is a portmanteau of the two major states that were united to create the country, Tanganyika and Zanzibar.

Technically the United Republic of Tanzania, the country unites a complicated patchwork of tribes and cultures and owes its existence to a typically horrifying colonial past, beginning with Vasco da Gama, who in 1500 arbitrarily claimed the territory for Portugal. By 1700, Saif bin Sultan had taken over, making Zanzibar the center of the Arab slave trade. Almost the entire population was enslaved, and over 700,000 natives were shipped out of the country for sale at distant ports. By 1850 the Belgians and Germans had arrived, with the Germans ultimately taking over the country and putting down armed rebellions with what at the time was typical restraint (i.e., brutality widely inflicted on whatever natives happened to be standing nearby). After World War I the English took over from the Germans, and after World War II the country was named a United Nations Trust Territory, removing England from direct control. A slow-moving but inevitable independence movement culminated in 1964 when Tanganyika united with Zanzibar and became Tanzania.

With a yearly GDP average of $600 per Tanzanian, the economy, though supported by strong mineral and agricultural resources, can't be called flourishing.[67] The average Tanzanian has no access to banking, and only 14 percent have reliable electricity. However, and this is not unusual for the region, cell phone usage is amazingly high: 73 percent of adults own one or more cell phone, and the percentage is climbing.[68] The country essentially skipped over the "landline" phase of existence, leveraging huge savings over more traditional first-world countries, whose accreted mass of wires and cables, once a great resource, now constitute a drag upon the economy, with giants such as AT&T actively petitioning the government for permission to get out of the unprofitable landline business.

With cell phones came applications such as mobile banking. And with mobile banking, Bitcoin steps into the spotlight.

The Bitcoin-based company BitPesa was founded in 2014, and allows customers to send Bitcoins to a Tanzanian or Kenyan cell phone, where the bitcoins are placed into a well-supported mobile-phone money account. From there the bitcoins can be spent directly with merchants who support the service or turned into Tanzania shillings (the local currency) at an exchange rate of 1 percent or less. This wasn't possible two years ago, much less ten. The so-called remittance market, in which money is sent home from expatriates living and working in countries with better pay/opportunities, is notorious for its high fees; MoneyGram transfers to Tanzania are in the 20 percent range, with Western Union well above 10 percent. This is money taken directly from the poorest among us and is priced to extract maximum value regardless of actual cost to the company: "To wire $500 to Mexico from Dallas costs $14. To send the same amount from New York costs $25."[69]

This is the expected capitalist behavior, which puts a premium on profit and isn't concerned with possible exploitation of the poor, who often don't have the time or ability to search around for money transfer alternatives (if they even exist in their location). It costs less to wire money to Mexico in Dallas because of supply and demand— presumably there are more remittance alternatives given Dallas's significant Mexican-American population, while in New York you have to take what you get. Something unusual, such as wiring pesos from Mexico to Tanzania, isn't feasible; it often involves two or three steps, losing 10 percent (or more) at each step, as pesos are turned into dollars and then into Tanzanian shillings. The total fees could reach 35 percent or higher, making the entire process a dubious proposition, only undertaken by the desperate.

The fact that Bitcoin is global and rigorously democratic in its usage is a vast improvement over traditional "location-based" price gouging. It doesn't matter where you are; BitPesa certainly doesn't know or care. As long as you have Bitcoins to send they'll happily assist in your transaction. You won't have to go to a grimy teller, squinting behind bullet-proof glass, in offices often found in neighborhoods not known for their safety or convenience. Instead, using BitPesa, you make the transfer in the safety of your own backyard, almost instantly, using your phone.[70]

Most Americans don't transfer money overseas,[71] and improvement in this market is relatively invisible. But the overall effect for those it does touch is substantial. Every time somebody uses Bitcoin to transfer money across the world, a small chunk of service fees (and other weaselly charges traditionally associated with this type of transaction) are swept away. Money skimmed off every remittance, once going to billion-dollar global corporations, is instead retained by those who actually worked to earn the money. Bitcoin functions, in this small example, as an equalizing agent, removing barriers set up over many years by institutions that profited greatly by making this sort of monetary movement difficult, time-consuming, and expensive, despite vastly improved methods (behind the scenes) supporting such transfers. It's hard to imagine how the remittance market could have been shaken up without something like Bitcoin; with vast profits steadily available, and little consumer outcry due to the relative powerlessness of those being served, change might otherwise have been impossible.

Central to Sarah Tyre's vision of the future is Bitcoin's ability to improve the lives of the poorest and most desperate citizens. Global economic improvement takes precedence over geeking out over Bitcoin's cryptographic sophistication or libertarian desires for a nongovernmental currency or a whole raft of associated political and philosophical arguments.

Sarah's ideology is both flexible and pragmatic. The goal is to lessen human suffering, but not at all costs: what you choose to do should be legal, ethical, and most importantly effective. This isn't the flip side of Ross Ulbricht's extreme libertarianism, where a theory is proffered as the only solution to a problem. For Sarah and others like her the ultimate goal is helping others, and she's happy to do whatever it takes to get there, using whatever methods are available. If that involves Bitcoin—so be it.

She summed it up this way:

> The people I work with and surround myself with are true believers in this technology. They could easily be making much, much more money working as developers for larger organizations or even other startups that are in slightly more mature and investable industries. If the Bitcoin ecosystem does not have reputable tech and responsible members, Bitcoin cannot meet its maximum potential. Personally, I enjoy working with those of a similar mindset who strive for innovation rather than profits—who choose collaborative exploration over self-interest. It sounds so cliché, but I mean that's the truth of it. I want to change the world.[72]

For those working in the Bitcoin space, the Winklevoss twins are viewed far differently than they are depicted in the mainstream press and social media venues. The Winklevoss twins are thought to be, if not true believers,[73] at least serious and mature players in the Bitcoin universe, having seen the possibilities before most and taken advantage of their prescience. It's not much of a stretch to wonder if the Winklevoss twins, through their work at setting up a regulated exchange and popularizing the currency at every opportunity, are not doing more—indirectly or not—for the global poor than many well-meaning Americans. Yes, Bitcoin pioneers and entrepreneurs are going to become rich and establish fortunes and occasionally behave badly like everyone else, with one major difference: Bitcoin profits are often diverted from existing institutions and partially redistributed to consumers as savings.

Thanks to Bitcoin, you can send money to Tanzania for a total transaction fee of 3 percent. Imagine what that rate will be in a few years, or ten. Bitcoin increases monetary efficiency and has the ability to place this power in the hands of consumers. It's not something happening behind a bank's closed doors, allowing them to transfer funds back and forth (across borders, across the world) at light speed, giving them a few additional percentage points of profit on top of whatever they already make. The frictionless nature of Bitcoin is there for all to see and leverage equally.

INCREMENTAL PROGRESS

In 1877 Thomas Edison patented an invention neither technologically complex nor arising from a significant mechanical or chemical advancement—each individual part of the machine could have been bought at any small-town hardware store—yet it shocked everyone exposed to it to a degree almost metaphysical. The phonograph wasn't a result of eons-long striving for an obvious goal, such as heavier-than-air flight; it wasn't an application of a cutting-edge technology to transportation, which defined the slow development of efficient steam locomotives; it wasn't a clever use of electricity, harnessed to generate a magnetic field or heat a filament to incandescent brightness or a thousand other useful tasks; no, the phonograph abruptly proved, in mechanical terms immune to counterargument, that sound could be recorded, stored, and played back with reasonably high fidelity.

Before 1877 this was thought impossible, and the phonograph had few predecessors either fanciful or material. Recorded sound wasn't part of early science-fiction,[1] which had a much easier time imagining flying to the moon or burrowing beneath the Earth's crust to discover a primordial world hidden in massive caves,[2] than a "speaking machine." Scientific interest in sound recording was similarly scarce; however, in 1857, a French printer named Édouard-Léon Scott de Martinville patented a machine he called a Phonautograph[3] that recorded sounds waves in a thin deposit of soot. The Phonautograph was simply intended, as its etymology indicates, to write sound onto paper, nothing more, and few (at the time) imagined it possible for the recorded waves to be used to replicate the sound that had created them.[4] Edison's sudden discovery of a practical method to playback recorded sound, arriving as soon as he started serious experimentation, was entirely unexpected—the idea itself so difficult to imagine that the likelihood of material success was thought, at the time, miniscule. The shock of discovery is best reported by Edison himself:

> From my experiments on the telephone I knew of the power of a diaphragm to take up sound vibrations, as I had made a little toy which when you recited loudly in the funnel would work a pawl connected to the diaphragm; and this, engaging a ratchet-wheel, served to give continuous rotation to a pulley. This pulley was connected by a cord to a little paper toy representing a man sawing wood. Hence, if one shouted: "Mary had a little lamb," etc., the paper man would start sawing wood. *I reached the conclusion that if I could record the movements of the diaphragm properly I could cause such records to reproduce the original movements imparted to the diaphragm by the voice, and thus succeed in recording and reproducing the human voice.*
>
> Instead of using a disk I designed a little machine, using a cylinder provided with grooves around the surface. Over this was to be placed tin-foil, which easily received and recorded the movements of the diaphragm. . . . [I]t was [soon] finished; the foil was put on; I then shouted "Mary had a little lamb," etc. I adjusted the reproducer, and the machine reproduced it perfectly. I was never so taken back in my life. Everybody was astonished. I was always afraid of things that worked the first time. Long experience proved that there were great drawbacks found generally before they could be made commercial; but here was something there was no doubt of.[5]

The phonograph was a bolt from the blue, instantly and hugely profitable, a physical manifestation of an idea so implausible it rarely if ever made it into the most fantastic dream-visions of futurists, prophets, and opium-eaters. That which was once deemed impossible could be purchased at a reasonable (and ever-diminishing) price at newly minted department stores the world over.

Bitcoin's invention couldn't have been more different. Not only was the concept of a digital currency fully described by the Cypherpunks in the 1980s, each individual piece of Bitcoin had to undergo independent development in order to reach a state capable of supporting

Satoshi's ultimate design. The internet had to be broadly distributed, easily available, and robust. Personal computers had to be powerful enough to solve the requisite mathematical problems with sufficient complexity to allow for theoretical (and real-world) security. Open-source software and non-centralized development had to prove itself capable of reliable long-term results. Hashing functions of sufficient randomness and complexity had to be publicly available and broadly trusted. A thousand other components were necessary, both tech-nological and theoretical, and ongoing experimentation was con-stant, from e-Gold (1996) to b-money (1998)[6] to Karma (2003)[7] to Bitcoin (2009)—with plenty more scattered between. Far from being unexpected, a cryptocurrency like Bitcoin was the explicit focus of research and development, and when the pieces were finally available Satoshi was able to step up and put them into place. Cryptocurrency fans and Cypherpunks and anyone interested in alternative curren-cies for political or theoretical reasons all viewed Bitcoin for what it was—the latest of a long string of experiments and (mostly) failures, the fulfillment of a longstanding dream: a mathematically secure and anonymous online currency.

The phonograph was huge leap forward, but strangely enough Edison's first prototype was remarkably close to the phonograph's developmental endpoint. If you took a record player from 1965 and sent it back in time to 1877 for Edison to inspect, he could have had taken it apart and understood its functioning within hours. The only "real" improvements in phonograph technology were enhanced etching of sound waves (in the form of vinyl records) and reading of sound waves (a diamond needle wiggling between electromagnets), which worked together to output electrically augmented (amplified) music. Edison's solution, writing and reading of sound waves onto a physical medium, was essentially unchanged, and some of his early models were capable of both recording live input and playing back pre-recorded sound, features record players firmly rejected (creating the recorded music industry in the process). It wasn't until the digital revolution that Edison's invention took a leap forward; send an iPod back in time and Edison would have viewed it with utter incompre-hension. Nevertheless, the phonograph had a hundred-year reign as the default technology for high-quality sound reproduction, an astonishing run given the massive technological changes happening in almost every other part of the economy.

Bitcoin isn't the modern digital version of the phonograph, a dazzling invention that in its birth essentially predicted its mature form. Bitcoin isn't seen by anyone close to the technology as the "final stage" of cryptocurrency, simply an early and successful example—yet one with clear flaws. These deficiencies are not of the sort that will undermine the currency; Bitcoin is remarkably stable and has survived over five years without anyone suffering a significant loss due to bugs or malevolent hacks to the network—this despite massive rewards for anyone capable of such a feat (tens of millions of dollars are at stake, possibly hundreds of millions).[8] Given its overall security record and current level of user confidence, Bitcoin has never looked healthier. Its value has stabilized; rapid price increases and decreases might be a thing of the past. Bitcoin's penetration into the US economy is continuing to grow; its global share is on the rise; more people are using bitcoins than ever before. Isn't Bitcoin the beginning and end of cryptocurrencies?

Not by a long shot. It's easy to find things to dislike about Bitcoin and easy to improve it—people have done so by the dozens. Because Bitcoin is open source, it's relatively straightforward to create an "alternative" Bitcoin by copying Bitcoin's source code, tweaking it, and releasing it to the public. This is sometimes done as a cash grab; a typical "pump and dump" scheme of this type was Auroracoin[9] in Iceland, which had a brief moment of popularity and rising prices during the long Nordic summer, during which the initial creators of Auroracoin sold out, realizing large gains, while the rest of the investors saw the currency price plummet, never to recover. Far more legitimate Bitcoin alternatives have also been created to fix obvious shortcomings, such as Bitcoin's dependence on the SHA-256 hashing function to mine bitcoins.

When viewed as a distributed computer (with each node doing its bit), the Bitcoin network, as a whole, is the most powerful supercomputer on the planet.[10] Yet almost all of its computing power is focused on mining, which uses the SHA-256 function to "solve" and secure blocks in the block chain. These block chain solutions have absolutely no value in any other field of human endeavor, as they are tied directly to the specific content of the mined blocks; Bitcoin is essentially wasting its remarkable computer power on the digital equivalent of twiddling its thumbs. Imagine a better system, where a Bitcoin-like currency does normal Bitcoin stuff but instead of locking down the blocks solely via SHA-256 it calculates immensely complicated multi-body orbital solutions; or plows through thousands of high-resolution medical scans, running a suite of diagnostic tests, searching for anomalies; or helps to calculate the dynamic forces pressing against a concrete barrier during a hurricane. There are endless projects for a massive supercomputer to dig into, and Bitcoin isn't doing any of it. As a result, many view its mining scheme as nothing more than a waste of electricity: turning power into heat via socially worthless calculations.[11]

Bitcoin's comparative weakness in this area gave rise to alternatives such as Primecoin,[12] similar to Bitcoin in many ways but using a different mining scheme: instead of "wasting" time running millions of SHA-256 operations, Primecoin miners search for prime numbers, in particular sequences of primes called Cunningham chains,[13] which when found both secure the Primecoin block chain and contribute to our overall understanding of prime number distribution. That might not sound like much of an improvement over Bitcoin's mining scheme, but prime numbers have many applications both within pure mathematics and without, and strictly speaking Primecoin is a clear improvement compared to Bitcoin as it retains all of Bitcoin's basic functionality while substituting a far more useful mining methodology. The only reason Primecoin isn't worth as much as Bitcoin is that it wasn't first and isn't being used as much and hasn't seen the same type of mass adoption.

Primecoin isn't the only alternative digital currency. More are popping up all the time, many with features that improve (in ways minor or major) upon Bitcoin's basic functionality.[14] While it's overwhelmingly likely none will quickly supplant Bitcoin in global value, it's not hard to imagine such an event occurring sometime in the near future. Bitcoin represents not an end but a beginning; it is the "proof of concept" for "proof of work" cryptocurrencies, and it has inspired (and will continue to inspire) a vast number of cryptocurrency alternatives.

Bitcoin's incremental development defined not only its birth and growth but its ultimate fate: obsolescence. Bitcoin should be understood not as a singular form of digital currency to be accepted or repudiated but the start of long-term public experimentation with cryptocurrencies of various types. It's also important to remember that Bitcoin's not just a currency; even if Bitcoin someday stops being used to buy and sell things, it's still bequeathed us the block chain, which might well be the more transformative technology in the long run. Beyond the technological details, Bitcoin allows us to imagine things that were, previously, either difficult to envision or easily discarded as unachievable. Imagine removing bank and credit card involvement from your financial life; discarding the national currency; reasserting one's ability to spend and purchase without constant tracking and oversight. Bitcoin's real power lies in broadening our theoretical and real-world horizons. Will citizens of a financially beleaguered country rise up one day and resist what is being foisted upon them, move to Bitcoin *en masse*, and leave their national currency (and corrupt or inept government) in ruins? It might never happen, but we can finally ask the question—and think seriously about its feasibility. Bitcoin, or its cryptocurrency progeny, are here to stay, and will continue to inspire entrepreneurs, visionaries, and hardscrabble devotees of realpolitik the world over.

ACKNOWLEDGMENTS

I would like to thank, first and foremost, my wonderful agent, Sheree Bykofsky; all those who took the time to explain to me, patiently and in plain English, how Bitcoin does and does not function (Ittay Eyal, Emin "Gun" Sirer, Alex Waters, Sarah Tyre, and many more); Amy Reading and Jay Farmer, for literary, emotional, and liquid support; the Constance Saltonstall Foundation, who kickstarted the project with a writing retreat; to my parents for a blissful and trauma-free childhood; Nancy and Tim Wilder for stepping up to the plate in various ways and hitting what were minimally triples and typically homeruns; Janet Rosen and Marcie Terman, who got me in touch with the incomparable Gavin Smith; Poornima Apte for advice and guidance; the Prometheus team (Steven and Peter and Jake and all the rest); and last but not least my long-suffering editor, Sheila Stewart, immensely competent at sifting silver from dross.

NOTES

INTRODUCTION: SPENDING SYMBOLS AND
BUYING POTATOES

    1. Seth Schiesel, "Payoff Still Elusive in Internet Gold Rush," *New York Times*, Jan. 2, 1997, http://www.nytimes.com/1997/01/02/business/payoff-still-elusive-in -internet-gold-rush.html.

    2. Ibid.

    3. Uninhabited by Americans, not Native Americans. The Northern Paiute had lived in the area for centuries, and a sudden influx of miners, with an insatiable demand for water and lumber, caused tensions to rise. By 1860, with emotions running high, the brothers Oscar and James Williams, traders at Williams Station (near Virginia City, center of the Comstock Lode), trigged the Pyramid Lake War. After kidnapping and raping two twelve-year-old Paiute girls and stuffing them in a hole beneath the cabin for safekeeping, the brothers were surprised by a band of Paiute looking for the missing children. One of the girls managed to loosen her gag and scream for help, resulting in their discovery and the immediate killing of the brothers. This led to panic among the settlers, who imagined the Northern Paiute on a generalized rampage, and they quickly organized a militia— promptly defeated by the Paiute, fighting in mountainous territory they knew far better than their opponents. After the settlers' defeat, the Federal and State governments got involved and quickly overwhelmed the Paiute with numerical and technological superiority, ending the war within the year.

    4. In *The Roar and the Silence: A History of Virginia City and the Comstock Lode* (University of Nevada Press, 1998), Ronald James lays out the rather gruesome details. Henry Comstock, after conning various miners out of their rightful claims, and making himself such a boastful presence in the boomtown that his name became unfairly associated with the strike, wasn't capable of handling the fortunes he swindled and soon went bankrupt. He committed suicide young and impoverished. Peter O'Riley, another codiscoverer of the lode, held onto his money better than most but soon became infected with gold mania. He spent his

fortune tunneling into the Sierra Nevada mountains looking for a gold deposit as large as Comstock's silver. Lightning of this sort never strikes the same person twice, and he found nothing of value, squandering his fortune in the process. He was soon diagnosed with "degenerative insanity" and died in a sanatorium. Patrick McLaughlin, an early claimant on what would later be a multimillion-dollar mine, sold out early, spent his small profits within the month, was quickly reduced to penury, and was buried in a pauper's grave. These sorts of stories are typical. It's a commonplace that when fate wishes to punish you, it gives you exactly what you desire. These are noteworthy examples.

5. Strangely enough, another Finney, Hal, was the first person to download the Bitcoin client, the first to install and run it, and the first to "mine" a bitcoin. In a terrible example of historical synchronicity, he was diagnosed with Amyotrophic Lateral Sclerosis shortly after mining his first bitcoin, and died in 2014. An immensely distinguished computer scientist, Finney was on the forefront of a shockingly high percentage of cryptographic advances in the last fifty years. A libertarian who carried Ayn Rand's *Atlas Shrugged* around with him in high school, he was an early cypherpunk and helped develop PGP (Pretty Good Privacy), now widely used for internet security, as well as for anonymous email "remailers" and a host of other applications. His final years were dedicated to Bitcoin's source code and related developments. By all accounts, Finney was a brilliant man whose intelligence never impinged upon his humanity—nor his humility. He was also the first person to describe a sophisticated version of a Bitcoin double-spending attack, requiring a mined block, which was subsequently named the "Finney Attack." (For Hal's original description of this (possible) Bitcoin exploit, see https://bitcointalk.org/index.php?topic=3441.msg48384#msg48384.)

6. In 2013, Alan Greenspan was forthright in his opinion: "It's a bubble. It has to have intrinsic value. You have to really stretch your imagination to infer what the intrinsic value of Bitcoin is. I haven't been able to do it. Maybe somebody else can." (Jeff Kearns, "Greenspan Says Bitcoin a Bubble Without Intrinsic Currency Value," *Bloomberg Business*, Dec. 4, 2013, http://www.bloomberg.com/news/articles/2013-12-04/greenspan-says-bitcoin-a-bubble-without-intrinsic-currency-value.) This isn't the first time Greenspan failed to wrap his head around a new invention; his refusal to regulate derivatives based on securitized real-estate instruments is widely credited with causing, or at least exacerbating, the 2008 Global Financial Crisis. (See Robert Lenzner, "Greenspan Finally Wakes Up to Fear and Euphoria as Market Forces," *Forbes*, Oct. 24, 2013, http://www.forbes.com/sites/robertlenzner/2013/10/24/what-alan-greenspan-learned-from-the-2008-crisis/.)

7. Michael Casey, "Sacramento Kings to Accept Bitcoin," *Wall Street Journal*,

Jan. 16, 2014, http://www.wsj.com/articles/SB10001424052702304603704579323352532979922.

8. Alex Walsh, "Bitcoins in Birmingham: Freshfully Now Accepts the Hot New Digital Currency," *AL.com*, Dec. 12, 2013, http://www.al.com/business/index.ssf/2013/12/bitcoins_in_birmingham_freshfu.html.

9. "Gross Profit for Visa (V) 2014," *Wikinvest*, http://www.wikinvest.com/stock/Visa_(V)/Data/Gross_Profit/2014.

10. Not an insult; the phrase describes those who wish to return to the gold standard.

11. For a critical view of gold bugs, see Paul Krugman, "The Gold Bug Variations," *Slate*, Nov. 23, 1996, http://www.slate.com/articles/business/the_dismal_science/1996/11/the_gold_bug_variations.html.

12. Much of the current anger is aimed at Obama and his administration's economic platform, rather than Bush I or Bush II or Clinton in his boom years, which makes one wonder what's really at the root of the most vociferous criticism.

13. Nobel-prize winning "liberal" economist Paul Krugman and "conservative" economist Martin Feldstein both agreed in 2010 that the 2009 stimulus had been too far too small. Feldstein admitted that "he, like some of the economists advising President Obama, underestimated the size of the economic problem in 2008–2009." The economic effect on the United States if its currency had remained pegged to the value of gold, making it impossible for the government to generate more than a tiny stimulus, boggles the mind.

(Eileen Appelbaum, "Panelists: Stimulus Was Too Small, More Action Needed to Jumpstart Economy," *CEPR Blog*, CEPR: Center for Economic and Policy Research, Oct. 6, 2010, http://www.cepr.net/blogs/cepr-blog/panelists-stimulus-was-too-small-more-action-needed-to-jumpstart-economy.)

CHAPTER 1: SATOSHI NAKAMOTO: WHAT HE INVENTED

1. In 1526, William Tyndale translated the Bible into English from various Greek and Hebrew sources. It was the first book to be printed (not transcribed) and was widely distributed throughout Europe. As the Roman Catholic Church deemed any biblical translation into English to be heresy, Tyndale was tracked down, seized, tried, and convicted. Sentenced to burn at the stake, various sympathetic authorities petitioned, successfully, for him to be strangled before his body was consigned to the flames. A mere two years later King Henry VIII, having broken from the Catholic church, authorized the creation of the Great Bible, the

first authorized edition of the Bible in English, which was heavily influenced by Tyndale's earlier translation. It is estimated that over 80 percent of the Great Bible, and a similar percentage of the King James Bible (appearing eighty years later), match Tyndale's original source. The King James Bible, widely considered to be the only masterpiece ever to arise from extensive committee meetings (involving forty-seven scholars working in six groups), nevertheless owes a huge debt to one man, Tyndale. The open-source development path of Bitcoin followed a similar course: a dedicated initial creator (Satoshi) released his creation into the world, and after it achieved wide distribution he stepped out of the limelight. Satoshi was no martyr, but it's notable that his code base was stable enough to serve as the foundation for a stable and reliable system.

2. Juola & Associates, "text analysis experts," famous for outing J. K. Rowling's authorship of *The Cuckoo's Calling* under a pseudonym, has done work on Satoshi's forum posts and other textual leavings for various journalists over the years. Results have been broadly negative when attempting to link Satoshi to a specific person, but Satoshi's writing is remarkably consistent as a corpus, indicating single authorship. For a typical example, see Andy Greenberg, "Nakamoto's Neighbor: My Hunt for Bitcoin's Creator Led to a Paralyzed Crypto Genius," *Forbes*, Mar. 25, 2014, http://www.forbes.com/sites/andygreenberg/2014/03/25/satoshi-nakamotos-neighbor-the-bitcoin-ghostwriter-who-wasnt/.

3. Benjamin Wallace, "The Rise and Fall of Bitcoin," *Wired*, Nov. 23, 2011, http://www.wired.com/2011/11/mf_bitcoin/.

4. Weekends and holidays didn't alter Satoshi's posting schedule, so it's unlikely this "silent interval" represented hours working at a job; if this were so, weekends (when Satoshi was off work) would have generated at least a few Bitcoin-related posts during the "silent interval" over the years. But that's not what's been found.

5. See Sergio Demian Lerner, "The Well Deserved Fortune of Satoshi Nakamoto, Bitcoin Creator, Visionary and Genius," *Bitslog*, Apr. 17, 2013, https://bitslog.wordpress.com/2013/04/17/the-well-deserved-fortune-of-satoshi-nakamoto, as well as associated articles. The author presents a convincing and well-received theory about Satoshi's early mining habits, total bitcoin holdings, and percentage still remaining unspent.

6. The price of a bitcoin is entirely determined by the market, in precisely the same way the value of a US dollar fluctuates in value against foreign currencies. A bitcoin is worth exactly what somebody is willing to pay for it, and bitcoins can be purchased at Bitcoin exchanges using most major currencies—i.e., you give them a thousand dollars, and they send a thousand dollars' worth of bitcoins to your Bitcoin e-wallet.

7. Or worse yet listen to as he gives an amusing and generally content-free ten-minute TED lecture.

8. In 2010, WikiLeaks released a vast trove of embarrassing information involving the Iraq War, the Afghanistan War, and unredacted US Diplomatic cables. The United States put heavy global pressure on various banks and financial institutions to halt or slow funding of WikiLeaks, causing significant strain to the organization.

9. Satoshi Nakamoto, "dfg: PC World Article on Bitcoin," *Bitcoin Forum*, Dec. 11, 2010, https://bitcointalk.org/index.php?topic=2216.msg29280#msg29280.

10. Except for one message, posted March 7, 2014, in which Satoshi stated, "I am not Dorian Nakamoto." Dorian Nakamoto was an American living in Temple City, California, who had been publicly identified as "Satoshi Nakamoto" in a March 6 article by *Newsweek* magazine—a hypothesis later resoundingly refuted.

11. On August 27, 2010, Satoshi responded to a very detailed message board thread, showing himself to be fully up to date regarding the Austrian School of economic thought. See Satoshi Nakamoto, "Bitcoin Does NOT Violate Mises' Regression Theorem," *Bitcoin Forum*, Aug. 27, 2010, https://bitcointalk.org/index .php?topic=583.msg11405#msg11405.

12. Before 2009, digital currencies were generally thought to be illegal, or unfeasible, or simply silly. In a 2008 article typical for the period, Stephen Johnson writes, regarding the short-lived digital currency Beenz, "Along with International banking regulations, the people behind Beenz also ignored the fact that you'd have to be effing crazy to invest any money in a completely unsecured fake currency created by a fly-by-night internet startup that couldn't even use the letter 'Z' correctly. Instead of using, say, your credit cards to buy porn. In the end, traditional currencies weren't shaken by the been." (Stephen Johnson, "Epic Fail: World Changing Technology," *G4*, June 19, 2008, http://www.g4tv.com/thefeed/ blog/post/686374/epic-fail-world-changing-technology/.)

13. Economic textbooks are full of such thought experiments; what follows is a mild and reasonable example.

14. Ludwig von Mises wasn't the first to come up with this theory of how currency developed, but he rigorously argued it so successfully that it slowly became the accepted economic view. For further details regarding Ludwig's thinking, and the so-called "Austrian School of Economics" in general (oft larded with heavy libertarian content), visit the Mises Institute ("Austrian Economics, Freedom, and Peace") at https://mises.org/.

15. All Satoshi quotes, unless otherwise noted, are from message board posts. Refer to http://satoshi.nakamotoinstitute.org/posts/ for a complete collection.

16. See http://satoshi.nakamotoinstitute.org/. The "massive overhead"

Satoshi criticizes refers to bank or credit card fees, which are often higher than the value of the transaction. For example, it's not feasible to purchase something with a credit card that costs a quarter, as the "minimum" transaction fee for credit card charges is greater than a quarter. Allowing such transactions would quickly bankrupt a merchant; thus these types of micropayments are impossible in many countries.

17. By the time 2015 rolled around, Lauriston Castle had become magnificent, fruit of endless additions and expansions, adding a wing here and a great hall there when its owners could afford it, and closely resembled something you would associate with the word "castle." It didn't when Law was born. A mediaeval stronghold located on the site had been destroyed in 1544 after bitter fighting, and a modest tower house was its 1590 replacement. For the most part a solid unadorned rectangle of stone, it featured two corbelled corner turrets bristling with arrow slits reminding everyone, nervously, of the previous castle's destruction, and it resembled a military installation far more than an elegant country estate.

18. Perfectly normal for the period; it was a rare upper-class family that lacked at least one profligate wastrel. Most were happy if they didn't have two or three.

19. John Philip Wood, *A Sketch of the Life and Projects of John Law of Lauriston, Comptroller General of the Finances in France* (London: Peter Hill and George Kearsley, 1791), p. 9.

20. Rue Quincampoix was the "Wall Street" of Paris at the time. Traders congregated in the street and, in chaotic and often hysterical scenes, swapped thousands of shares every hour.

21. Antoin E. Murphy, *John Law: Economic Theorist and Policy-Maker* (Oxford: Oxford University Press, 1997), p. 2.

22. E-Gold is discussed extensively in the next chapter.

23. For a good summary, refer to "Money From Nothing," *The Economist*, Mar. 15, 2014, http://www.economist.com/news/finance-and-economics/21599053 -chronic-deflation-may-keep-bitcoin-displacing-its-fiat-rivals-money.

24. Steve Forbes, "Bitcoin: Whatever It Is, It's Not Money!" *Forbes*, Apr. 16, 2013, http://www.forbes.com/sites/steveforbes/2013/04/16/bitcoin -whatever-it-is-its-not-money/.

CHAPTER 2: SATOSHI NAKAMOTO:
HOW BITCOIN WORKS

1. Bobby (anonymous), telephone interview with author, May 3, 2015.

2. This is an excellent Bitcoin address to use for testing; send bitcoins to this

wallet, tiny fractions or multiple thousands—any amount will be gratefully received by its owner (me).

3. She would give a Bitcoin exchange twenty dollars and her bitcoin address, and then would send twenty dollars' worth of bitcoins to her e-wallet (minus commission).

4. Email addresses used to look pretty ugly, if we are honest about it and remember the old days, how weird the @ looked stuck in the middle with a .com at the end.

5. As of mid-2015.

6. This is a problem that's been solved, or is rapidly in the process of being solved. Bitcoin exchanges allow you to purchase bitcoins with cash or credit cards, or sell your existing bitcoins for some flavor of fiat currency. The Coinbase exchange and the Winklevoss twins' Gemini exchange are based in the United States, and both claim to be legal and regulated. They are likely to be fighting it out for market share in the near future.

7. Stolen in traditional ways, that is. If a thief purloins your laptop, containing your e-wallet, it's unlikely you will lose any bitcoins because the thief won't know and can't guess your password. There are other ways to lose bitcoins of course. A few trusting people actually use "Web Wallets," which are Bitcoin wallets hosted by somebody running a server somewhere. Typically the company hosting the Web Wallet has access to all their customer's passwords and (in theory) bitcoins, raising the possibility of large-scale theft. Software e-wallets, running on a computer or phone, don't transmit passwords over the internet; the password/passphrase lock is strictly local. It's possible and really common (and a good idea) to "copy" an e-wallet to a backup drive or other computer. You're able to access/use the same e-wallet from multiple locations; a thief stealing one of the e-wallets doesn't impact your use of the other ones. It's the same idea as running multiple email clients on multiple devices—you can use any of them to access your email, and if one is stolen it doesn't affect your email unless the thief figures out the password and starts tampering.

8. This simplified example requires most of the participants to be honest. Under this scheme it would be possible to write down a fictional transaction and have it propagate through many villages before the person being stolen from even realizes what's going on. For example, if Fred writes down "Julie gives Fred 1000 VCNs" one morning (and she really hasn't), by evening everyone on the island, except perhaps Julie, who angrily refuses to write it on her personal chalkboard since she knows it's false, would have this transaction listed, and it would "seem" to be valid. Bitcoin gets around this problem of tampering with transactions by essentially "locking down" the chalkboards every few minutes, and requiring a

permission password (from the person losing VCNs) before any transaction can be submitted. This is impossible to achieve with chalkboards, but easy with computers.

9. Because every Bitcoin node has all the Bitcoin transactions ever transmitted, the network is extremely robust. Were all Europe to lose electricity, Bitcoin would still be up and running (if a bit slower), since the rest of the world's nodes could still communicate with each other and they all share up-to-date transaction data. In fact, all the electricity in the world could fail except for one country—for example, Iceland—and Bitcoin would likely struggle on, using nodes located in Iceland that were still active. As the rest of the world slowly regained electricity, and the internet expanded, Bitcoins nodes in other countries would suddenly burst into life, contact the nodes in Iceland that had never failed, and copy the latest transactions (coming from inside Iceland) to their records. If electricity or the internet goes down on a worldwide basis, the Bitcoin network will slowly struggle back to life as electricity is restored, without loss of data or missing any new transactions (since none could be made). Should electricity / the internet be forever banished from our world, Bitcoin and every other currency under the sun will become equally worthless, and what will matter most will be guns, gold, and goods. Canned goods. Lots and lots of canned goods.

10. Bitcoin functions like a checking account with the following caveats: 1) there is no bank in the middle, charging fees and tracking the flow of money, 2) Bitcoin is nearly instantaneous, while checks (in particular bounced checks) sometimes take days/weeks to resolve. In addition, checks don't include a guarantee of adequate funds; they must be accepted on faith. Bitcoin transactions can't be processed without the guarantee that the sender in fact has sufficient bitcoins to send.

11. You have to prove you have Bitcoins to spend before you are allowed to spend them. You prove you have Bitcoins by pointing to the public ledger and showing where you have received Bitcoins in the past that haven't yet been spent. If you want to send one hundred BTC, it's unlikely that you will happen to have a series of Bitcoin transactions on the public ledger that add up to exactly one hundred BTC; it's far more likely the total will be off by a little or a lot. Your ledger might indicate bitcoin inflow of 50 BTC, 25.5 BTC, and 30 BTC, totaling 105.5 BTC. You use these transactions, worth 105.5 BTC, to prove you have the right to send 100 BTC (since 100 BTC < 105.5 BTC). After being sent, your e-wallet is returned the difference—in this case 5.5 BTC. This is why many Bitcoin transactions (the vast majority) include a return amount. Note that in odd cases this return amount can be vastly bigger than the payment amount. If your only bitcoin inflow was a massive 1000 BTC payment for a house, and you want to spend .1 BTC for a really good hamburger, you will end up sending .1 BTC to the restaurant, and receiving 999.9BTC as a return.

12. Found at https://bitcoin.org/bitcoin.pdf.

13. Forgetting your password is a very bad thing. There isn't any central authority you can petition. Nobody else knows your password (assuming it's a local software e-wallet). Any bitcoins in an e-wallet made inaccessible due to password amnesia are forever lost. You could hire a firm to attempt to hack your e-wallet, but it's unlikely they will make much progress unless they are given a few decades. To avoid this fate, write your password down and put it somewhere secure, like on a slip of paper in the middle of Moby Dick, with another copy secreted in your in-law's basement, ensuring that if your house burns down the password will survive. Professional Bitcoin traders have multiple backup systems in place, many featuring storage vaults and duplicates of duplicates.

14. While this discussion has been technical, I've simplified the messier details. For example, the e-wallet does not actually broadcast its public key, rather its public key hash, a shorter encoded form. For full details, read the developer documentation suite found at https://bitcoin.org.

15. We are not expected to reach 21 million Bitcoin for over a hundred years, and any deflation occurring after that could easily be offset by a slight tweak to the Bitcoin code, allowing just enough replacement bitcoins to be mined to replace those estimated to be no longer useable (for a variety of reasons). Until that point Bitcoin is a purely inflationary currency, though at quite a low (adjusted) rate.

16. BC_Acolyte (pseudonym), phone interview with author, May 2015.

17. The mining reward is lowered at fixed intervals; it's currently 25 BTC and will drop to 12.5 BTC in 2016.

18. For details, refer to the very readable introductory text *A History of Byzantium*, by Timothy E. Gregory (Hoboken, NJ: Wiley-Blackwell, 2010).

19. Bitcoin transaction blocks are similarly fluid; new Bitcoin transactions are sent to the network and "pooled" in a queue. Miners grab a handful of these transactions, create a transaction block out of them, and work to mine the block. If they succeed, any transactions included in the block are added to the block chain, while those not selected from the pool are still available to be placed in a new block and mined. Most miners are mining slightly different transaction blocks, some with more transactions, others with fewer, but in the long run all the transactions in the queue eventually make it into (some) block and into the block chain. The precise order of the mining events isn't important, nor are the contents of any given block. What matters is the aggregate effect, agreed upon by all nodes.

20. They jointly published the well-known "Selfish Miner" paper (http://arxiv.org/abs/1311.0243); Ittay is solely responsible for "The Miner's Dilemma" (http://arxiv.org/abs/1411.7099). They poke holes in the Bitcoin network's overall security as well as suggest easy fixes, and both reward close reading.

21. Modern is associated, as always, with long lengths of glass supported by metal and cushioned by rubber bumpers. Hot bright lights illuminate dusty corners. How it will look in twenty years, I think we can all imagine; nothing ages so quickly as "modern" design.

22. The US government is on record as attempting to breach/attack the Tor network in order to identify "criminal" or "terrorist" users. See Thomas Fox-Brewster, "Leaked Emails: How Hacking Team and US Government Want to Break Web Encryption Together," *Forbes*, July 6, 2015, http://www.forbes.com/sites/thomasbrewster/2015/07/06/us-gov-likes-hacking-team/.

23. All quotes in this chapter from Ittay and Gun are from my personal interview, August 2015.

24. Christian Decker supplied me with a brief first-hand account via email: "At the time I was doing measurements in the Bitcoin network to analyze the scalability of the network and find whether we can improve it unilaterally and reduce the number of BlockChain forks. This meant forwarding blocks to a large number of nodes in the network, and some sites assumed that we were the origin of the blocks and people started speculating whether ETH Zurich was attempting to sabotage the network. This seems to have drawn a bull's-eye on my back and there was a very targeted attack from Russia against my computer doing the forwarding, and this eventually resulted in the theft of my bitcoins. I reported a loss equivalent to 100,000 Swiss Francs to the police, but by the time Reuters picked it up the Bitcoin exchange rate had increased 100-fold. The coins were all mined so I didn't lose my life-savings, and my interest in improving Bitcoin is still going strong." Christian here proves himself to be far more level headed and forgiving than many others would be, including myself, at the loss of what was ultimately a substantial fortune.

25. A web site that produces random numbers on demand; they claim their random numbers are generated ". . . [by] atmospheric noise, which for many purposes is better than the pseudo-random number algorithms typically used in computer programs." For more information, visit www.random.org.

26. The paper can be found here: http://research.microsoft.com/pubs/204914/734.pdf. It's incredibly interesting, particularly the table listing various "bogus" customized destination addresses, containing unspendable bitcoins.

27. Obviously the intent was academic, not criminal, and they were not going to steal any bitcoins.

28. This occurred long before Nadia's group even looked into the subject, so it wasn't an "inside job."

CHAPTER 3: SATOSHI NAKAMOTO:
A ROCKET-POWERED LAUNCH

1. All of Satoshi's writings can be found at http://satoshi.nakamotoinstitute
.org, and this quote in particular at http://satoshi.nakamotoinstitute.org/emails/
cryptography/4/.

2. http://satoshi.nakamotoinstitute.org/emails/cryptography/12/.

3. Libertarian Party, http://www.lp.org/.

4. "Libertarianism is good because it helps conservatives pass off a patently
probusiness political agenda as a noble bid for human freedom. Whatever we may
think of libertarianism as a set of ideas, practically speaking, it is a doctrine that
owes its visibility to the obvious charms it holds for the wealthy and the powerful.
The reason we have so many well-funded libertarians in American these days is not
because libertarianism suddenly acquired an enormous grassroots following, but
because it appeals to those who are able to fund ideas. Like social Darwinism and
Christian Science before it, libertarianism flatters the successful and rationalizes
their core beliefs about the world. They warm to the libertarian idea that taxation
is theft because they themselves don't like to pay taxes. They fancy the libertarian
notion that regulation is communist because they themselves find regulation
intrusive and annoying. Libertarianism is a politics born to be subsidized. In the
'free market of ideas,' it is a sure winner." (Thomas Frank, *The Wrecking Crew: How
Conservatives Rule* [New York: Metropolitan Books, 2008], p. 115.)

5. Retirement accounts are not intended to return high yields, as financial
risk is directly linked to profit. Using retirement funds to chase profits is a
guaranteed recipe for long-term disaster, as any serious financial planner will tell
you. Opening up retirement funds for speculation siphons funds from retirement
accounts into other parts of the economy, most notably the financial services
industry. It's unlikely to the point of impossibility that individuals, working alone,
without much financial education or market experience, will somehow manage
to outperform the status quo, earning more for retirement than they would
have under the current, extremely conservative and safe system. Privatization of
social security opens the door for the unwise to lose their retirement savings—
some would argue that's their right, of course, but it's worth noting society still
picks up the bill for bad decisions. Penniless and starving retirees will burden
the governmental safety net, resulting in a long-term trade of social support
(at end of life) for marginal increase of freedom early in life (decision to pull
out of a retirement fund or unwisely invest it). While it's true a few prospective
retirees will invest their money well, and thanks to luck or skill end up with more
retirement money than the average social security recipient, these types will be

far less numerous than the losers. It's not unreasonable for society to balk at such an unfair tradeoff, and require both participation and ceded control. The same sort of logic is associated with the notorious "motorcycle helmet argument"—that is, loss of small personal freedom (letting the wind blow through one's hair while riding) versus the often horrific long-term medical costs for those involved in helmetless accidents, often paid by state or local governments. Most states have said, emphatically, "No."

6. Julian Assange, a noted Cypherpunk supporter, founded the highly encrypted and secure WikiLeaks site as a place for citizens to publicly post examples of governmental malfeasance, inspired by Louis Brandeis' well-known maxim, "Sunlight is . . . the best of disinfectants"(i.e., transparency inhibits corruption).

7. Eric Hughes, "A Cypherpunk's Manifesto," Activism.net, Mar. 9, 1993, http://www.activism.net/cypherpunk/manifesto.html.

8. Ibid.

9. John Gilmore, "Privacy, Technology, and the Open Society," speech, Conference on Computers, Freedom, and Privacy, March 28, 1991, Burlingame, CA.

10. For details about this amazing story, start with: Steven Levy, "Battle of the Clipper Chip," *New York Times*, June 12, 1994, http://www.nytimes.com/1994/06/12/magazine/battle-of-the-clipper-chip.html.

11. John Gilmore, quoted on "Introduction to FreeS/WAN," *Linux FreeS/WAN*, http://www.freeswan.org/freeswan_trees/freeswan-1.97/doc/politics.html.

12. See Bruce Sterling, *The Hacker Crackdown: Law and Disorder on the Electronic Frontier* (New York: Bantam Books, 1992). Read the author-authorized Gutenberg e-book here: http://www.gutenberg.org/ebooks/101.

13. The history of phone phreaks is utterly fascinating and includes a substantial subgroup composed of technologically savvy but blind enthusiasts. Since nobody knows you are blind when you are on the phone, many proto-phreaks got their start as children messing around with phones and dial tones. For a basic introduction, leading to further intriguing articles, see "Phone Phreaking," *Telephone Tribute*, http://www.telephonetribute.com/phonephreaking.html.

14. The company is very much alive and well. For details, see http://www.sjgames.com/general/about-sjg.html.

15. GURPS stands for (of course) "**G**eneric **U**niversal **R**ole**P**laying **S**ystem."

16. Bruce Sterling, "Gurps' Labour Lost," *Electronic Frontier Foundation*, 1991, https://w2.eff.org/Misc/Publications/Bruce_Sterling/gurps_labor_lost.article.

17. Discussed in the next chapter; it is a secure and encrypted "alternative internet."

18. Kim Zetter, "Bullion and Bandits: The Improbable Rise and Fall of E-Gold," *Wired*, June 9, 2009, http://www.wired.com/2009/06/e-gold/.

19. *Washington Journal*, "Discussion with Christopher Hitchens and David Frum," C-SPAN, Dec. 11, 1996, https://www.youtube.com/watch?v=VW3t SBDOIDU (starting at roughly 26:00 minutes into this clip).

20. This idea is most notably put forth by Noam Chomsky, who isn't alone in his take: "What's called libertarian in the United States . . . is a special U. S. phenomenon, it doesn't really exist anywhere else—a little bit in England— [it] permits a very high level of authority and domination but in the hands of private power. Private power should be unleashed to do whatever it likes. The assumption is that by some kind of magic, concentrated private power will lead to a more free and just society." (Michael S. Wilson and Noam Chomsky, "Noam Chomsky: The Kind of Anarchism I Believe In, and What's Wrong with Libertarians," *AlterNet*, May 28, 2013, http://www.alternet.org/civil-liberties/ noam-chomsky-kind-anarchism-i-believe-and-whats-wrong-libertarians.)

21. The libertarian flavors I describe are relatively well-represented in the current debates, and I use their most common names. Refer to the following for basic details:

Mainstream American Libertarian:

Molly Ball, "America's Libertarian Moment," *The Atlantic*, Aug. 18, 2013, http://www.theatlantic.com/politics/archive/2013/08/americas-libertarian -moment/278785/.

Anarcho-Libertarians:

Gerard Casey, *Libertarian Anarchy: Against the State* (New York: Continuum, 2012). Social Libertarians:

Joseph W. Kopsick, "What Is Social Libertarianism?" *The Aquarian Agrarian*, Jan. 26, 2011, http://aquarianagrarian.blogspot.com/2011/01/what-is-social -libertarianism.html.

22. Dorothy Parker once said about *Atlas Shrugged*, "This is not a book to be tossed aside lightly. It should be thrown with great force."

23. Ayn Rand, "Brief Summary," *The Objectivist*, vol. 10, Sept. 1971, http:// aynrandlexicon.com/ayn-rand-ideas/ayn-rand-q-on-a-on-libertarianism.html.

24. Reagan Foundation, "The President's News Conference, August 12, 1986," *YouTube* video, 37:25, June 22, 2010, https://www.youtube.com/watch?v=1ySHt DHrLJY. In the news conference, Reagan discusses governmental interference in the agricultural economy.

25. Bruce Bartlett, "Tax Cuts and 'Starving the Beast,'" *Forbes*, May 7, 2010, http://www.forbes.com/2010/05/06/tax-cuts-republicans-starve-the-beast -columnists-bruce-bartlett.html.

26. Dick Cheney, "Dick Cheney on Budget & Economy," *OnTheIssues*, http:// www.ontheissues.org/Celeb/Dick_Cheney_Budget_+_Economy.htm.

27. Henry David Thoreau, "Where I Lived and What I Lived For," chap. 2 in *Walden*, http://thoreau.eserver.org/walden02.html.

28. For a libertarian take on Thoreau, with quotes such as: "How does it become a man to behave toward the American government today? I answer, that he cannot without disgrace be associated with it," see Jeff Riggenbach, "Henry David Thoreau: Founding Father of American Libertarian Thought," *Mises Institute*, July 15, 2010, https://mises.org/library/henry-david-thoreau -founding-father-american-libertarian-thought.

29. Wendy McElroy, "Henry Thoreau and 'Civil Disobedience,'" *The Thoreau Reader*, 2005, http://thoreau.eserver.org/wendy.html.

30. This and other Ross Ulbricht's quotes (unless otherwise noted) are from the Silk Road forums, archived at: http://antilop.cc/sr/.

31. Dorian Cope, "10th October 1837: The Death of Charles Fourier," *On This Deity*, http://www.onthisdeity.com/10th-october-1837-%E2%80%93 -the-death-of-charles-fourier/.

32. Charles Fourier, *On Trade*, trans. Friedrich Engels, https://www.marxists .org/reference/archive/fourier/works/ch28.htm.

33. Ibid.

34. Charles Sears, *The North American Phalanx: An Historical and Descriptive Sketch* (New York: John M. Pryse, 1886).

35. The spiritualists carefully demolished the single large brick building the Fourierists had managed to construct on a tall hill and rebuilt it, brick by brick, closer to the banks of the Ohio River—against the firm advice of all their neighbors. A month after they finished moving it the Ohio River flooded with such force and violence that the building was surrounded by water and swallowed up: the brick walls caved in, killing sixteen, ending the new collective by drowning all the participants in the icy Ohio. Thus ended the second Utopian experiment in five years, and for a hundred years thereafter the site was considered a ghost town.

36. Rosabeth Moss Kanter, *Commitment and Community: Communes and Utopias in Sociological Perspective* (Cambridge, MA: Harvard University Press, 1972), 123.

37. Josiah Warren, *Equitable Commerce: A New Development of Principles for the Harmoneous Adjustment and Regulation of the Pecuniary, Intellectual, and Moral Intercourse of Mankind, Proposed as Elements of New Society* (Utopia, OH: Amos E. Senter, 1849), 7.

38. Paul Glover was well aware of Josiah Warren: "A few weeks later I saw a sample 'Hour' note issued by British industrialist Robert Owen in 1847. This Hour was negotiable only at Owens' company store and based, I discovered in 1993, on Josiah Warren's 'Time Store' notes of 1827." Paul Glover, "A History of Ithaca HOURS," *Ithaca Hours*, Jan. 2000, http://www.paulglover.org/0001.html.

39. See http://www.paulglover.org/ for more details about Paul's rather amazing career as teacher and community organizer.

40. Paul Glover, "Real Money vs. Funny Money," *Ithaca Hours*, http://www.paulglover.org/9203.html.

41. Ibid.

42. This is enforced by the community; while nothing is stopping a person from hoarding and lending Ithaca Hours (with interest), it's been generally agreed that such behavior isn't going to be supported and such a "bank" would have few, if any, customers.

43. Paul Glover, "Labor: The New Gold Standard," *Ithaca Hours*, http://www.paulglover.org/1107.html.

44. A poor result for both economics and poetry.

45. Ezra Pound, *An Introduction to the Economic Nature of the United States* (London: Peter Russell, 1950); https://archive.org/details/AnIntroductionToThe EconomicNatureOfTheUnitedStates.

46. A historical example of a demurrage currency is found in *bracteate* coins, used in German-speaking areas of Europe from 1000 to 1500 CE. Every two or three years all bracteates had to be returned to the issuer, who replaced them with newly minted coins at an (expected) exchange penalty of between 10 and 20 percent of value. This was a convenient way to collect taxes, as well as spur currency velocity, since hoarding coins resulted in biannual depreciation.

47. Silvio Gesell, a German economist writing in 1918, claimed in *The Natural Economic Order* that currency velocity was critical for economic growth, and slowing or stagnating velocity would necessarily result in economic depression. A translation can be found at http://www.geokey.de/literatur/doc/neo.pdf.

48. Bernard Lietaer, "The Wörgl Experiment: Austria (1932–1933)," *Currency Solutions for a Wiser World*, Mar. 27, 2010, http://www.lietaer.com/2010/03/the-worgl-experiment/.

49. "The miracle of Wörgl came to a sudden end. In January 1933 an injunction to prohibit the experiment was issued by the Austrian authorities against the community of Wörgl. The Austrian National Bank was behind this; it saw its monopoly on money threatened. The community of Wörgl appealed against the decision but was not successful. The use of AB notes continued illegally in Wörgl until late 1933 when the Austrian State threatened to use force. The miracle of Wörgl ceased on 15 September 1933 amidst comments from the Swiss government that the Wörgl example could undermine the monopoly of the Swiss Central Bank as well. Unterguggenberger was even prevented from lecturing in Switzerland afterwards." (George Reiff, "Free Economy and the Miracle of Wörgl," *Prof. Dr. George Reiff,* http://www.george-reiff.eu/miscellaneous/sub-section-about-germany/free-economy-and-the-miracle-of-worgl/.)

50. For more information, all of which is fascinating, see www.community currenciesinaction.eu.

51. Full details can be found at: Susan Steed and Leander Bindewald, "Money with a Purpose," *NEF (New Economics Foundation)*, May 18, 2015, http://www.new economics.org/publications/entry/money-with-a-purpose.

52. For more information about this exciting currency, see http://www.itha cash.org.

53. Free State Project: Liberty in our Lifetime, https://freestateproject.org/.

54. Aaron Blake, "Poll: 22 Percent of Americans Lean Libertarian," *Washington Post*, Oct. 29, 2013, http://www.washingtonpost.com/blogs/post-politics/wp/2013/10/29/poll-22-percent-of-americans-lean-libertarian/.

55. Pew Research Center: U.S. Politics and Policy, "Section 3: Demographics and News Sources," *Beyond Red vs. Blue: The Political Typology*, May 4, 2011, http://www.people-press.org/2011/05/04/section-3-demographics-and-news-sources/.

56. Michele Dumas, "101 Reasons to Move to New Hampshire," *Free State Project*, 2002, https://freestateproject.org/about/101-reasons-move-new-hampshire.

57. See http://www.bookofsatoshi.com/ for details.

58. Phil Champagne, *The Book of Satoshi* (e53 Publishing, 2014), p. 155.

59. Phil Champagne, telephone interview with author, April 16, 2015.

60. For a good introduction to all things Linux, see Glyn Moody's *Rebel Code: Linux and the Open Source Revolution* (New York: Basic Books, 2009).

61. Satoshi Nakamoto, "Re: Wikileaks contact info?" *Satoshi Nakamoto Institute*, Dec. 5, 2010, http://satoshi.nakamotoinstitute.org/posts/bitcointalk/523/.

62. The technical details are a bit more complicated, as I eventually found out. An empty block can be mined and a reward issued; the real problem is that every transaction block points to a previous transaction block and includes a hash of it in its header; the genesis block lacks a previous transaction block since it's the start of the block chain—which should render it invalid. Satoshi had to do a little one-time magic to get the initial block to issue a reward.

63. "Genesis Block," *Bitcoin Wiki,*. Nov. 5, 2015, https://en.bitcoin.it/wiki/Genesis_block.

64. The equivalent of the US Secretary of the Treasury.

65. Francis Elliott and Gary Duncan, "Chancellor Alistair Darling on Brink of Second Bailout for Banks," *The Times* [London], Jan. 3, 2009, http://www.thetimes.co.uk/tto/business/industries/banking/article2160028.ece.

66. Tim Haab, "A Libertarian Economist's Take on the Bailout," *Environmental Economics*, Sept. 30, 2008, http://www.env-econ.net/2008/09/a-libertarian-e.html.

67. Satoshi Nakamoto, "Bitcoin Open Source Implementation of P2P Currency," *Satoshi Nakamoto Institute*, Feb. 11, 2009, http://satoshi.nakamoto institute.org/posts/p2pfoundation/1/.

68. The Glass–Steagall Act limited commercial bank securities activities; for example, commercial banks were barred from buying and selling stocks using customer deposits, fearing that a bank might lose all the deposits following bad investments—which seems, in retrospect, incredibly likely. It also created the FDIC as a guard against bank runs, which has proven to be a cheap investment immensely effective in times of crisis.

69. Steve Sailer, "2002: Bush's Speech to the White House Conference on Increasing Minority Homeownership," *Steve Sailer: iSteve*, Sept. 24, 2008, http://isteve.blogspot.com/2008/09/2002-bushs-speech-to-white-house.html.

70. Ibid.

71. Edmund L. Andrews, "Greenspan Concedes Error on Regulation," *New York Times*, Oct. 23, 2008, http://www.nytimes.com/2008/10/24/business/economy/24panel.html.

72. Louise Story, "On Wall Street, Bonuses, Not Profits, Were Real," *New York Times*, Dec. 17, 2008, http://www.nytimes.com/2008/12/18/business/18pay.html.

73. The English government at least purchased common and preferred stock in troubled banks, giving them partial ownership after the crisis passed. The English "bank bailout" was essentially a partial nationalization of troubled banks, which might pay for itself in the long term (or even make a profit). The American bailouts, by comparison, consisted of purchasing (rancid) mortgage-backed securities that American banks were unable to shift.

74. Leaping from the frying pan, trusting somebody else to save you from the fire.

75. Long-standing libertarian complaint, first formulated during President Andrew Jackson's "Bank War" against the Second Bank of the United States in 1834.

76. "OKCupid Starts Accepting Bitcoin Using Coinbase!" *Coinbase Blog*, Apr. 16, 2013, https://blog.coinbase.com/2013/04/16/okcupid-starts-accepting-bitcoin-using-coinbase/.

CHAPTER 4: ROSS ULBRICHT: INTO THE DARK

1. This was one of the first documents I stumbled across in my early exploration of the Dark Web.

2. Presumably Bangkok's Goddess Tuptim Shrine, though others exist. The Bangkok shrine is widely regarded as the best example of *intentional* phallic architecture in the world. For details, see Andy Deemer, "The Cockiest Shrine in Bangkok," *Asia Obscura*, Jan. 14, 2012, http://asiaobscura.com/2012/01/the-cockiest-shrine-in-bangkok.html.

3. The lead *Twilight* movie vampiric heartthrob, once considered edgy and outré, now slightly passé.

4. Ross Ulbricht's net worth was estimated to be $100 million; Silk Road was up and running for roughly three years, giving him an annual income of at least $30 million during this period. At the time of his arrest, he had twenty million dollars' worth of bitcoins in various e-wallets. For details, see Jim Edwards, "Silk Road's 'Dread Pirate Roberts' Used $20 Million Bitcoin Fortune to Order 6 Assassinations, According to Feds," *Business Insider*, Nov. 22, 2013, http://www .businessinsider.com/silk-road-boss-ordered-6-assassinations-and-owned-20-million -in-bitcoins-feds-claim-2013-11.

5. The "Free Ross Ulbricht" foundation, a legal fund for his defense, can be found here: http://freeross.org/.

6. Ryan Mac, "Who Is Ross Ulbricht? Piecing Together the Life of the Alleged Libertarian Mastermind Behind Silk Road," *Forbes*, Oct. 2, 2013, http:// www.forbes.com/sites/ryanmac/2013/10/02/who-is-ross-ulbricht-piecing-together -the-life-of-the-alleged-libertarian-mastermind-behind-silk-road.

7. Andy Greenberg, "Ross Ulbricht's Mother Calls Silk Road Allegations 'Absurd,' Launches Defense Fund," *Forbes*, Nov. 20, 2013, http://www.forbes.com/ sites/andygreenberg/2013/11/20/ross-ulbrichts-mother-calls-silk-road -allegations-absurd-launches-defense-fund/.

8. Andy Greenberg, "Alleged Silk Road Creator Ross Ulbricht Pleads Not Guilty on All Charges," *Forbes*, Feb. 7, 2014, http://www.forbes .com/sites/ andygreenberg/2014/02/07/alleged-silk-road-creator-ross-ulbricht-pleads -not-guilty-on-all-charges/.

9. At least not directly; it'll take quite a while as jobs are lost and the economy collapses.

10. "Former National Security Agency director Michael Hayden on Monday marveled at the puny nature of the surveillance reforms put in place two years after NSA whistleblower Edward Snowden revealed a vast expansion of intrusive U.S. government surveillance at home and abroad. Hayden mocked the loss of the one program that was reined in—the NSA's bulk collection of metadata information about domestic phone calls— calling it 'that little 215 program.'" Dan Froomkin, "Hayden Mocks Extent of Post-Snowden Reform: 'And This Is It After Two Years? Cool!'" *The Intercept*, June 17, 2015, https://firstlook.org/theintercept/2015/06/17/ hayden-mocks-extent-post-snowden-surveillance-reform-2-years-cool/.

11. "Companies are provided monetary incentive to spy and share that information with the government and blanket liability once they do under the USA Freedom Act—even if that breaks that law. . . . Once companies receive [this

assurance], they'll have almost no reason to weigh in on meaningful surveillance reform." Andrea Peterson, "It's Nearly Two Years After Snowden and Privacy Advocates Are Divided on How to Fix NSA Spying," *Washington Post*, Spr. 29, 2015, https://www.washingtonpost.com/blogs/the-switch/wp/2015/04/29/its-nearly -two-years-after-snowden-and-privacy-advocates-are-divided-on-how-to-fix-nsa -spying/.

12. For more details about the NSA Prism program, as detailed by Snowden's confidential files release, see Tom Ritter, "About the Tor/NSA Slide Decks," *Ritter. Vg*, Oct. 7, 2013, https://ritter.vg/blog-tor-nsa-slide-decks.html.

13. To install Tor on your computer and start poking around the Dark Web, go to https://www.torproject.org/index.html.en and download and install a client.

14. It's curious that the rabidly anti-regulation libertarian crowd quietly accepted regulation when it was, as they say, market driven. If the problem, therefore, isn't regulation *per se* but the regulation's origins (or possibly the extent of regulatory reach), what's wrong with modifying current regulations instead of agitating for complete removal?

15. Apparently delicious, dark, moist, and savory Cannabis buds. According to expert users, "I prefer dense bud, purely because of the crunchy noise it makes in my grinder."

16. Enabling online drug sales was certainly not Satoshi's major goal in creating Bitcoin. It might have been a necessary byproduct, but wasn't a major (or minor) focus.

17. Or wasn't the DEA itself, which as we shall see is a major vector of attack for law enforcement.

18. For details, refer to the fantastic resource http://www.gwern.net/Silk%20 Road, whose author should be given some sort of award for public service.

19. Pretty much all of them.

20. Which is precisely what happened when Silk Road was shut down by the authorities. Within weeks a new Dread Pirate Roberts appeared, launched Silk Road II, and the process started all over again.

21. The current Dread Pirate confesses after a failed attack by his apprentice (Westley): "'I am not the Dread Pirate Roberts,' he said, 'my name is Ryan. I inherited this ship from the previous Dread Pirate Roberts just as you will inherit it from me. The man I inherited from was not the real Dread Pirate Roberts either; his name was Cummerbund. The real original Dread Pirate Roberts has been retired fifteen years and has been living like a king in Patagonia.'" (William Goldman, *The Princess Bride: S. Morgenstern's Classic Tale of True Love and High Adventure* [New York: Houghton Mifflin Harcourt, 2007], 194.)

22. Its etymology according to the Oxford English Dictionary: "Of uncertain

origin: sometimes taken as a euphemistic alteration of turd." Its etymology according to folk: "nerd" derives from "knurd," which is "drunk" spelled backward. Its etymology according to Merriam-Webster: "perhaps from *nerd,* a creature in the children's book *If I Ran the Zoo* (1950) by Dr. Seuss." And according to an online etymology dictionary: "probably an alteration of 1940s slang *nert* 'stupid or crazy person,' itself an alteration of *nut.*" Clearly, no one knows. . . .

23. It's been posited and convincingly argued that nerd culture marks itself as "superwhite"—the racial element isn't tangential but central. (See Mary Bucholtz, "The Whiteness of Nerds: Superstandard English and Racial Markedness," *Journal of Linguistic Anthropology,* 11, no. 1 [June 2001]: 84–100, http://www.jstor.org/ stable/43103956, for details.) This does not imply black nerds are impossible; it's claimed they are aligning themselves with "superwhite" cultural values.

24. Though many are, granted, hidden behind superhero masks. But many aren't.

25. Noam Cohen, "We're All Nerds Now," *New York Times,* Sept. 13, 2014, http://www.nytimes.com/2014/09/14/sunday-review/were-all-nerds-now.html.

26. A similar transformation occurred with the word "gay" after it was embraced by the homosexual community to such an extent that bigots no longer had any fun shouting it from passing cars and pickups.

27. One of the oldest, largest, and most-respected Unix-based text-only adventure games, *Nethack,* termed "the best video game ever" by more than one online reviewer, features a creature called a "mail daemon." Unlike the normal demons, devils, dragons, and dingoes your hardy adventurer fights in the game, the mail daemon's only role is to deliver real mail messages to the player in the form of a mediaeval scroll. This should be understood as a canonical example of nerd humor.

28. A good discussion can be found here: Erik Germ, "6 Awesome Easter Eggs Hidden in Programs You Use Every Day," *Cracked,* Jan. 15, 2013, http://www .cracked.com/article_20174_6-awesome-easter-eggs-hidden-in-programs-you-use -every-day.html.

29. "Management [of Atari] was known to partake of the ganja as well, helping to release some of the stress of running a company expanding at a breakneck pace. While that may sound incredible in this day of random drug screenings and 'no tolerance immediate terminations,' it was hardly the first instance of drugs in the workplace. John Markoff covered the intersection of drugs and the high tech industry in *What the Dormouse Said,* painstakingly recounting the use of LSD amongst engineers in the 1960s to expand their creativity." (Marty Goldberg and Curt Vendel, *Atari Inc.: Business Is Fun* [Carmel, NY: Syzygy Press, 2012], 102.)

30. "[Atari Management] found some unique ways to help workers let off steam—and the permissible atmosphere allowed workers to find their own ways for release. . . . [These] could include riding a skateboard through the rows of PONGs being manufactured or taking advantage of the many after parties." (Goldberg and Vendel, *Atari Inc.*, 101.)

31. Goldberg and Vendel, *Atari Inc.*, 317.

32. The Atari culture was described as, "A bunch of free thinking, dope smoking, fun loving people. We sailed boats, flew airplanes, smoked pot and played video games." (Goldberg and Vendel, *Atari Inc.*, 102.) More worrisome, "In 1978, there were 23 employee arrests, 77 employee discharges, and five security incidents." A typical example: "[In 1978] . . . two Atari pinball employees were so intoxicated on the job that their employment was terminated." (Ibid., 338.)

33. "The Federal Drug Kingpin Law," *CNN: Law Center,* June 18, 2001, http:// cgi.cnn.com/2001/LAW/06/18/garza.kingpin.law/index.html?related.

34. Unless otherwise noted, all Ross Ulbricht quotes come from the Silk Road forums, which can be found here: http://antilop.cc/sr/. Ross is also being a little coy here; Silk Road wasn't regulated by the market, but by Ross's personal whims. Weapon sales were banned on Silk Road because Ross didn't want weapons being sold on Silk Road, and that's pretty much the only reason.

35. First stated June 1971, by United States President Richard Nixon. The idea was to formulate an all-out assault on "public enemy number one," drug use.

36. "Libertarian Party: 40 Years Is Enough—End the Drug War," *Libertarian Party,* June 17, 2011, https://www.lp.org/news/press-releases/libertarian-party -40-years-is-enough-end-the-drug-war.

37. Fabian Franklin, *What Prohibition Has Done to America* (New York: Harcourt, Brace, 1922), 99.

38. Mike Riggs, "[Updated With Correction]: Forty Years of Drug War Failure Represented in a Single Chart," *Reason.com,* Oct. 11, 2012, http://reason.com/ blog/2012/10/11/forty-years-of-drug-war-failure-in-a-sin.

39. Ross Ulbricht, Silk Road forum post, http://antilop.cc/sr/users/dpr/ messages/20120429-0604-445-If_prohibition_is_lifted.txt.

40. "Popping Pills: Prescription Drug Abuse in America," *National Institute on Drug Abuse,* https://www.drugabuse.gov/related-topics/trends-statistics/ infographics/popping-pills-prescription-drug-abuse-in-america#1.

41. To show how things stood, the 1819 Cotton Mills and Factories Act cracked down on child labor by limiting nine-year-old workers to no more than twelve hours work per day. It makes one wonder how long they worked before this act reduced their hours.

42. Ross Ulbricht, Silk Road forum post, http://antilop.cc/sr/users/dpr/ messages/20121003-0610-367-Re_DPR_s_Book_Club_Reading_Assignment_1.txt.

43. For a very interesting international take, see Mark Weisbrot, Robert Naiman, and Natalia Rudiak, "Can Developing Countries Afford to Ban or Regulate Child Labor?" *Political Economy Research Institute*, University of Massachusetts—Amherst, Peri. umass.edu,. 2015. http://www.peri.umass.edu/fileadmin/pdf/child.PDF.

44. With a self-described focus on politics, culture, and Christian ethics, Ms. Bruenig's articles and essays can be found in *The New Republic*, *The Atlantic*, *The Boston Review*, *Al Jazeera America*, the *Los Angeles Review of Books*, *The American Conservative*, *The Daily Beast*, *The Nation*, *Salon*, and many more.

45. Elizabeth Bruenig, "Libertarians Have a History of Horrifying Views on Parenting," *The New Republic*, Feb. 4, 2015, http://www.newrepublic.com/article/120965/rand-paul-libertarians-have-long-had-horrifying-view-parenting.

46. At this point of Bitcoin's life, anonymous Bitcoin exchanges (such as Mt. Gox) could be used to convert cash into Bitcoins and back again.

47. Andy Greenberg, "Meet the Dread Pirate Roberts, the Man Behind Booming Black Market Drug Website Silk Road," *Forbes*, Aug. 14, 2013, http://www.forbes.com/sites/andygreenberg/2013/08/14/meet-the-dread-pirate-roberts-the-man-behind-booming-black-market-drug-website-silk-road/.

CHAPTER 5: ROSS ULBRICHT: THE RISE AND FALL OF SILK ROAD

1. Most of the participants watched a pirated BitTorrent stream of the movie. It should come as no surprise that many libertarians view intellectual property rights as constituting an artificial governmental infringement upon freedom of speech and action; see Boldrin and Levine's *Against Intellectual Monopoly* for a typical libertarian take on the subject: Michele Boldrin and David K. Levine, "Against Intellectual Monopoly," *Economic and Game Theory*, Nov. 11, 2005, http://levine.sscnet.ucla.edu/general/intellectual/against.htm.

2. All Ross Ulbricht quotes are from his Silk Road forums unless otherwise noted. For a complete archive, see http://antilop.cc/sr/.

3. It's still available, check it out at https://www.linkedin.com/in/rossulbricht.

4. Some would say "discovered," as the equation matches fact remarkably well when using objects humans typically throw. But not feathers, highly susceptible to air resistance, so the equation's far from perfect. Strictly speaking, no scientific theory is ever *discovered*; there isn't a glowing equation written by Nature, which a wild-haired scientist unlocks from a chest labeled "Truth lies within"—everything is hypothesized, and open to future change as more data

arrives. Extraordinarily well-documented theories such as evolution are generally called "discoveries," as broadly speaking they have been proven correct, even if the details are in flux. Others, such as string theory, are called "theories" because they lack a hundred years of supporting research and evidence.

5. Maybe *this* time it will be different?

6. Mandy Hofmockel, "Students Debate Current Issues," *Daily Collegian*, Dec. 4, 2008, http://www.collegian.psu.edu/archives/article_1cb3e5e4-6ed2-5bb8-b980 -1df989c663f9.html.

7. Katharine Lackey, "Paul to Visit PSU," *Daily Collegian*, Mar. 26, 2008, http://www.collegian.psu.edu/archives/article_239513a3-a577-5732-bab0 -9cc27c5d4610.html.

8. "The notion of mandated health insurance is inherently anti-libertarian," etc. See Josh Blackman, "The Libertarian Challenge to Obamacare," *Reason.com*, Sept. 24, 2013, http://reason.com/archives/2013/09/24/the-libertarian -challenge-to-obamacare.

9. A rather interesting Yelp discussion about Good Wagon Books can be found here: http://www.yelp.com/topic/austin-good-wagon-books.

10. "Good Wagon Books," Yelp Austin, Aug. 22, 2010, http://www.yelp.com/ topic/austin-good-wagon-books.

11. Ibid.

12. "This was an industry despised even by Republicans for exploiting society's least advantaged by charging them outrageously high fees." (Timothy Noah, "Legal Usury: The Skeevy Business of Payday Loans," *Slate*, Oct. 5, 2010, http://www.slate. com/articles/business/the_customer/2010/10/legal_usury.html.)

13. It's not coincidental that the only two companies Ross Ulbricht ever founded, both with the stated goal of "doing good," both attracted broad public condemnation. Both shared the same weakness: theoretically unobjectionable but socially dubious aims.

14. Tiffany Kelly, "On OkCupid, Ross Ulbricht Was a 'Scientist Turned Entrepreneur,'" *Ars Technica*, Jan. 29, 2015, http://arstechnica.com/tech -policy/2015/01/on-okcupid-ross-ulbricht-was-a-scientist-turned-entrepreneur/.

15. *The Secret* was an unexpected self-help bestseller, which hypothesized a universal "Law of Attraction" aligning the "magnetic frequency of thoughts" with the objects those thoughts concern. The best way to make money is to think about money 24/7. For further foolishness, briefly browse a used copy of *The Secret*, by Rhonda Byrne (New York: Atria Books, 2006).

16. United States v. Ross William Ulbricht, transcript, 14 CR 68 (Southern Dist. of NY, Jan. 21, 2015). A copy can be found here: http://antilop.cc/sr/ files/2015_01_21_Ulbricht_trial_transcript_W2_D2.pdf.

17. From the government's criminal complaint against Ross (http://antilop. cc/sr/files/DPR_Silk_Road_NY_UlbrichtCriminalComplaint.pdf).

18. ShadowOfHarbringer, forum post, "A Heroin Store," *Bitcointalk.org*, Jan. 30, 2011, https://bitcointalk.org/?topic=175.70;wap2.

19. Joe Mullin, "At Silk Road Trial, Federal Agent Explains How He Trapped Ulbricht," *Ars Technica*, Jan. 14, 2015, http://arstechnica.com/tech-policy/ 2015/01/silk-road-trial-federal-agent-explains-how-he-trapped-ulbricht/.

20. In 2014 the Mt. Gox Bitcoin exchange collapsed following external (possibly) or internal (more likely) theft of over 600 million dollars' worth of Bitcoin. The Bitcoin community was shaken to the core as many lost not only their money but their confidence in the currency. See the discussion on Bitcoin regulation for further details.

21. Preet Bharara to Hon. Kevin N. Fox, "Re: *United States v. Ross William Ulbricht*, 13 Mag. 2328," Nov. 20, 2013, http://antilop.cc/sr/files/DPR_Silk_Road _Gov_Bail_Response_to_Bail_Request.pdf.

22. "Moving to Austin," *Shroomery*, Feb. 12, 2012, http://www.shroomery.org/ forums/showflat.php/Number/15796830#15796830.

23. United States v. Ross William Ulbricht, "Government Exhibit 240 B," 14 CR 68 (Southern Dist. of NY), http://antilop.cc/sr/exhibits/253456476-Silk-Road -exhibits-GX-240B.pdf.

24. Ibid. The price of Bitcoin was spiking and had Ross waited longer before selling he could have made much higher profits. Of course, there wasn't any way for him to know this at the time.

25. A well-known web service "solution stack," incorporating the **L**inux operating system, the **A**pache HTTP Server, the **M**ySQL relational database management system, and the **P**HP programming language. Put them together and you get LAMP, allowing developers to quickly and easily build stable and reliable websites.

26. United States v. Ross William Ulbricht, "Government Exhibit 240 B."

27. Ibid.

28. Nicola Kean, "Senators Target Mail-Order Drug Site," *Upstart Business Journal*, June 6, 2011, http://upstart.bizjournals.com/news/wire/2011/06/06/ senators-want-to-shut-down-mail-order-drug-site.html?page=all.

29. United States v. Ross William Ulbricht, "Government Exhibit 240 B."

30. Sarah Jeong, "The Dread Pirate's Confidante," *Forbes*, January 22, 2015, http:// www.forbes.com/sites/sarahjeong/2015/01/22/the-dread-pirates-confidante/.

31. Andy Greenberg, "Ulbricht Confessed to Running Silk Road, His College Friend Testifies," *Wired*, Jan. 22, 2015, http://www.wired.com/2015/01/ richard-bates-ross-ulbricht-silk-road/.

32. Or a run-of-the-mill drug dealer with basic computer skills.

33. Antilop.cc, http://antilop.cc/sr/users/inigo(SR2)/messages/20131209
-2112-18-Re_HELP_Where_to_buy_weapon_now_that_BMR_is_not_allowing_new
_depostis.txt.

34. Joshuah Bearman, "The Untold Story of Silk Road, Part 1," *Wired*, May 23, 2015, http://www.wired.com/2015/04/silk-road-1/.

35. Sarah Jeong, "Criminal Charges Against Agents Reveal Staggering Corruption in the Silk Road Investigation," *Forbes*, Mar. 31, 2015, http://www.forbes.com/sites/sarahjeong/2015/03/31/force-and-bridges/.

36. One of them was recently found guilty: Joe Mullin, "Corrupt Silk Road Agent Carl Force Sentenced to 78 Months," *Ars Technica*, Oct. 19, 2015, http://arstechnica.com/tech-policy/2015/10/corrupt-silk-road-agent-carl-force-sentenced-to-78-months/.

37. Government v. Ross William Ulbricht, "Document 227-1; Exhibit A," http://antilop.cc/sr/exhibits/2015_03_31_exhibit_A_chatlogs_dpr_nob_inigo_cimon.pdf.

38. Jeong, "Criminal Charges Against Agents Reveal Staggering Corruption."

39. Ross Ulbricht was convicted of being the Dread Pirate Roberts and sentenced to serve jail time for seven drug convictions of the following lengths: "20 years, one for five years, one for 15 years and two for life, to be served concurrently with no possibility of parole." (Nicky Woolf, "Silk Road: Ross Ulbricht Files Appeal Against Convictions and Sentencing," *Guardian*, June 5, 2015, http://www.theguardian.com/technology/2015/jun/05/silk-road-ross-ulbricht-appeal-convictions-sentencing.)

However, while Ross Ulbricht was charged in Maryland for various murder-for-hire schemes, the trial has not yet begun as of this writing, thus Ross has not yet been convicted of hiring hit men and contracting murder, despite the Dread Pirate Roberts chats and messages to this effect being read in open court during his drug trial: Andy Greenberg, "Read the Transcript of Silk Road's Boss Ordering 5 Assassinations," *Wired*, Feb. 2, 2015, http://www.wired.com/2015/02/read-transcript-silk-roads-boss-ordering-5-assassinations/.

Consequently, DPR (Dread Pirate Roberts) is shorthand for criminal activity charged but not yet proven committed by Ross Ulbricht, despite written evidence.

40. Since Nob knew details about the investigation and Curtis Green's arrest, he was already privy to Curtis's actual location and address. This made Nob useful to Ross.

41. From the Maryland criminal complaint, http://www.ice.gov/doclib/news/releases/2013/131002baltimore.pdf.

42. Greenberg, "Read the Transcript of Silk Road's Boss Ordering 5 Assassinations."

43. This is a ludicrous detail, and it's almost impossible to believe DPR actually thought black-suited ninja-inspired "assassin squads" really existed. Amazingly, he did.

44. Itself a banality, but horrifically appropriate given the circumstance.

45. As described by Edward Herman, following Hannah Arendt's lead in her *Eichmann in Jerusalem: A Report on the Banality of Evil*. Edward S. Herman, "The Banality of Evil," *Information Clearing House*, http://www.informationclearinghouse.info/article7278.htm.

46. Greenberg, "Read the Transcript of Silk Road's Boss Ordering 5 Assassinations."

47. From unredacted trial exhibits: http://antilop.cc/sr/exhibits/2015_03_31_unredacted_silkroad_log_file.pdf.

48. Ibid.

49. From the Silk Road forums, archived on antilop.cc: http://antilop.cc/sr/users/kmfkewm/html/kmfkewm_posts_page_218_start_3255.html.

50. The library is a small example of brutalism in concrete (naturally) and glass, more glass than was typically allowed in these types of buildings, and nearly making up for the stained and uninspiring concrete covering the front and sides of the building, representing nothing more than cowardice on the part of the architects for whom "less is more" was taken to be a cost-savings principle allowing them to escape the natural and cosmopolitan requirement to paint, or decorate minimally with ornamentation, an exterior that otherwise resembled the hard-worn and tainted cafeteria floor of a municipal insane asylum.

51. It would be possible, I suppose, to graph the general decline of printed books by the size and scope of public library collections, and given San Francisco's status as the ultimate technophile hotbed such shrunken bookshelves are to be expected.

52. Which would be absurd, but given Ross's poor history with computer security not entirely out of the question.

53. This refers to Murray Newton Rothbard, the leading proponent of anarcho-capitalism, who argues that the complete removal of governmental meddling in a "free market" will *necessarily* improve society. This isn't a small government philosophy, it's *no* government philosophy.

54. Such as the 1838 Mormon War in Missouri, killing twenty-one, a result of ongoing harassment of Mormons for their religious beliefs, which ended with the Mormons being expelled from Missouri and their property confiscated. It was one of a number of such episodes, culminating in Brigham Young's decision to remove to Utah in the year following their founder Joseph Smith's slaughter by a mob (while jailed on charges of property destruction). Lots of bad behavior occurred

on both sides, though it's hard to argue Mormons didn't suffer the brunt of the pain.

55. The scientific method is a wonderful invention, a delightful theory, and has improved humanity's existence to an almost unbelievable degree, yet it's surely not the only way humans are able to discover useful facts about the world—or themselves.

56. Roy F. Baumeister, *Evil: Inside Human Violence and Cruelty* (New York: Macmillan, 1999), p. 181.

57. Ibid., p. 171.

58. "Statism" is a curse uttered by libertarians, which in this context usually means "the state (government) controls some or all of an economy." Currently, every economy on Earth qualifies as *statist.*

59. For example, Richard Feynman, Nobel Prize winner (Physics, 1965), a noted bongo player, socially adept (some would say predatory) seducer, confident and inspiring lecturer, etc.

60. William Shockley, inventor of the transistor, dipping into eugenics and campaigning for sterilization of everyone with a sub-100 IQ; Kary Mullis, inventor of the PCR (polymerase chain reaction) technique, who is convinced HIV does not cause AIDS; Linus Pauling (vastly accomplished chemist and biochemist) and his opinions about the curative properties of vitamin C, etc.

CHAPTER 6: THE WINKLEVOSS TWINS:
BORN ON THIRD BASE, HIT A DOUBLE

1. A curiously appropriate actor to select. Armie Hammer not only resembles the twins in his height (6'5"), broad breadth, and clean-cut WASPY good looks, but shares a privileged and blessed childhood—his great-grandfather, Armand Hammer, ran Occidental Petroleum for decades, and was a well-known figure on the world stage. After his death Armie's family inherited millions, allowing them to move to the Cayman Islands for five years before returning to the United States and settling in Los Angeles. Armie's father was involved in many business ventures, such as Armand Hammer Productions (a film production company), and in general the family prospered.

2. It's not particularly likely, but it's also far from impossible. Zuckerberg's treatment of Facebook cofounder Eduardo Saverin was by all accounts deeply self-serving, as Zuckerberg apparently attempted to "cut" him out of his fair share of Facebook after making it big. Saverin sued, but the case never went to trial and was settled out of court. Saverin is worth over two billion, most of it resulting from his Facebook settlement.

3. Max Read, "Idiot Dick Facebook Twins Now Own One Percent of All Bitcoin," *Gawker*, Apr. 11, 2013, http://gawker.com/5994433/idiot-dick-facebook-twins-now-own-one-percent-of-all-bitcoin.

4. J. Webster, "The Winklevoss Twins Are Now 'Venture Capitalists,'" *Market Squeeze*, Apr. 28, 2012, http://www.marketsqueeze.com/2012/04/the-winklevoss-twins-are-now-venture-capitalists/.

5. Mike Vilensky, "The Winklevoss Twins Are Just As Angry With Mark Zuckerberg Today As They Were When They Sued Him the First Time," *New York Magazine*, Dec. 31, 2010, http://nymag.com/daily/intelligencer/2010/12/winklevoss_twins_still_mad.html.

6. Dana Vachon, "The Code of the Winklevii," *Vanity Fair*, Nov. 30, 2010, http://www.vanityfair.com/news/2011/12/winklevosses-201112.

7. Ibid.

8. It's instructive to compare the public reception of "famous for no reason" celebrities (or "famous for a leaked porn video" celebrities) to the Winklevoss twins, who have by any stretch of the imagination accomplished far more in their lives, regardless of upbringing.

9. Pablo Torre writes: "By the time they have been retired for two years, 78% of former NFL players have gone bankrupt or are under financial stress because of joblessness or divorce. Within five years of retirement, an estimated 60% of former NBA players are broke." Pablo S. Torre, "How (and Why) Athletes Go Broke," *Sports Illustrated*, Mar. 23, 2009, http://www.si.com/vault/2009/03/23/105789480/how-and-why-athletes-go-broke.

10. Rick Hampson, –"No Fairy Tale Life for Lottery Winner," *USA Today*, Dec. 22, 2004, http://usatoday30.usatoday.com/news/nation/2004-12-22-lottery-tragedy_x.htm.

11. Situations change more readily than personality. Let's remember Ross Ulbricht in this context; money and world-wide acclaim convinced Ross of his righteousness and the righteousness of his cause—leading directly to extremism.

12. Simon Johnson, "Perhaps the Most Boring Important Topic in Economics," *The Baseline Scenario*, March 31, 2014, http://baselinescenario.com/2014/03/31/perhaps-the-most-boring-important-topic-in-economics/.

13. "Is Pension Work Boring?" *Actuarial Outpost*, April 26, 2008, http://www.actuarialoutpost.com/actuarial_discussion_forum/archive/index.php/t-136591.html.

14. As reported by Plutarch in *Plutarch's Lives of the Noble Greeks and Romans*.

15. Vachon, "Code of the Winklevii."

16. See Robert A. Margo, "Employment and Unemployment in the 1930s," *Journal of Economic Perspectives* 7, no. 2 (spring 1993): 41–59; https://fraser.stlouisfed.org/docs/meltzer/maremp93.pdf.

17. Despite assiduous research, I've been unable to determine exactly how Howard Sr. accumulated enough money to be on the bank's board of directors. The simple answer is that many of the companies he started must have prospered mightily.

18. Vachon, "Code of the Winklevii."

19. The sordid story goes something like this: crippled man (using the terminology of the day) falls for a girl, who lives with him for a while but eventually dumps him for another man. This doesn't sit well. When the spurned lover learns the pair can be found walking nightly at a local park, he takes a taxi and waits for them to show up. What you expect to happen did: the cripple steps out from behind a tree (rather, leans over to one side) and the girl sees him, produces a loud cinematic scream, and runs as fast as she can, failing to win an impromptu sprint versus two .45 bullets, which enter her back and do all sorts of gruesome damage while passing through. Naturally her new beau leaps up and runs in the opposite direction, but he's plugged three times in the back. Detective Leonard was called to the scene and he tracked down the murderer, took the (literally) smoking gun out of his pocket, and recorded his subsequent confession.

20. During the 2008 presidential campaign, Romney refused to discuss "economic inequality," arguing that anyone who even broaches the subject is simply being petty: "You know, I think it's about envy. I think it's about class warfare." Romney naturally defends the status quo: "I believe in a merit nation, an opportunity nation where people by virtue of their education, their hard work and risk taking and their dreams—maybe a little luck—could achieve great things." Note that even Romney, in a full-throated defense of merit, is forced to grant a little wiggle room to "luck." Which covers, I suppose, being born to a father who had saved American Motors from bankruptcy and was a nationally known and highly respected public figure. (Tami Luhby, "Romney: Income Inequality Is Just 'Envy,'" *CNN Money*, Jan. 12, 2012, http://money.cnn.com/2012/01/12/news/economy/Romney_envy/.)

21. Hal Gershowitz and Stephen Porter, "Education in America: The Real Death Spiral," *Of Thee I Sing 1776*, Nov. 10, 2013, http://www.oftheeising1776.com/education-in-america-the-real-death-spiral.

22. "Per Pupil Spending Varies Heavily Across the United States," United States Census Bureau, June 2, 2015, https://www.census.gov/newsroom/press-releases/2015/cb15-98.html.

23. Sandra Y. L. Korn, "Aid Isn't Enough," *Harvard Crimson*, Sept. 27, 2012, http://www.thecrimson.com/column/the-red-line/article/2012/9/27/harvard-real-diversity/.

CHAPTER 7: THE WINKLEVOSS TWINS:
THE FOG OF SUCCESS

1. For example, the Bitcoin Center NYC (http://bitcoincenternyc.com/about
-bitcoin-center/) is the largest in the country and features extensive educational and
outreach support, as well as more typical trading/business startup backing.

2. Suniya S. Luthar, "The Problem With Rich Kids," *Psychology Today*, Nov. 5,
2013, https://www.psychologytoday.com/articles/201310/the-problem-rich-kids.

3. Suniya S. Luthar, Samuel H. Barkin, and Elizabeth J. Crossman, "'I
Can, Therefore I Must': Fragility in the Upper-Middle Classes," *Development and
Psychopathology, 25th Anniversary Special Issue*, Nov. 2015, http://www.pubfacts.com/
detail/24342854/I-can-therefore-I-must-fragility-in-the-upper-middle-classes.

4. Ibid.

5. Erin Sherbert, "Facebook Hollywood Saga Comes to an End: Winklevii
Twins Lose in Court," *SF Weekly*, Apr. 11, 2011, http://www.sfweekly.com/the
snitch/2011/04/11/facebook-hollywood-saga-comes-to-an-end-winklevii-twins-lose
-in-court.

6. Sally Thompson, "The Liberty Lectures," *Adam Smith Institute*, Dec. 10,
2010, http://www.adamsmith.org/blog/philosophy/the-liberty-lectures/.

7. For more details about cons, both long and short, refer to Amy Reading's
*The Mark Inside: A Perfect Swindle, a Cunning Revenge, and a Small History of the Big
Con* (New York: Knopf Doubleday, 2013).

8. McGregor was notorious during his time in the British Army for insisting
his men wear full dress uniforms at all times, regardless of climate or condition. He
wasn't a popular officer.

9. Even after the con was exposed, Gregor MacGregor continued to issue
bonds and sell Poyaisian real estate in France and England until he eventually
retired to Venezuela. He was put on trial for fraud a number of times but never
convicted or imprisoned and kept much of what he managed to swindle from the
investing class of greater Europe.

10. Nathan Mayer Rothschild's net worth is estimated to have been close to
$500 billion: "When Nathan died in 1836, his personal fortune was equivalent
to 0.62% of the British national income." (Niall Ferguson, *The Ascent of Money: A
Financial History of the World* [New York: Penguin, 2008], 84.)

11. He founded Stanford University in 1885 with a donation of $38,754,000;
this is worth well over a billion in today's money.

12. Chloe Sorvino, "The Gilded Age Family that Gave it All Away: The
Carnegies," *Forbes*, Jul. 8, 2014, http://www.forbes.com/sites/chloesorvino/
2014/07/08/whats-become-of-them-the-carnegie-family/.

13. Associated Press, "Henry Ford Is Dead at 83 in Dearborn," *New York Times*, Apr. 8, 1947, http://www.nytimes.com/learning/general/onthisday/bday/0730 .html.

14. Well, maybe.

15. Fluctuating on the open market like any commodity (and most curren-cies), increasing in price when people buy more, and falling off when people sell.

16. Colleen Taylor, "Cameron and Tyler Winklevoss File for $20 Million IPO of Their 'Bitcoin Trust,'" *TechCrunch*, Jul. 1, 2013, http://techcrunch.com/2013/07/ 01/cameron-and-tyler-winklevoss-file-for-20-million-ipo-of-their-bitcoin-trust/.

17. Brian Womack, "Winklevoss Twins Create Fund to Invest in Bitcoin Market," *Bloomberg*, Jul. 2, 2013, http://www.bloomberg.com/news/articles/ 2013-07-02/winklevoss-twins-create-fund-to-invest-in-bitcoin-market.

18. Colleen Taylor, "With $1.5M Led by Winklevoss Capital, BitInstant Aims to Be the Go-To Site to Buy and Sell Bitcoins," *TechCrunch*, http://techcrunch .com/2013/05/17/with-1-5m-led-by-winklevoss-capital-bitinstant-aims-to-be-the-go -to-site-to-buy-and-sell-bitcoins/.

19. Alec Liu, "Who's Building Bitcoin? An Inside Look at Bitcoin's Open Source Development," *Motherboard*, May 7, 2013, http://motherboard.vice.com/ blog/whos-building-bitcoin-an-inside-look-at-bitcoins-open-source-development.

20. Kashmir Hill, "Bitcoin Companies and Entrepreneurs Can't Get Bank Accounts," *Forbes*, Nov. 15, 2013, http://www.forbes.com/sites/kashmirhill/ 2013/11/15/bitcoin-companies-and-entrepreneurs-cant-get-bank-accounts/.

21. United States Attorney's Office: Southern District of New York, "Man-hattan U.S. Attorney Announces Charges Against Bitcoin Exchangers, Including CEO of Bitcoin Exchange Company, For Scheme to Sell and Launder Over $1 Million in Bitcoins Related to Silk Road Drug Trafficking," news release, Jan. 27, 2014, http://www.justice.gov/usao-sdny/pr/manhattan-us-attorney-announces -charges-against-bitcoin-exchangers-including-ceo.

22. Sydney Ember, "Charles Shrem, Bitcoin Supporter, Pleads Guilty in Court," *DealBook*, Sept. 4, 2014, http://dealbook.nytimes.com/2014/09/04/ charles-shrem-bitcoin-supporter-pleads-guilty-to-federal-charge.

23. Ibid.

24. Neil Sardesai, "Andreas Antonopoulos Leaves Bitcoin Foundation Over 'Complete Lack of Transparency,'" *CryptoCoinsNews*, Jul. 10, 2014, https://www.cryptocoinsnews.com/andreas-antonopoulos-leaves-bitcoin -foundation-complete-lack-transparency/.

25. "Written Testimony of Cameron and Tyler Winklevoss to the New York State Department of Financial Services," NYDFS Virtual Currency Hearing, Jan. 28, 2014, http://www.dfs.ny.gov/about/hearings/vc_01282014/Winklevoss.pdf.

26. Concerning Jed McCaleb: "[S]omething like 75 percent of the 40 people interviewed for this story used the word 'genius'—he knew plenty about decentralized peer-to-peer networks and operating beyond traditional boundaries of property and government control." (Michael Craig, "The Race to Replace Bitcoin," *Observer*, Feb. 5, 2015, http://observer.com/2015/02/the-race-to-replace-bitcoin/.)

27. mtgox [Jed McCaleb], "New Bitcoin Exchange (Mtgox.Com)," *Bitcoin Forum*, Jul. 18, 2010, https://bitcointalk.org/index.php?topic=444.msg3866 #msg3866.

28. mtgox [Jed McCaleb], "Mtgox Is Changing Owners," *Bitcoin Forum*, Mar. 6, 2011, https://bitcointalk.org/index.php?topic=4187.0;all.

29. Rachel Abrams and Nathaniel Popper, "Trading Site Failure Stirs Ire and Hope for Bitcoin," *DealBook*, Feb. 25, 2014, http://dealbook.nytimes.com/2014/02/25/trading-site-failure-stirs-ire-and-hope-for-bitcoin/.

30. I'm ignoring theft committed by heads of state, who can bring both police and army to bear. It's not a fair comparison.

31. Jonathan Soble, "Mark Karpeles, Chief of Bankrupt Bitcoin Exchange, Is Arrested in Tokyo," *DealBook*, Aug. 1, 2015, http://www.nytimes.com/2015/08/02/business/dealbook/mark-karpeles-mt-gox-bitcoin-arrested.html?_r=0.

32. See http://blog.vaultoro.com/author/joshua/ for details about both Mr. Scigala and his "transparent" exchange.

33. Joshua Scigala, email correspondence with author, August 11, 2015.

34. Ibid.

35. Ibid.

36. Andreas Antonopoulos, quoted in Andy Greenberg, "Bitcoin Shrugs Off Mt. Gox's Death Rattle," *Forbes*, Feb. 28, 2014, http://www.forbes.com/sites/andygreenberg/2014/02/28/bitcoin-shrugs-off-mt-goxs-death-rattle/.

37. Jacob Cohen Donnelly, "Bitcoin 2014: Bitcoin's Biggest Nightmare, the Collapse of Mt. Gox," *Blockchain Agenda*, Dec. 28, 2014, http://insidebitcoins.com/news/bitcoin-2014-bitcoins-biggest-nightmare-the-collapse-of-mt-gox/28074.

38. Helping new Bitcoin startups form, get funding, and hone their business model.

39. "Coin Apex: Bitcoin Ventures," *Coin Apex*, http://www.coinapex.com/ventures.

40. Alex Waters, telephone interview with author, August 2015.

41. Ibid.

42. Ibid.

43. A simple system for websites to "push" frequently updated content to users.

44. Waters, telephone interview.

45. Ibid. Alex Waters isn't financially involved with the Winklevoss twins, except as possible Bitcoin competitors.

46. Michael Carney, "Coinbase Wins the Race to Launch the First Regulated US Bitcoin Exchange," *Pando*, Jan. 25, 2015, https://pando.com/2015/01/25/coinbase-wins-the-race-to-launch-the-first-regulated-us-bitcoin-exchange/.

47. Kayla Ruble, "A Nasdaq for Bitcoin: VICE News Interviews the Winklevoss Twins About the Future of Cryptocurrency," *VICE News*, Feb. 16, 2015, https://news.vice.com/article/a-nasdaq-for-bitcoin-vice-news-interviews-the-winklevoss-twins-about-the-future-of-cryptocurrency.

48. Jon Southurst, "Winklevoss Twins Plan Regulated US Bitcoin Exchange," *CoinDesk*, Jan. 23, 2015, http://www.coindesk.com/winklevoss-twins-plan-regulated-us-bitcoin-exchange/.

49. Diana Ngo, "Weekend Roundup: First Publicly Traded US Bitcoin Derivatives Exchange Set to Launch, New BTMs In The US, UK," *CoinTelegraph*, Mar. 1, 2015 http://cointelegraph.com/news/113578/weekend-roundup-first-publicly-traded-us-bitcoin-derivatives-exchange-set-to-launch-new-btms-in-the-us-uk.

50. Gavin Smith, telephone interview with author, July 2015.

51. Ibid.

52. A sad list of busted and hacked exchanges can be found here: Peter Yeh, "Hacks, Scams and Shut Downs: A Sad, Incomplete History of Bitcoin Exchanges," *ANIMAL*, Apr. 3, 2014, http://animalnewyork.com/2014/hacks-scams-shut-downs-sad-incomplete-history-bitcoin-exchanges/.

In general, most Bitcoin exchanges have not lasted more than a year, ending in complete loss of all associated bitcoins.

53. Smith, telephone interview.

54. Ibid.

55. Corynne McSherry, "U.S. Government Seizes 82 Websites: A Glimpse at the Draconian Future of Copyright Enforcement?" *Electronic Frontier Foundation*, Nov. 29, 2010, https://www.eff.org/deeplinks/2010/11/us-government-seizes-82-websites-draconian-future.

56. From the *Oxford English Dictionary*, 1993 edition: "A reduction in the use or role of banks and savings institutions as intermediaries between lenders and borrowers."

57. At the time of the interview. The precise value of the Bitcoin market is public knowledge, since the total number of bitcoins issued can be added up and multiplied by the current price.

58. Smith, telephone interview.

59. "HMT Call for Information on Digital Money: Citi," *CoinDesk*, Dec. 3,

2014, http://www.scribd.com/doc/266008779/Citi-Response-to-the
-HMT-Call-for-Information-on-Digital-Money.

   60. Simon Johnson, "Money-Laundering Banks Still Get a Pass From
U.S.," *Bloomberg View*, Mar. 31, 2013, http://www.bloomberg.com/news/
articles/2013-03-31/money-laundering-banks-still-get-a-pass-from-u-s-.

   61. Suzanne Rose, "Senate Hearings on Money Laundering Highlight
Criminality of U.S. Banks," *Executive Intelligence Review*, Dec. 17, 1999, http://www
.larouchepub.com/eiw/public/1999/eirv26n50-19991217/eirv26n50
-19991217_066-senate_hearings_on_money_launder.pdf.

   62. Michael Hudson, "Big Banks Are Knee-Deep in the Dirty Money-
Laundering Business," *AlterNet*, May 2, 2013, http://www.alternet.org/
investigations/big-banks-are-knee-deep-dirty-money-laundering-business.

   63. Johnson, "Money-Laundering Banks Still Get a Pass from U.S."

   64. Smith, telephone interview.

   65. Sarah Tyre, telephone interview with author, August 2015.

   66. Ibid.

   67. "Tanzania GDP Per Capita: 1988–2015," *Trading Economics*, http://www
.tradingeconomics.com/tanzania/gdp-per-capita.

   68. "Cell Phones in Africa: Communication Lifeline," *Pew Research Center*,
Washington, DC, Apr. 15, 2015, http://www.pewglobal.org/2015/04/15/cell
-phones-in-africa-communication-lifeline/.

   69. "Over the Sea and Far Away," *Economist*, May 19, 2012, http://www
.economist.com/node/21554740.

   70. The sticking point is, again, getting bitcoins in the first place. It's still
difficult (though getting easier) to reliably purchase bitcoins. As Bitcoin exchanges
expand and become cheaper, transaction fees for "buying bitcoins" will drop (they
are already moving downward), with the savings going to those who need it most.

   71. Although roughly six million families regularly do.

   72. Tyre, telephone interview.

   73. And they might be.

CONCLUSION: INCREMENTAL PROGRESS

   1. Rather, works that fit comfortably (or could after some squeezing) in the
genre ultimately named "science fiction."

   2. Written sometime in the 1620s, Francis Godwin's *The Man in the Moone:
or a Discourse of a Voyage Thither* involves geese capable of orbital flight, a fanciful
trip to the moon, and the discovery of an alien race living there (the Lunars);

in 1788 the famous (or infamous) Giacomo Casanova (whose "escapades and amours," according to the Oxford English Dictionary, were so notorious his name is now part of the English language) published a massive five-volume work of science fiction, *Icosaméron*, embracing the "hollow Earth" hypothesis, in which a brother and sister fall into the Earth and discover a subterranean utopia populated by Mégamicres, a race of multicolored, hermaphroditic dwarves. Hijinks most definitely followed.

    3. For a fascinating discussion of how the machine worked, and the later transformation of the recorded waveforms into actual sound following computer digitalization, see the article "Retrieving Sound from Soot—Our Evolving Approaches," at Firstsounds.org (http://firstsounds.org/sounds/approach.php).

    4. With one remarkable exception: an amateur French scientist named Charles Cros wrote a paper on April 30, 1877, outlining the theoretical possibility of turning a sound trace back into a sound; and by October 10, 1877, an account of his idea, and mechanical plans for putting it into practice, was published. Edison had already been working on his invention for months at this point and by November was giving successful demonstrations of what would later be called a phonograph—a case of independent invention, made more remarkable by the general paucity of interest and research into the possibility of recorded sound. This seems to be a case where the mechanical ease and straightforward nature of the ultimate solution outweighed cultural and historical resistance. For more details about Charles Cros, see Jacques Attali's *Noise: The Political Economy of Music* (Manchester, UK: Manchester University Press, 1985), pp. 90–92.

    5. He also reported: "'The workman [asked to do the] sketch [of my new invention] was John Kruesi. I didn't have much faith that it would work, expecting that I might possibly hear a word or so that would give hope of a future for the idea. Kruesi, when he had nearly finished [the sketch], asked what it was for. I told him I was going to record talking, and then have the machine talk back. *He thought it absurd. . . .*' No wonder that John Kruesi, after he heard the little machine repeat the words that had been spoken into it, ejaculated in an awestricken tone: 'Mein Gott im Himmel!' No wonder the [other workmen] joined hands and danced around Edison, singing and shouting. No wonder that Edison and his associates sat up all night fixing and adjusting it so as to get better and better results—reciting and singing and trying one another's voices and listening with awe and delight as the crude little machine repeated the words spoken or sung into it." (William Henry Meadowcroft, *The Boy's Life of Edison* [New York: Harper & Brothers, 1911], p. 177.)

    6. An important precursor to Bitcoin, published on the Cypherpunks mailing list in 1998. For details: http://www.weidai.com/bmoney.txt.

7. An early cryptocurrency with "proof of work" baked into the system: Vivek Vishnumurthy, Sangeeth Chandrakumar, and Emin Gün Sirer, "KARMA: A Secure Economic Framework for Peer-to-Peer Resource Sharing," conference paper, 2003, http://www.cs.cornell.edu/people/egs/papers/karma.pdf.

8. Hundreds of thousands of bitcoins have, in aggregate, been stolen out of individual e-wallets or taken as a result of outright fraud (the Mt. Gox exchange is a good example of this), but these are a result of humdrum theft, not a weakness in the underlying Bitcoin network. No bitcoins have been lost by being "reassigned" to somebody else directly in the block chain, or been hacked in a way (ultimately) unrelated to user error (or at least, unwise user decisions). As always, use a very strong passphrase for any Bitcoin e-wallet and don't send money and/or bitcoins to unregulated exchanges half a globe away without expecting something bad to happen.

9. "Auroracoin: One of the Biggest Pump and Dumps in Cryptocurrency History," *Cryptocurrency Times*, May 14, 2014, http://www.usacryptocoins.com/thecryptocurrencytimes/uncategorized/auroracoin-one-of-the-biggest-pump-and-dumps-in-cryptocurrency-history/.

10. Larry X, "Bitcoin Network 8 Times More Powerful Than Top 500 World's Supercomputers Combined," *The Bitcoin*, Jun. 12, 2013, http://thebitcoin.org/bitcoin-network-8-times-more-powerful-than-top-500-worlds-supercomputers-combined/.

11. On the other hand, it's probably less energy-intensive than mining actual gold out of the ground, refining it, stamping it, and distributing it, as "real currencies" in the past had been forced to do.

12. "About Primecoin," *Primecoin*, 2014, http://primecoin.io/about.php#advantages-xpm.

13. For details, refer to Chris Caldwell, "The Prime Glossary: Cunningham Chain," *The Prime Pages*, http://primes.utm.edu/glossary/page.php?sort=CunninghamChain.

14. There are hundreds of cryptocurrencies being traded on online markets; for examples, see "Crypto-Currency Market Capitalizations," http://coinmarketcap.com/.

INDEX

Adorno, Theodore, 199
aerarium militare, 217, 219
American Dream, 212–13
Andresen, Gavin, 241
Argentina inflation crisis, 262–63
Armory, the, (website), 177
astroturfing, 168–69
Atari, 142–45
Augustus (Roman emperor), 218–19
auletrides, 215
Auroracoin (pump and dump scheme), 274

bank bailouts
    effect of, 117
    message in genesis block, 109
    moral hazard, 110
baronsyntax. *See* Bates, Richard
Bastrop State Park (fungal wonder-land), 169
Bates, Richard, 164–65, 173–74
    baronsyntax transcripts, 174–75
Baumeister, Roy F., 197
Bello Coffee, 185
Bitcoin
    addresses, 44
    birth, 11
    controlled outside politics, 36
    insubstantiality, 51
    mining, 23, 42, 61–62
    price spike, 9
    public ledger, 48–49, 62, 246
    regulation, 242, 249–50
    theft, 76
    ultimate fate, 276
BitInstant, 240–42
BitPesa, 267–68
Blankenship, Loyd, (master hacker), 82

block chain, 53, 58–62, 74
b-money, 273
Bobby interview, 42
Bruenig, Elizabeth, 153
Brunswick School, 207, 227
Brutalism, 304n50
Bush, George W., 113
Byzantine General's Problem, 66

CCIA (Community Currencies in Action), 102–103
CDOs (collateralized debt obligations), 114
CDSs (Credit Default Swaps), 115
Champagne, Phil, 104–106
Cirrus (Silk Road mole), 186
Citibank, Bitcoin objections, 259
cocaine import and sale, 178
"Code of the Winklevii, The," 209–10
Coin Apex, 248
Coinbase, 252
Communes, proximate and dispersed, 93
Comstock silver lode, 10
ConnectU, 240
counterfeiting
    Bitcoin solution to, 51
    fiat currency, 131–32
    traditional penalties, 47
credit card numbers
    payment guarantees, 13
    privacy concerns, 43
    unreality of, 14
currency
    boring grey alternative, Satoshi's proposed, 29
    ideal, 48
    fundamental features, 27

theory of origin, conventional, 26–27
theory of origin, Satoshi rejection
    of, 27–29
velocity and devaluation, 101
cypher clock, 69
Cypherpunks
    defined, 80
    privacy fight, 82
    manifesto, 81
    mathematical basis of trust, 111
    ultimate victory, 83

Dark Web, 124–33
Decker, Christian, 74
demurrage, 103, 101
derivatives, 115–16
Donnelly, Jacob, 245
DPR. *See* Dread Pirate Roberts
Dread Pirate Roberts, the, 139–40
    book club, 159
    extorted by hacker, 181
    ignores blackmail attempt, 185
    origin of name, 139
    pays for assassination of Curtis, 181
    pays for assassination of four
        dealers, 182
    war on drugs, 155
    See also Ulbricht, Ross

Easter eggs, 141–42
e-cash, 43
Edison, Thomas, 271–72
e-Gold, 38, 60, 84, 273
Engels, Friedrich, 94
Equitable Commerce (Warren), 97, 99
e-wallet
    defined, 17
    format of data, 50–51
    use, sending, receiving, 44–46
exchanges, Bitcoin, 42, 44, 242–43,
    246–47, 254
extortion, FBI use of, 181, 185
Eyal, Ittay, 72–73

Facebook, 208–209, 231, 234, 238–39
Faiella, Robert M., 242

faith
    Bitcoin use engenders, 39
    credit card companies, 14
    effect on currency of loss thereof,
        15
    fiat currency requires, 30
FBI, 158, 174–75, 184–85, 189
    Slinker & Stinker, corrupt federal
        agents, 178–81
fiat currency
    defined, 30
    early failure of, 37
    inflation, 107
    typical functioning, 47
Finney, Hal, 280n5
First Global Credit, 254–55
First National Bank of Mercer, 222
flexible spending account (FSA) scam,
    154
Fourier, Charles, 94–96, 101, 115, 161
Franklin, Fabian, 148
free market, idealism, 80, 87, 100, 116,
    151–55, 199, 234
Free State Project, 103–104
French Maid (Silk Road alias), 184

Gemini (Bitcoin exchange), 252
genesis block, 51, 108–10
Gilmore, John, 80
Glass books protocol, 245
Glen Park library, 187
Glover, Paul, 99
gold bugs, 16, 37, 281n11
gold rush, internet, 9
gold standard
    defined, 15
    enthusiasts, 16
    inflexibility during recession, 17
    leaving, 38
    leveraging, 34
Good Wagon Books, 166–67, 170
Greateastern Insurance Corporation, 222
Green, Curtis
    arrested, suborned, 179
    beaten and tortured (virtually), 180
    "flush" account on Silk Road, 178

killed (virtually), 181, 200
    Silk Road administrator, 178
Greenspan, Alan, 116, 280n6
Greenwich Country Day School, 207, 227

hackers
    government crackdown and over-
        reach, 82–83
    Mt. Gox theft, 244
    privacy concerns, 43
    Silk Road, 170–71, 183
Hammer, Armie, 208
hash function, cryptographic, 53, 57,
    62, 64
healthcare, libertarian argument
    against, 163
Heninger, Nadia, 75
Hinkle, Mark, 147
Hitchens, Christopher, 85
hit men
    advertising for hire, 132
    DPR hires, 180
Hughes, Eric, 80

inflation
    Argentina crisis, 262
    Bitcoin resists catastrophic, 107
    Bitcoin slowly inflating, 287n15
    gold standard, effect on, 16
    Ithaca Hours resists, 100
    John Law's fiat currency experi-
        ment, 36
    post-WWI Germany hyper, 15
Information Superhighway, 125–26
Interstate Auto Auctions, 222
Ithaca Hours, 99–100
Ithacash, 103

Karma (virtual currency), 273
Karpelès, Mark, 244–45
key cryptography, public and private
    keys, 53–58
Kingpin Statute, 145

language analysis, Satoshi's corpus, 22
Law, John, 31–35

Leonard, Francis J., 224
Leonard, Mildred (née Lotz), 223
libertarianism
    basis of Silk Road, 124
    child labor dispute, 153
    defined, and types, 85–86
    healthcare, 163
    Rand, Ayn, and, 89
    Satoshi's embrace of, 80
    Ulbricht's embrace of, 92, 202, 269
    utopia, Silk Road as libertarian, 162
Linux, 141, 146
Louis XIV, 33
Louisiana land grab, 35
Luthar, Suniya S., 233

Macaulay, Thomas Babington, 216
MacGregor, Gregor, 235–36
Manchin, Joe, 172
Marco Polo, 176
McCaleb, Jed, 243–44
McLuhan, Marshall, 18
"might makes right," 194
Miron, Jeffrey, 110
Mississippi
    bubble, 36
    Company, 35
money laundering, 259–61
Morris, Scott, 103
mortgage-backed securities, 112–13
Mt. Gox, 168, 243–44
MySpace, 238

National Security Agency (NSA), 128,
    131
nerd
    contrarian impulses, 146
    origins, 142–45
    overlap with libertarians, 144
Nob (Silk Road username)
    extorts money from Ross, 179
    identity, 179
    sets up fake assassination, 180
    Silk Road administrator, 179
North American Phalanx, 96

Occupy Wall Street, 117
Ockham's razor, 23
OkCupid, 118, 121
On Trade (Fourier), 94
Operation Dime Store, 176
Operation Sundevil, 82
Owen, Robert, 98

Paul, Ron, 88–89, 163
PayPal, 43
pensions, fascinating history of, 214–17
phonograph, invention of, 272
Pittsburgh Life Insurance Company, 222
Pound, Ezra, 101
Primecoin, 275
privacy
    Bitcoin's evolution, 256–58
    harvesting data, 43
    internet guarantees none, 128
    mathematical basis of, 81
    regulation inhibits, 241
    Satoshi's objections to current
        state, 30
    Tor enables, 164
Prohibition, 148–49
pseudoscience, 161
Publius Horatius Cocles, "Horatius," 216

Rand, Ayn, 88–89
random numbers (used to generate
    computational keys), 75
Read, Max, 209
Reagan, Ronald, 90
Redandwhite (Hell's Angel member
    and hit man), 181–83
restrictions, Silk Road sales, 158
Reykjavik Metropolitan Police, 184
Rockaway Beach, 223
Rothbardian anarcho-capitalism, 192
Rothschild, Nathan, 235

Satoshi
    anonymous, meaning or lack
        thereof, 24
    "Bitcoin: A Peer-to-Peer Electronic
        Cash System" (Satoshi), 53

Book of Satoshi, The (Champagne),
    104–106
contrarian currency impulses,
    25–30
mining statistics, 23
possible identities, 21–23
time stamps of message board
    posts, 23
scam. *See* Mt. Gox
school funding, 226–27
Schumer, Charles, 172
Scigala, Joshua, 245–47
Scigala, Philip, 245
Scotland, Bank of, 31
Secret, The (Byrne), 167
selfish mining, 74
SHA-256 hashing scheme, 105, 274–75
Shrem, Charlie, 242, 243
shrooms, 137, 168–70
Silk Road, 122, 136, 138
    development, 168–70
    Gawker article, 171
    self-regulation, 158
Sirer, Emin "Gun," 72–73
Smith, Gavin, 254–57
SMS (Short Message Service), 128
Snowden, Edward, 128, 296n10
social currency, 103
Social Network, The (film), 208
Solon of Athens, 215
State of Nature theory, 93
Steve Jackson Games, 82–83

Tanzania, United Republic of, 266
Thoreau, Henry David, 91–92
Tony76 (notorious Silk Road scammer),
    182
Tor (The Onion Router), 129–31
Torvalds, Linus, 106, 141, 146
trust
    failure by Wall Street, 110
    fiat currency, 31
    network security, 74
    required by traditional currencies, 30
    Silk Road, 133–36
Twentieth Century Corporation, 222

Twitter, 238
Tyre, Sarah, 263–65, 269

Ulbricht, Ross
    child labor, support of, 151–52
    deviation from Scientific Princi-
        ples, 160–61
    idealism, 190
    "Growth of EuO Thin Films
        by Molecular Beam Epitaxy"
        (thesis), 162
    libertarian philosophy, 92
    LinkedIn Profile, 159
    love of customers, 191
    OkCupid profile, 121
    online community, 191
    scientific method, perverted,
        159–61
    upbringing, 123–24
Universal Wholesale, 222
Unterguggenberger, Michael, 101

Vachon, Dana, 220
V for Vendetta (film), libertarian take on,
    122
Vilensky, Mike, 209
von Mises, Ludwig, 25, 283n14

War on Drugs, 147, 149–50, 155, 158, 178
Warren, Josiah, 96–99

Waters, Alex, 241, 248–50
Webster, J., 209
Whittaker, Jack, 212
WikiLeaks, 24, 106
Winklevoss Jr., Howard Edward, 207,
    213–14, 217
    Pension Mathematics with Numerical
        Illustrations (Winklevoss), 217
Winklevoss Sr., Howard Edward, 220
Winklevoss, Carol (Leonard), 207
Winklevoss, Marian Virginia (Minnis),
    221
Winklevoss, Tyler and Cameron
    ancestral history, 220–25
    Bitcoin discovery and investment,
        240
    education, 207, 231, 233
    embraced by Bitcoin community,
        269
    Facebook, 234–35, 239
    Gemini exchange, 253
    poor public image, 209–10
    privileged upbringing, 225, 227–28
    regulation of Bitcoin, support, 242,
        252–53
    Social Network, The (film), 208
    wealth of family, 214–15
Wörgl, Miracle of, 101–102

Zuckerberg, Mark, 208